blue monday™

ABSOLUTE BEGINNERS

cover colors by
GUY MAJOR

lettering by
SEAN KONOT

gray tones by
GUY MAJOR
JEROMY COX (CHAPTER 1), AND **CHERYLYN CRILL**

book design by **KEITH WOOD**
edited by **JAMIE S. RICH**

blue monday™

ABSOLUTE BEGINNERS

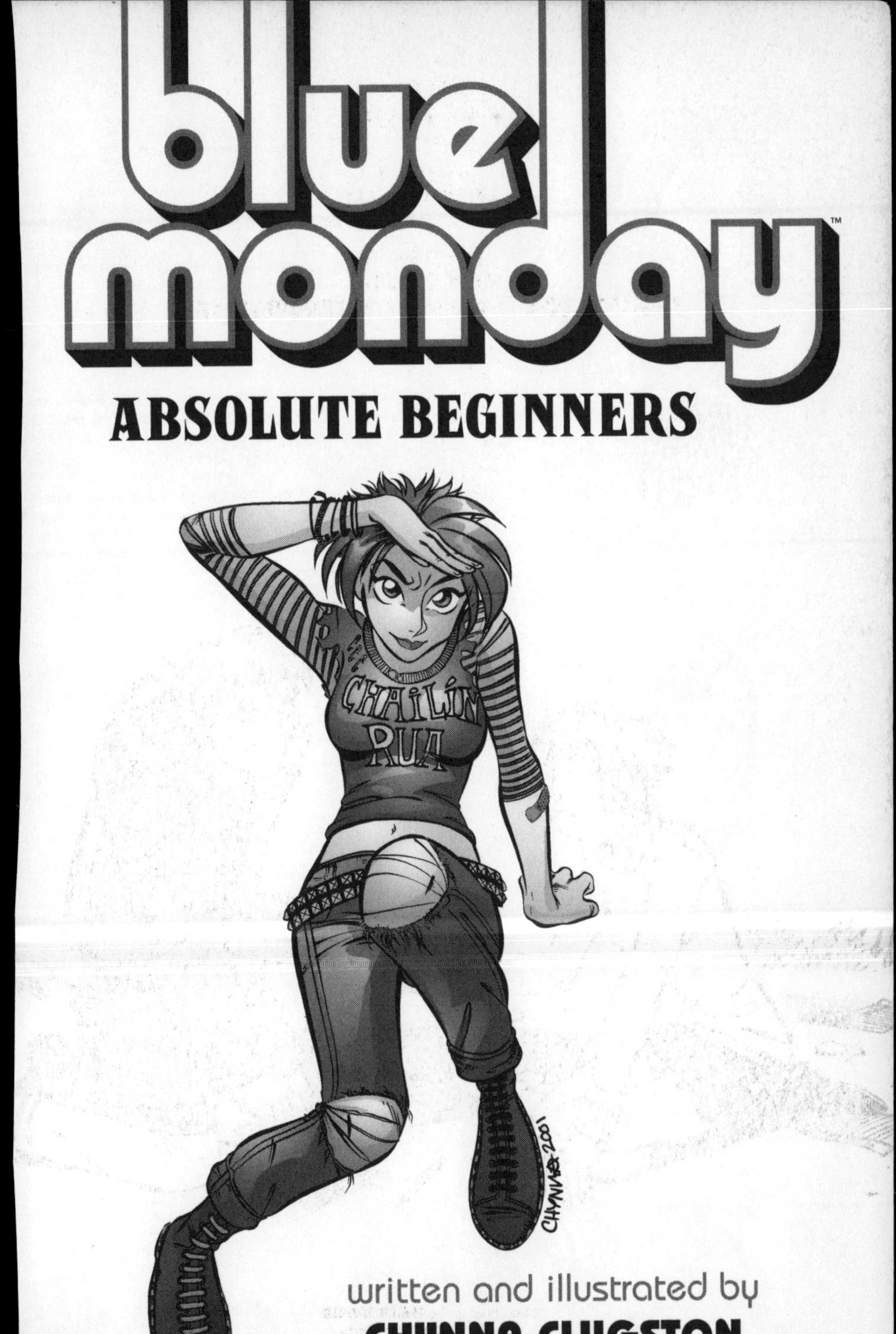
CHAILÍN RUA

written and illustrated by

CHYNNA CLUGSTON

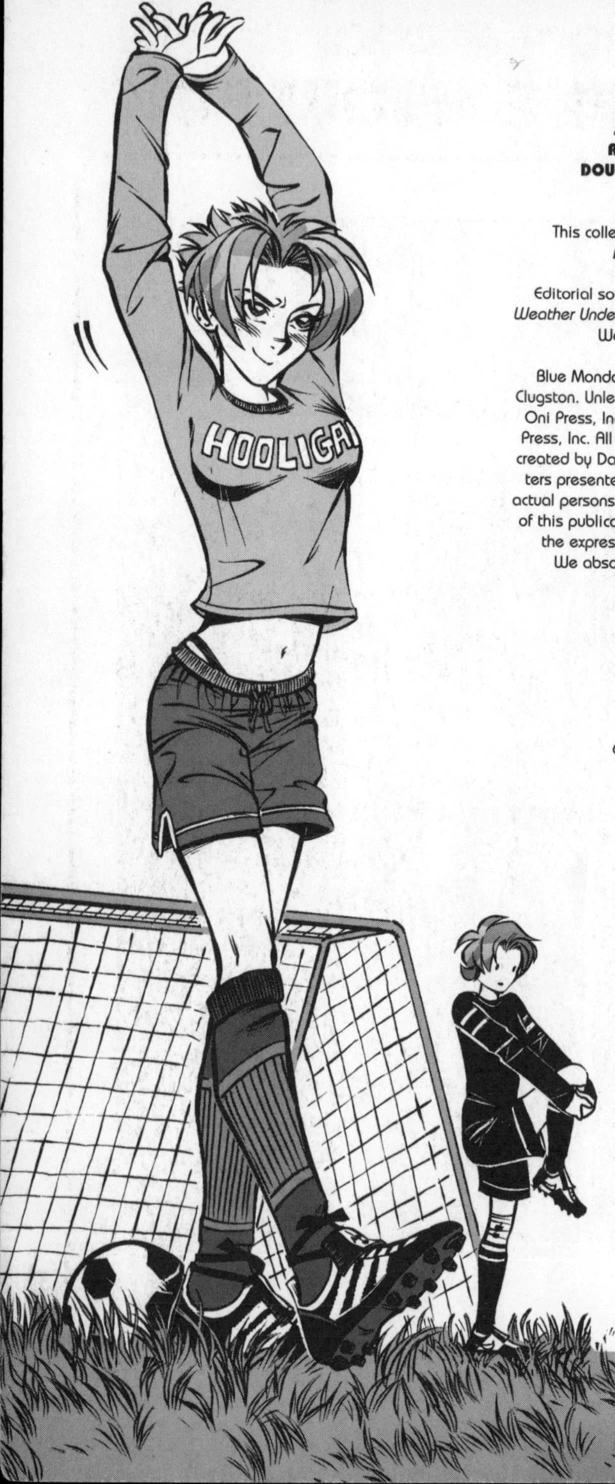

Published by Oni Press, Inc.
JOE NOZEMACK publisher
JAMES LUCAS JONES editor in chief
RANDAL C. JARRELL managing editor
DOUGLAS E. SHERWOOD editorial assistant

This collects issues 1-4 of the Oni Press comics series *Blue Monday: Absolute Beginners*™.

Editorial soundtrack: Garbage, *beautifulgarbage;* Geneva *Weather Underground;* Trash Can Sinatras, *On A B Road...Ag* Weezer, *Weezer* (a.k.a. *The Blue Album*)

ONI PRESS, INC.
6336 SE Milwaukie Avenue, PMB30
Portland, OR 97202
USA

www.onipress.com
www.bluemondaycomics.com

First edition: December 2001
ISBN-13: 978-1-929998-17-3
ISBN-10: 1-929998-17-1

3 5 7 9 10 8 6 4
PRINTED IN CANADA.

chapter one:
"SOMETHING ABOUT YOU"

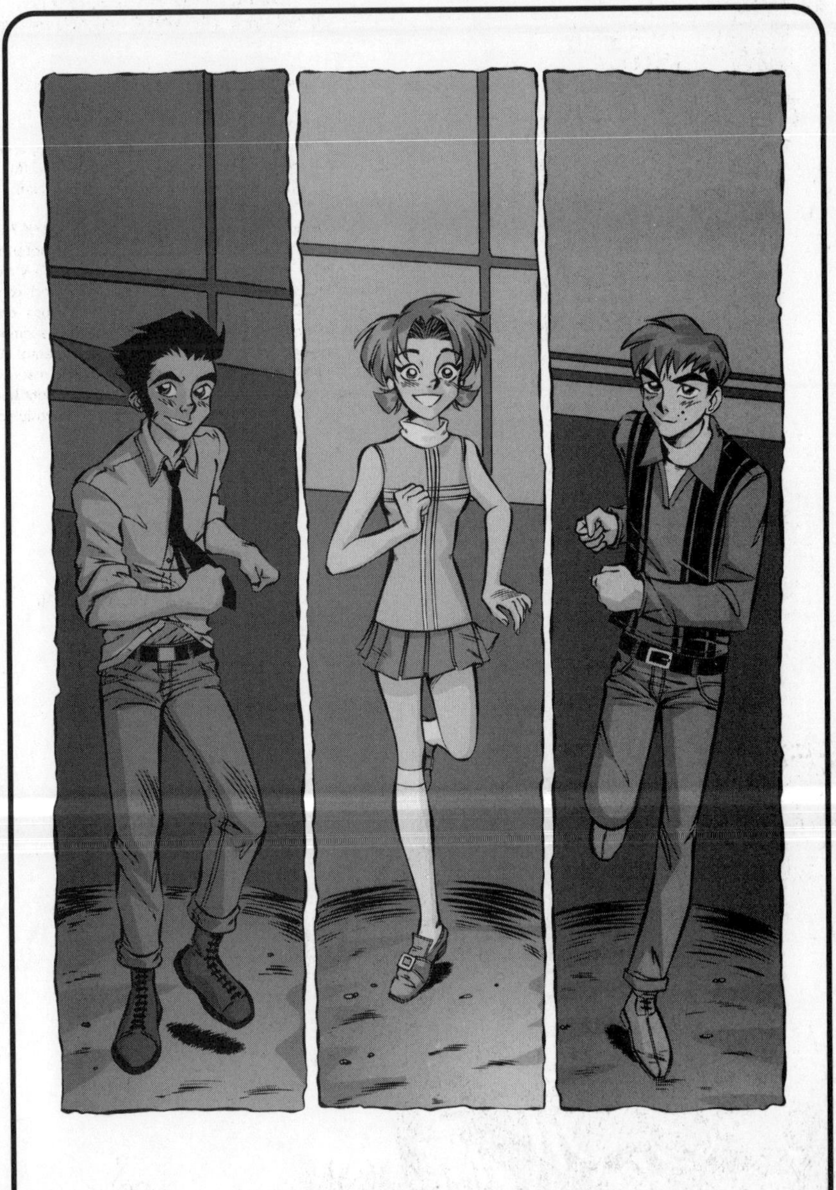

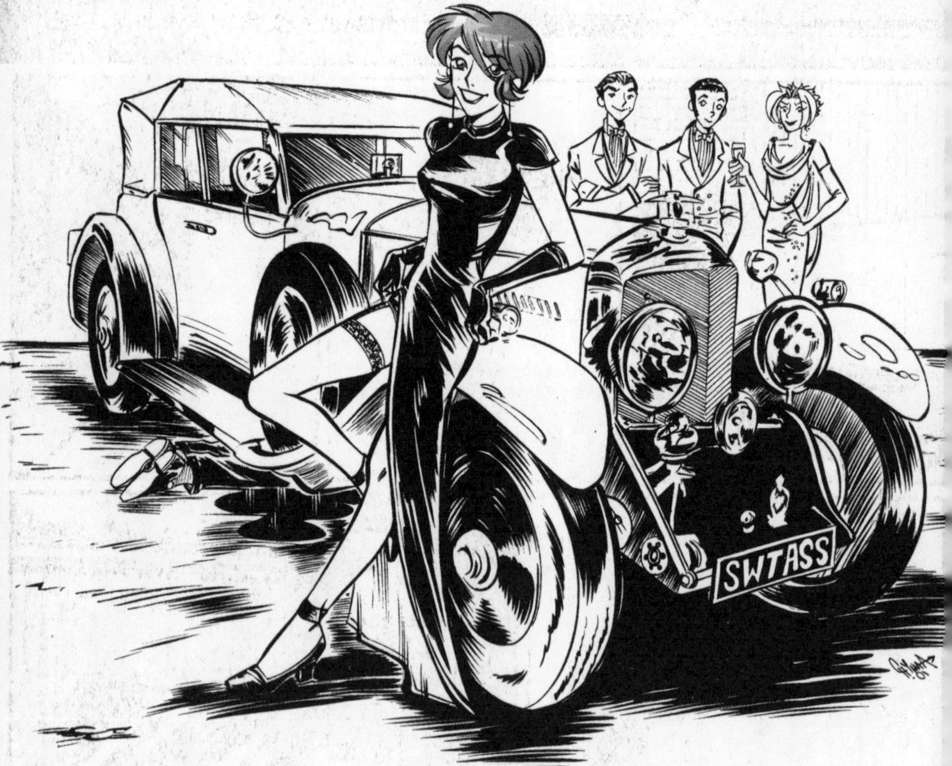
SWTASS

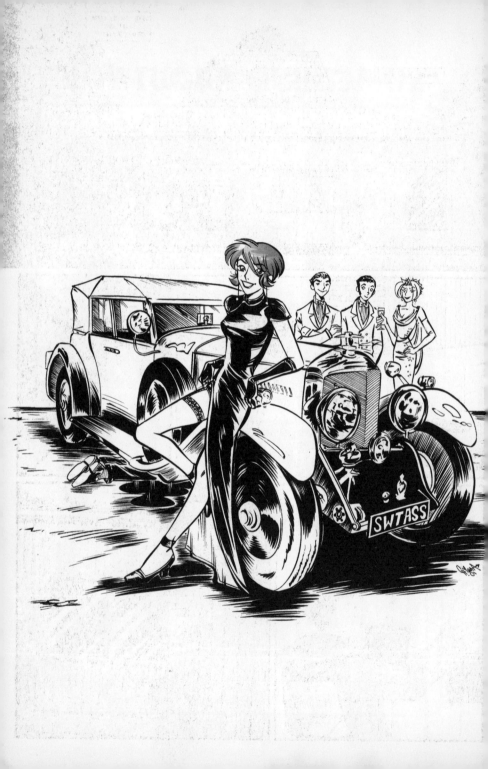

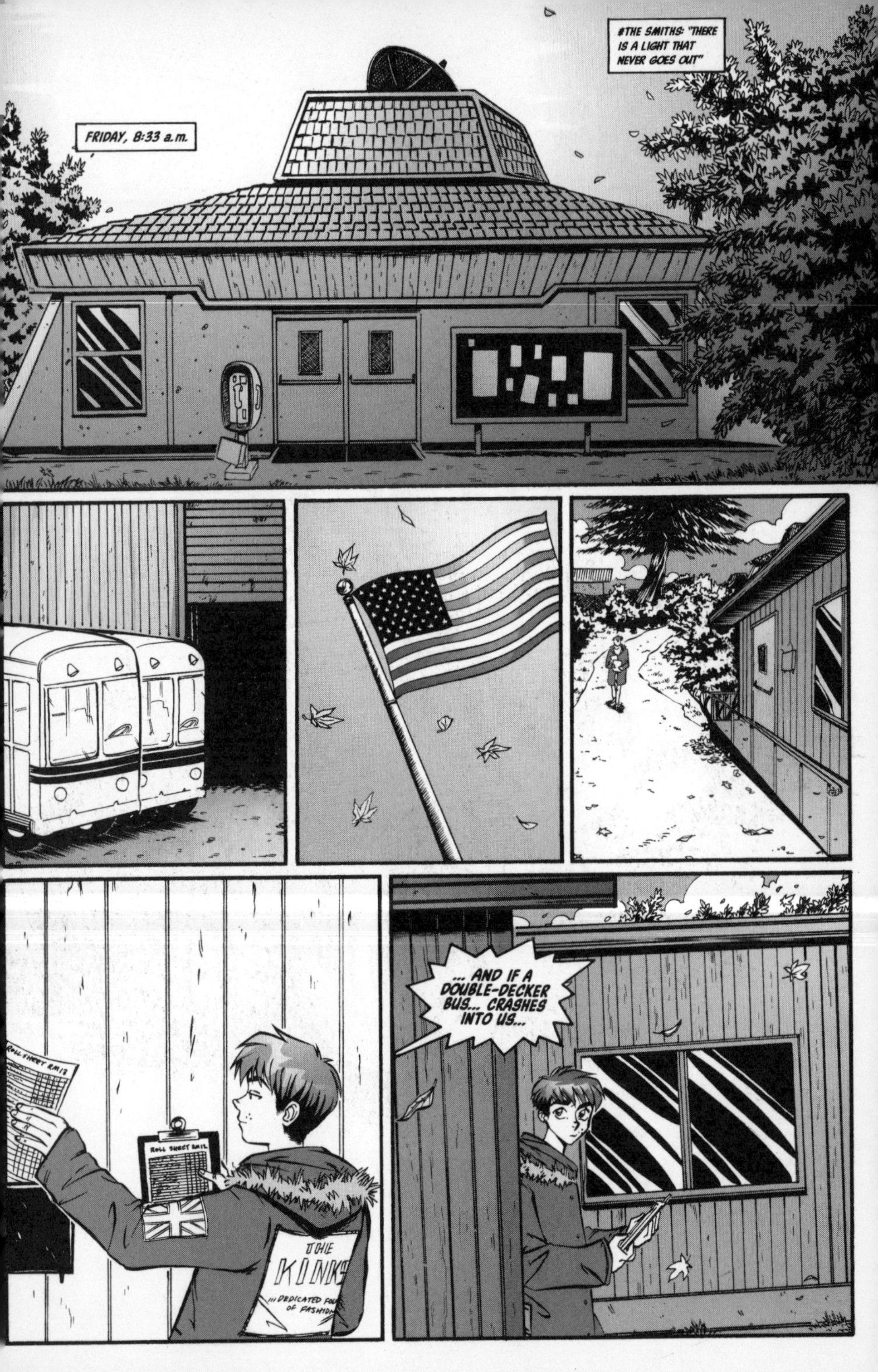
#THE SMITHS: "THERE IS A LIGHT THAT NEVER GOES OUT"
FRIDAY, 8:33 a.m.
... AND IF A DOUBLE-DECKER BUS... CRASHES INTO US...
THE KINKS
... DEDICATED FOL OF FASHION

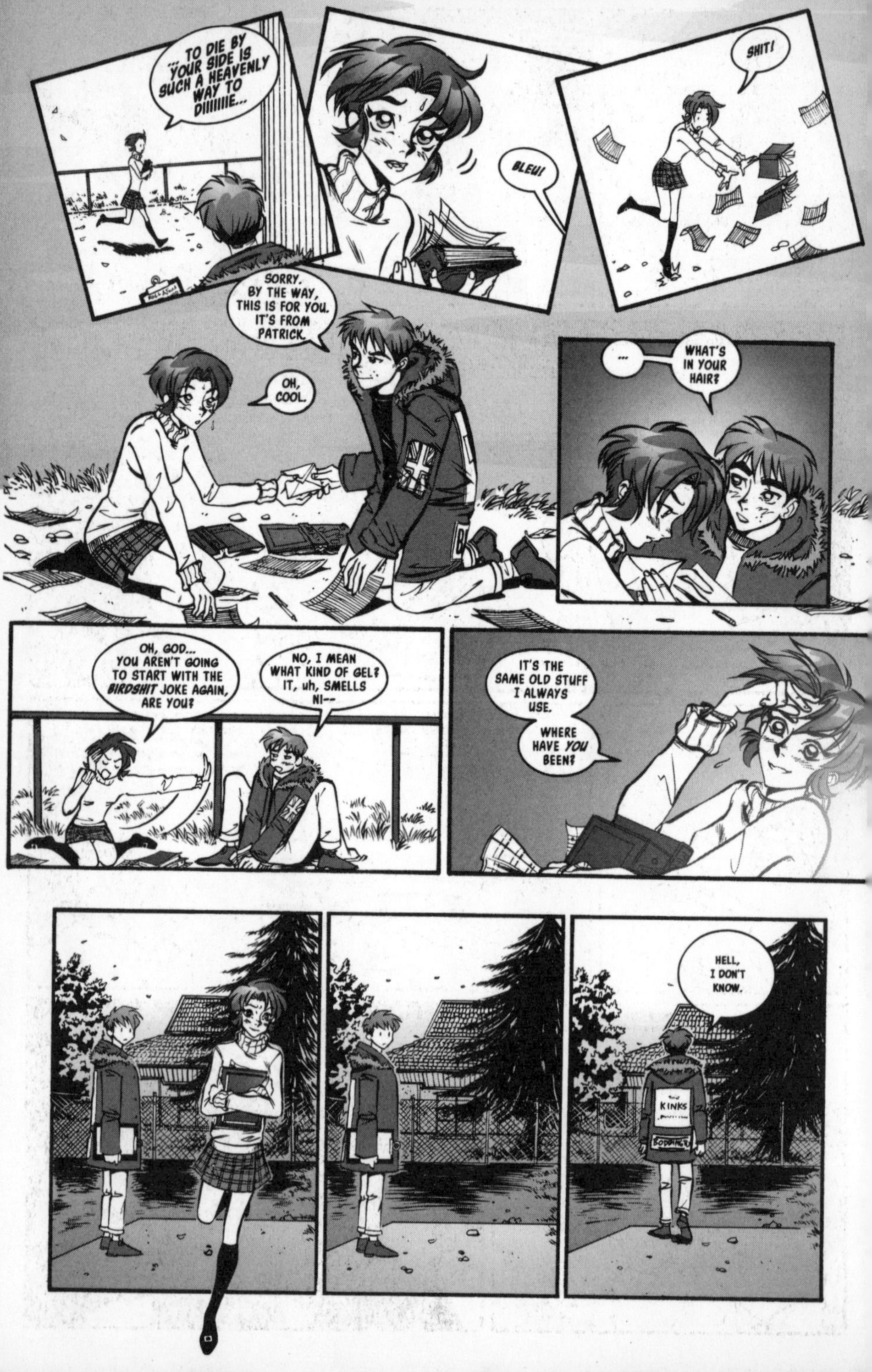
...TO DIE BY YOUR SIDE IS SUCH A HEAVENLY WAY TO DIIIIIIE...
BLEU!
SHIT!
SORRY. BY THE WAY, THIS IS FOR YOU. IT'S FROM PATRICK.
OH, COOL.
...
WHAT'S IN YOUR HAIR?
OH, GOD... YOU AREN'T GOING TO START WITH THE *BIRDSHIT* JOKE AGAIN, ARE YOU?
NO, I MEAN WHAT KIND OF GEL? IT, uh, SMELLS NI--
IT'S THE SAME OLD STUFF I ALWAYS USE.
WHERE HAVE *YOU* BEEN?
HELL, I DON'T KNOW.
KINKS

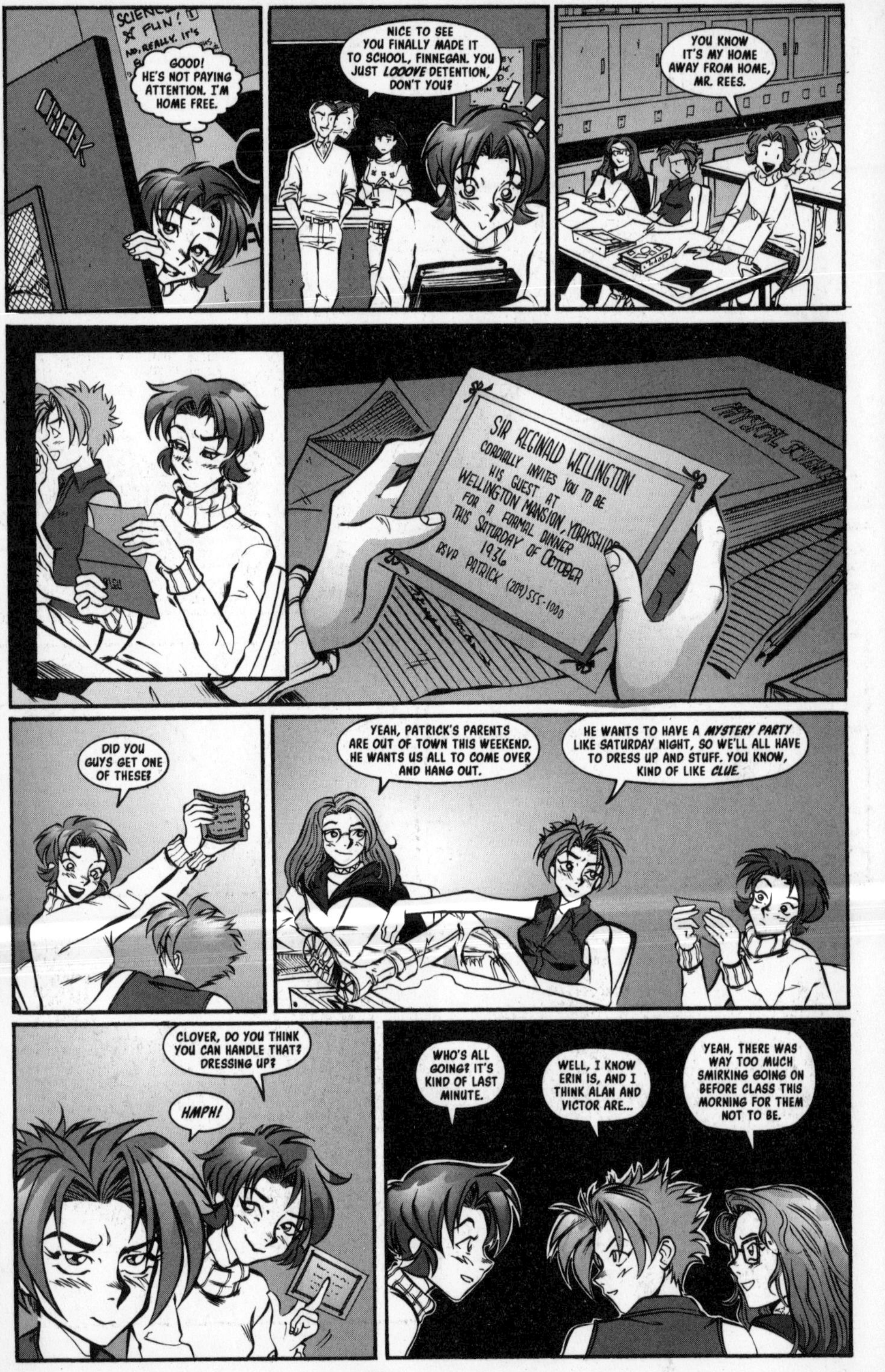

CREEK
GOOD! HE'S NOT PAYING ATTENTION. I'M HOME FREE.
NICE TO SEE YOU FINALLY MADE IT TO SCHOOL, FINNEGAN. YOU JUST LOOOVE DETENTION, DON'T YOU?
YOU KNOW IT'S MY HOME AWAY FROM HOME, MR. REES.
SIR REGINALD WELLINGTON
CORDIALLY INVITES YOU TO BE HIS GUEST AT
WELLINGTON MANSION, YORKSHIRE
FOR A FORMAL DINNER
THIS SATURDAY OF OCTOBER
1936
RSVP PATRICK (209) 555-1000
DID YOU GUYS GET ONE OF THESE?
YEAH, PATRICK'S PARENTS ARE OUT OF TOWN THIS WEEKEND. HE WANTS US ALL TO COME OVER AND HANG OUT.
HE WANTS TO HAVE A MYSTERY PARTY LIKE SATURDAY NIGHT, SO WE'LL ALL HAVE TO DRESS UP AND STUFF. YOU KNOW, KIND OF LIKE CLUE.
CLOVER, DO YOU THINK YOU CAN HANDLE THAT? DRESSING UP?
HMPH!
WHO'S ALL GOING? IT'S KIND OF LAST MINUTE.
WELL, I KNOW ERIN IS, AND I THINK ALAN AND VICTOR ARE...
YEAH, THERE WAS WAY TOO MUCH SMIRKING GOING ON BEFORE CLASS THIS MORNING FOR THEM NOT TO BE.

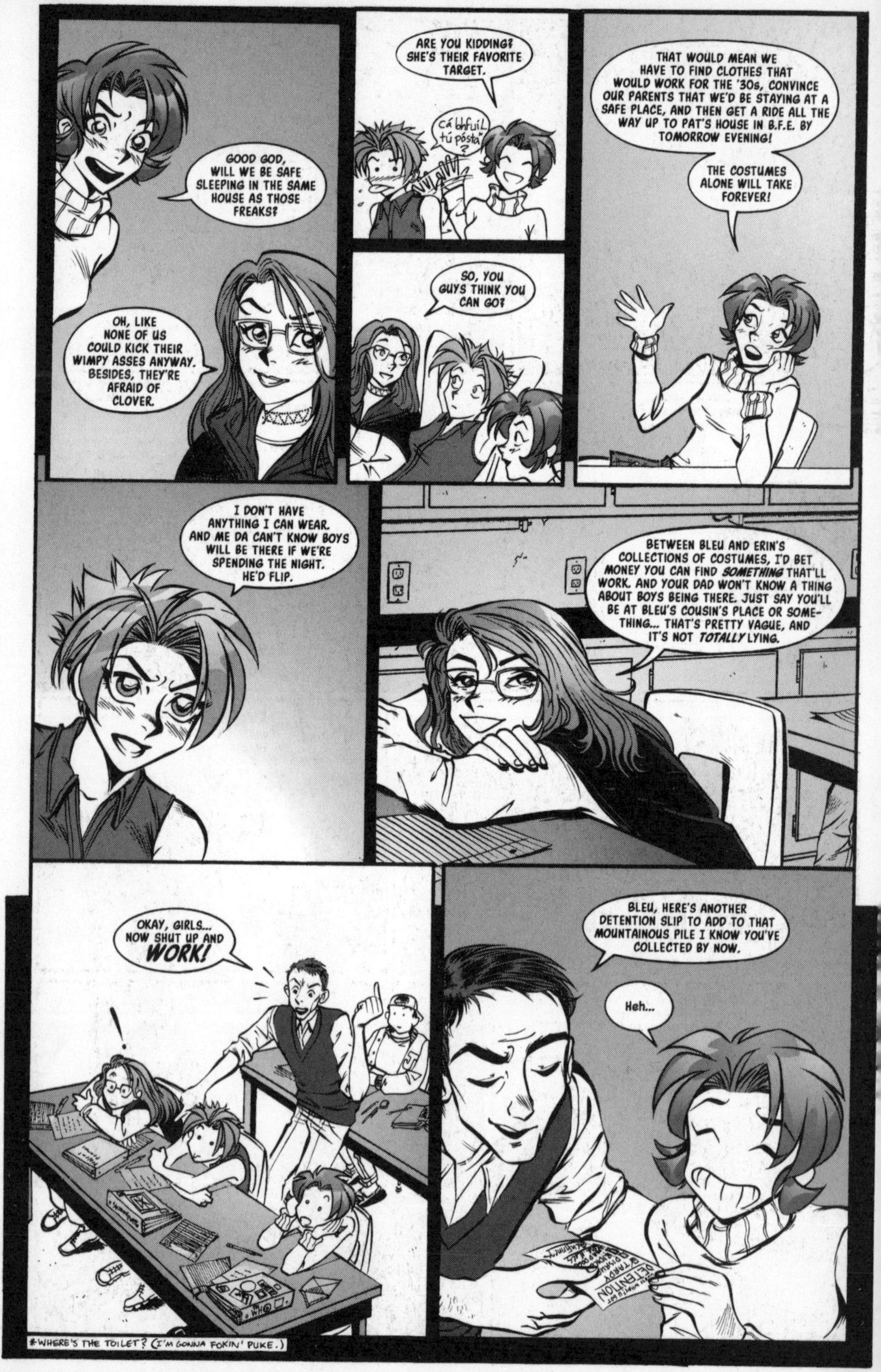
GOOD GOD, WILL WE BE SAFE SLEEPING IN THE SAME HOUSE AS THOSE FREAKS?
OH, LIKE NONE OF US COULD KICK THEIR WIMPY ASSES ANYWAY. BESIDES, THEY'RE AFRAID OF CLOVER.
ARE YOU KIDDING? SHE'S THEIR FAVORITE TARGET.
Cá bhfuiL tú pósta*?
SO, YOU GUYS THINK YOU CAN GO?
THAT WOULD MEAN WE HAVE TO FIND CLOTHES THAT WOULD WORK FOR THE '30s, CONVINCE OUR PARENTS THAT WE'D BE STAYING AT A SAFE PLACE, AND THEN GET A RIDE ALL THE WAY UP TO PAT'S HOUSE IN B.F.E. BY TOMORROW EVENING!
THE COSTUMES ALONE WILL TAKE FOREVER!
I DON'T HAVE ANYTHING I CAN WEAR. AND ME DA CAN'T KNOW BOYS WILL BE THERE IF WE'RE SPENDING THE NIGHT. HE'D FLIP.
BETWEEN BLEU AND ERIN'S COLLECTIONS OF COSTUMES, I'D BET MONEY YOU CAN FIND SOMETHING THAT'LL WORK. AND YOUR DAD WON'T KNOW A THING ABOUT BOYS BEING THERE. JUST SAY YOU'LL BE AT BLEU'S COUSIN'S PLACE OR SOMETHING... THAT'S PRETTY VAGUE, AND IT'S NOT TOTALLY LYING.
OKAY, GIRLS... NOW SHUT UP AND WORK!
!
BLEU, HERE'S ANOTHER DETENTION SLIP TO ADD TO THAT MOUNTAINOUS PILE I KNOW YOU'VE COLLECTED BY NOW.
Heh...
DETENTION
TARDY
*WHERE'S THE TOILET? (I'M GONNA FOKIN' PUKE.)

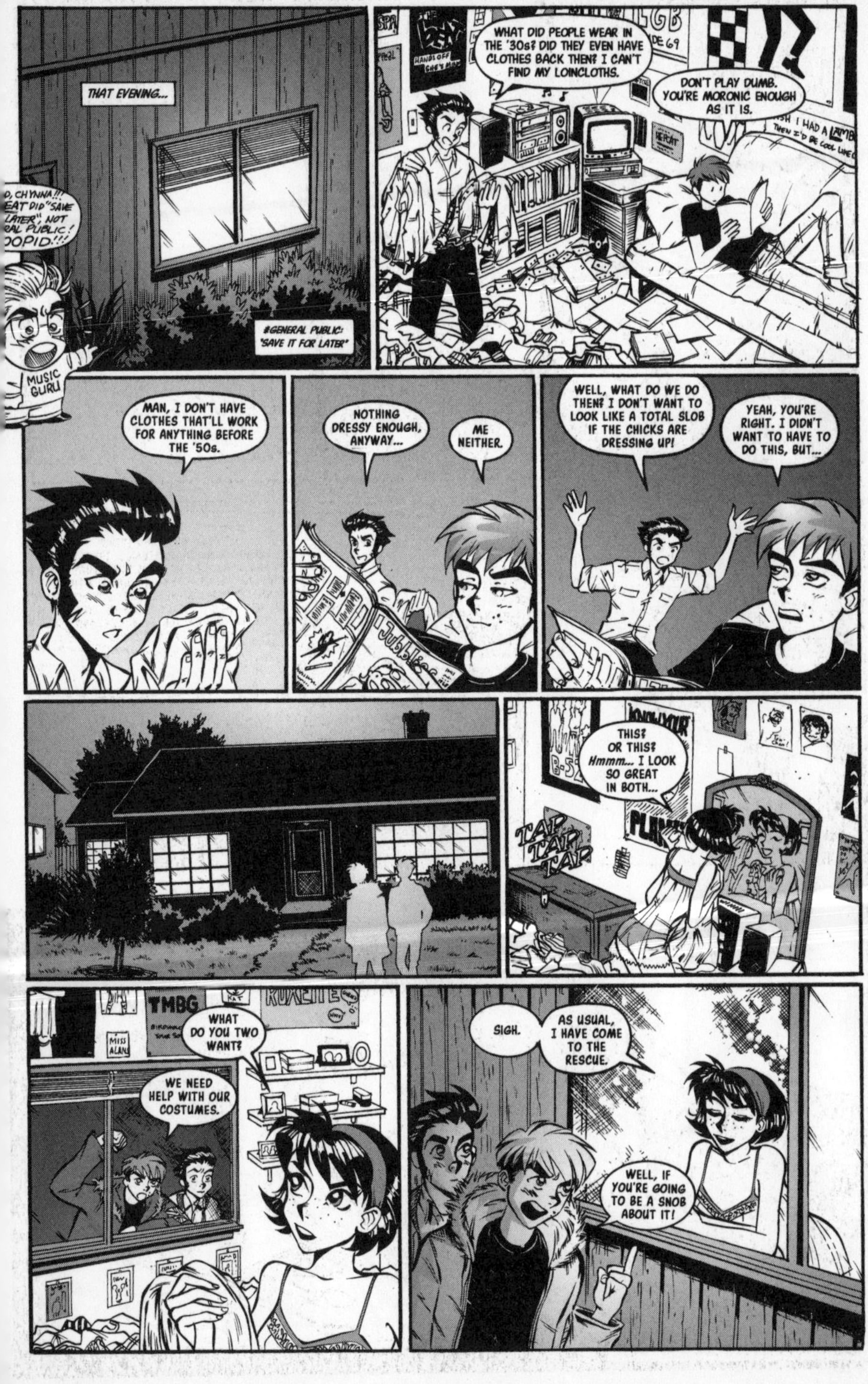

THAT EVENING...
#GENERAL PUBLIC: "SAVE IT FOR LATER"
WHAT DID PEOPLE WEAR IN THE '30s? DID THEY EVEN HAVE CLOTHES BACK THEN? I CAN'T FIND MY LOINCLOTHS.
DON'T PLAY DUMB. YOU'RE MORONIC ENOUGH AS IT IS.
MUSIC GURU
MAN, I DON'T HAVE CLOTHES THAT'LL WORK FOR ANYTHING BEFORE THE '50s.
NOTHING DRESSY ENOUGH, ANYWAY...
ME NEITHER.
WELL, WHAT DO WE DO THEN? I DON'T WANT TO LOOK LIKE A TOTAL SLOB IF THE CHICKS ARE DRESSING UP!
YEAH, YOU'RE RIGHT. I DIDN'T WANT TO HAVE TO DO THIS, BUT...
THIS? OR THIS? Hmmm... I LOOK SO GREAT IN BOTH...
TAP TAP TAP
WHAT DO YOU TWO WANT?
WE NEED HELP WITH OUR COSTUMES.
SIGH.
AS USUAL, I HAVE COME TO THE RESCUE.
WELL, IF YOU'RE GOING TO BE A SNOB ABOUT IT!

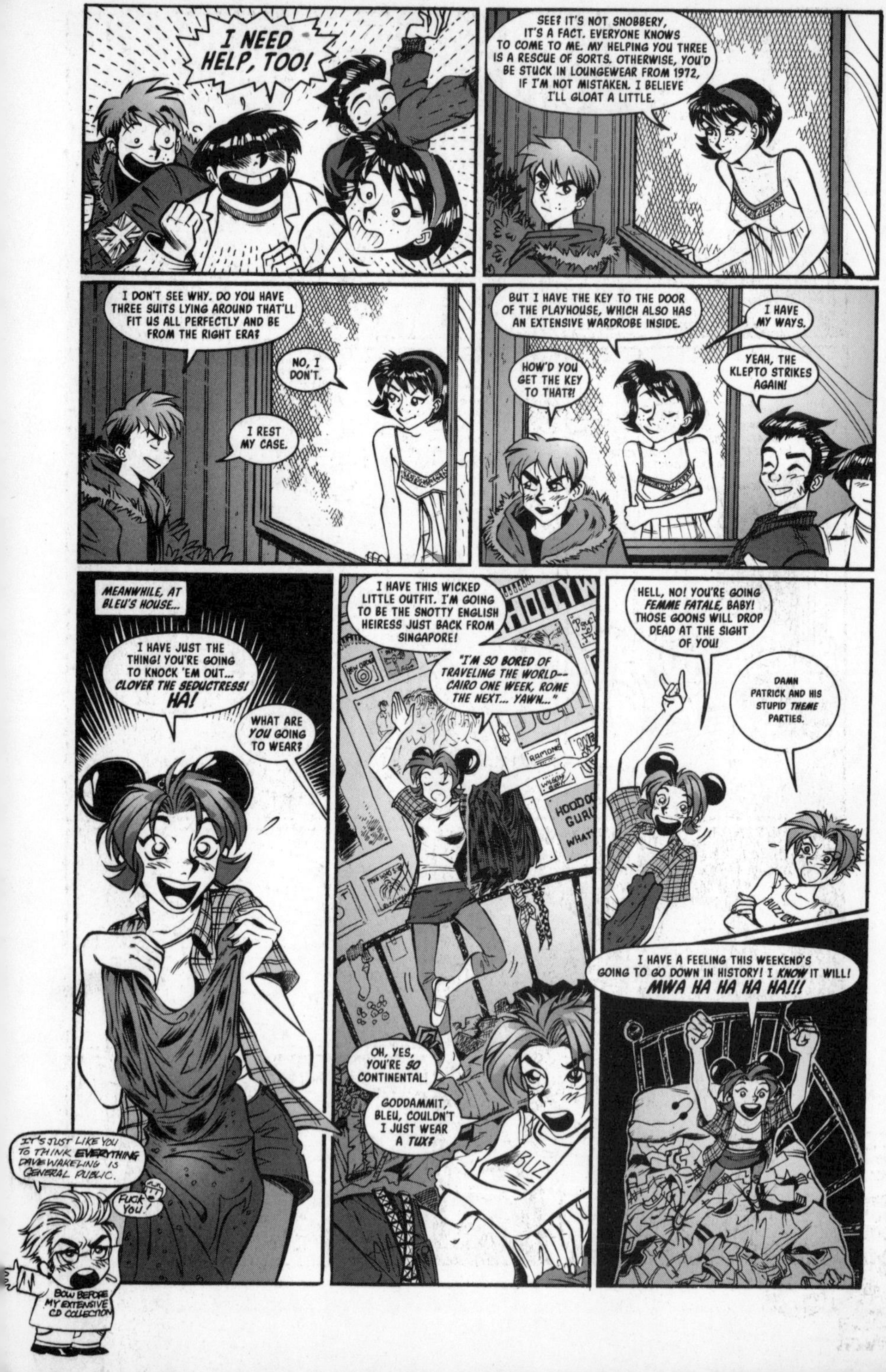
I NEED HELP, TOO!
SEE? IT'S NOT SNOBBERY, IT'S A FACT. EVERYONE KNOWS TO COME TO ME. MY HELPING YOU THREE IS A RESCUE OF SORTS. OTHERWISE, YOU'D BE STUCK IN LOUNGEWEAR FROM 1972, IF I'M NOT MISTAKEN. I BELIEVE I'LL GLOAT A LITTLE.
I DON'T SEE WHY. DO YOU HAVE THREE SUITS LYING AROUND THAT'LL FIT US ALL PERFECTLY AND BE FROM THE RIGHT ERA?
NO, I DON'T.
I REST MY CASE.
BUT I HAVE THE KEY TO THE DOOR OF THE PLAYHOUSE, WHICH ALSO HAS AN EXTENSIVE WARDROBE INSIDE.
HOW'D YOU GET THE KEY TO THAT?!
I HAVE MY WAYS.
YEAH, THE KLEPTO STRIKES AGAIN!
MEANWHILE, AT BLEU'S HOUSE...
I HAVE JUST THE THING! YOU'RE GOING TO KNOCK 'EM OUT... CLOVER THE SEDUCTRESS! HA!
WHAT ARE YOU GOING TO WEAR?
I HAVE THIS WICKED LITTLE OUTFIT. I'M GOING TO BE THE SNOTTY ENGLISH HEIRESS JUST BACK FROM SINGAPORE!
"I'M SO BORED OF TRAVELING THE WORLD-- CAIRO ONE WEEK, ROME THE NEXT... YAWN..."
OH, YES, YOU'RE SO CONTINENTAL.
GODDAMMIT, BLEU, COULDN'T I JUST WEAR A TUX?
HELL, NO! YOU'RE GOING FEMME FATALE, BABY! THOSE GOONS WILL DROP DEAD AT THE SIGHT OF YOU!
DAMN PATRICK AND HIS STUPID THEME PARTIES.
I HAVE A FEELING THIS WEEKEND'S GOING TO GO DOWN IN HISTORY! I KNOW IT WILL! MWA HA HA HA HA!!!
IT'S JUST LIKE YOU TO THINK EVERYTHING DAVE WAKELING IS GENERAL PUBLIC.
FUCK YOU!
BOW BEFORE MY EXTENSIVE CD COLLECTION

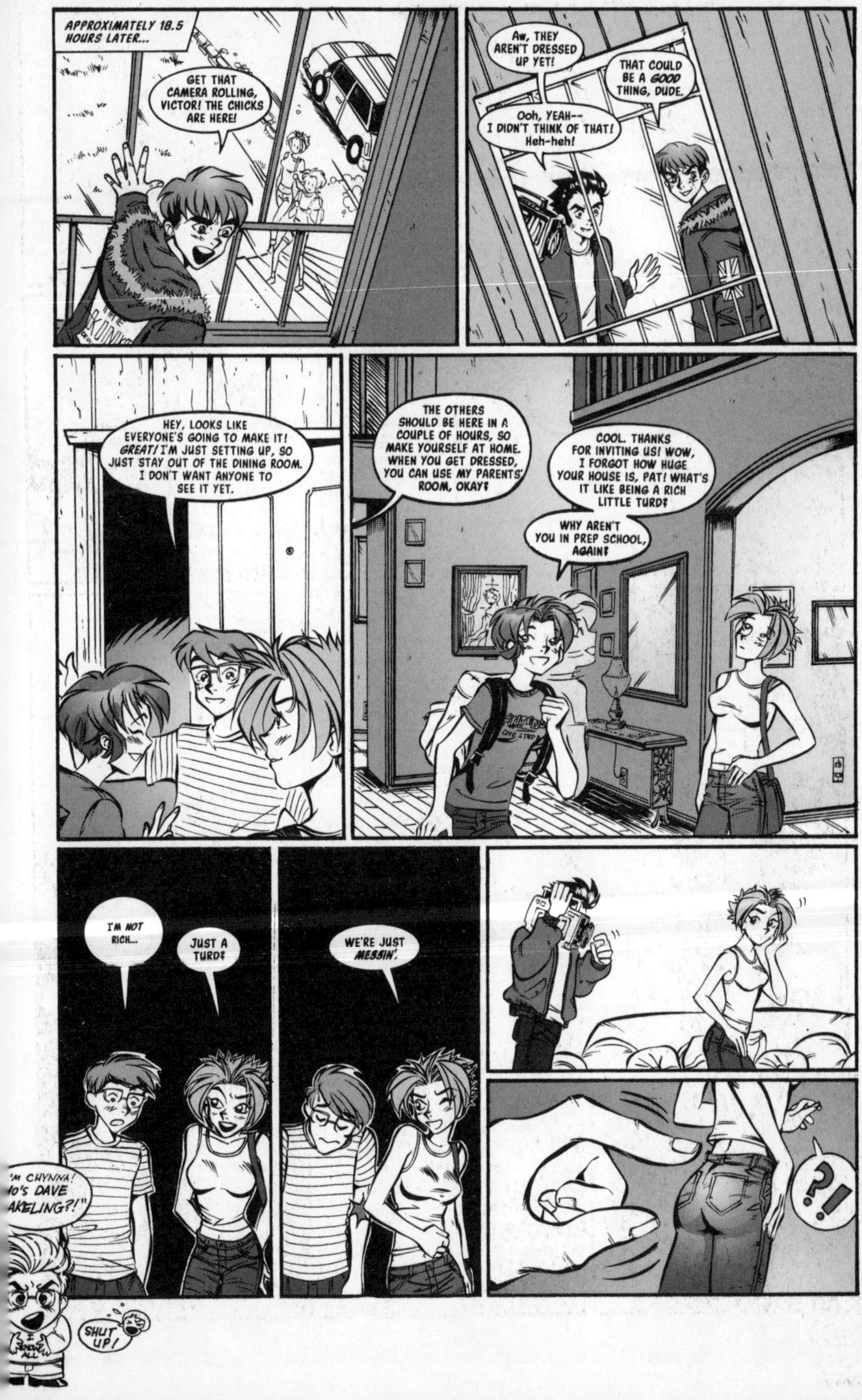
APPROXIMATELY 18.5 HOURS LATER...
GET THAT CAMERA ROLLING, VICTOR! THE CHICKS ARE HERE!
Aw, THEY AREN'T DRESSED UP YET!
THAT COULD BE A GOOD THING, DUDE.
Ooh, YEAH-- I DIDN'T THINK OF THAT! Heh-heh!
HEY, LOOKS LIKE EVERYONE'S GOING TO MAKE IT! GREAT! I'M JUST SETTING UP, SO JUST STAY OUT OF THE DINING ROOM. I DON'T WANT ANYONE TO SEE IT YET.
THE OTHERS SHOULD BE HERE IN A COUPLE OF HOURS, SO MAKE YOURSELF AT HOME. WHEN YOU GET DRESSED, YOU CAN USE MY PARENTS' ROOM, OKAY?
COOL. THANKS FOR INVITING US! WOW, I FORGOT HOW HUGE YOUR HOUSE IS, PAT! WHAT'S IT LIKE BEING A RICH LITTLE TURD?
WHY AREN'T YOU IN PREP SCHOOL, AGAIN?
I'M NOT RICH...
JUST A TURD?
WE'RE JUST MESSIN'.
?!
'M CHYNNA! HO'S DAVE AKELING?!"
SHUT UP!

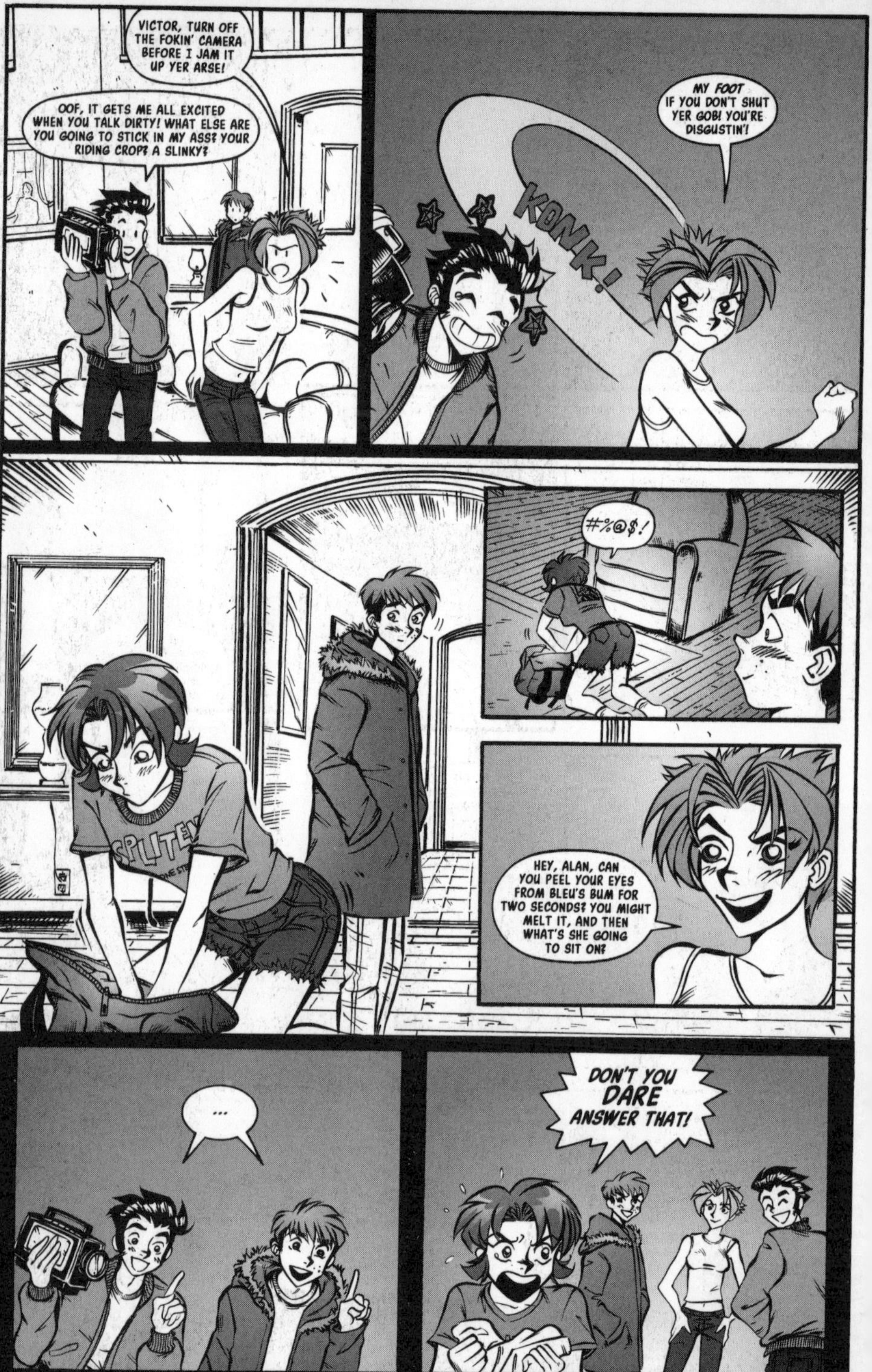
VICTOR, TURN OFF THE FOKIN' CAMERA BEFORE I JAM IT UP YER ARSE!
OOF, IT GETS ME ALL EXCITED WHEN YOU TALK DIRTY! WHAT ELSE ARE YOU GOING TO STICK IN MY ASS? YOUR RIDING CROP? A SLINKY?
MY FOOT IF YOU DON'T SHUT YER GOB! YOU'RE DISGUSTIN'!
KONK!
#%@$!
HEY, ALAN, CAN YOU PEEL YOUR EYES FROM BLEU'S BUM FOR TWO SECONDS? YOU MIGHT MELT IT, AND THEN WHAT'S SHE GOING TO SIT ON?
...
DON'T YOU DARE ANSWER THAT!

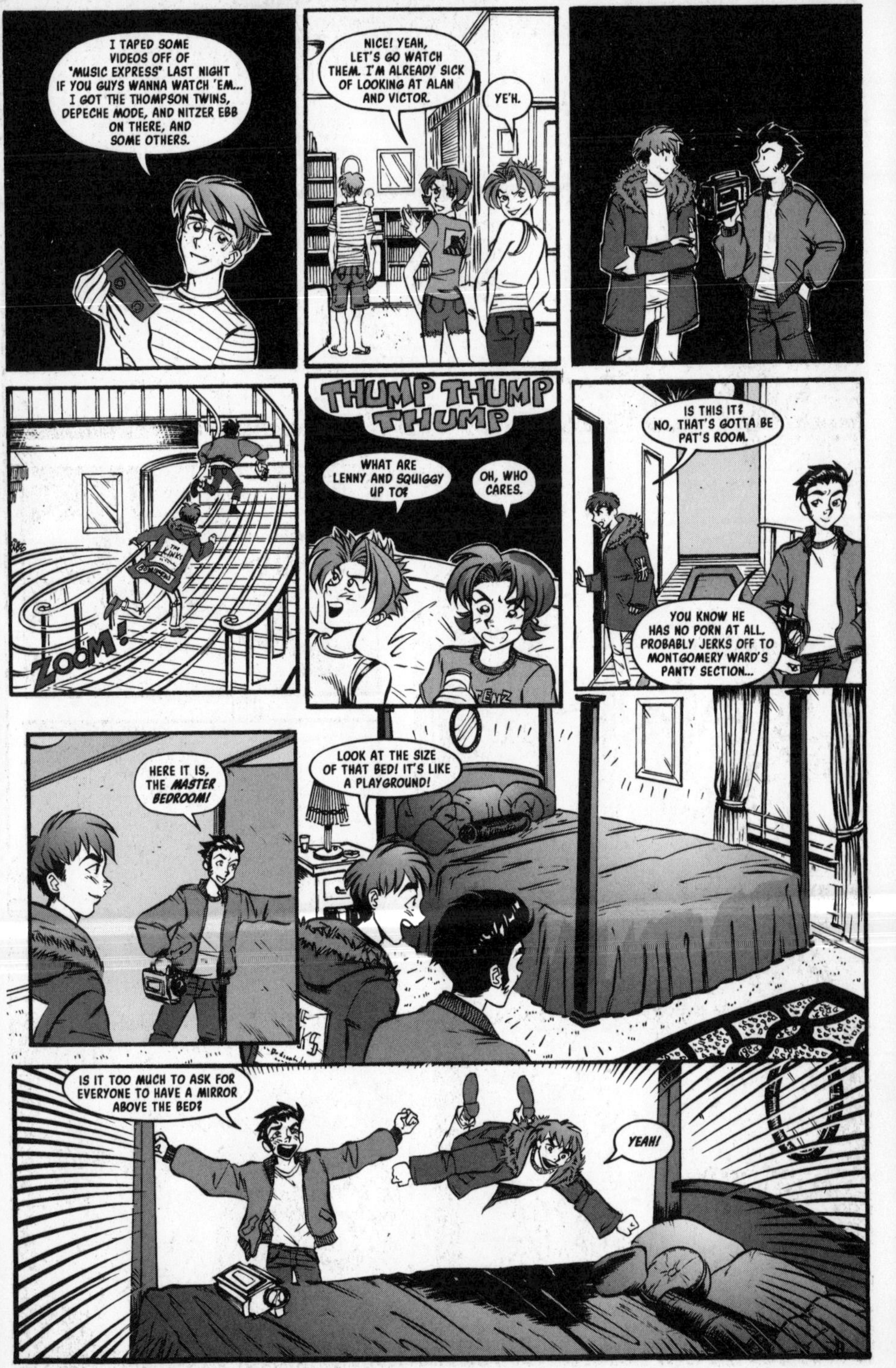
I TAPED SOME VIDEOS OFF OF "MUSIC EXPRESS" LAST NIGHT IF YOU GUYS WANNA WATCH 'EM... I GOT THE THOMPSON TWINS, DEPECHE MODE, AND NITZER EBB ON THERE, AND SOME OTHERS.
NICE! YEAH, LET'S GO WATCH THEM. I'M ALREADY SICK OF LOOKING AT ALAN AND VICTOR.
YE'H.
ZOOM!
THUMP THUMP THUMP
WHAT ARE LENNY AND SQUIGGY UP TO?
OH, WHO CARES.
IS THIS IT? NO, THAT'S GOTTA BE PAT'S ROOM.
YOU KNOW HE HAS NO PORN AT ALL. PROBABLY JERKS OFF TO MONTGOMERY WARD'S PANTY SECTION...
HERE IT IS, THE MASTER BEDROOM!
LOOK AT THE SIZE OF THAT BED! IT'S LIKE A PLAYGROUND!
IS IT TOO MUCH TO ASK FOR EVERYONE TO HAVE A MIRROR ABOVE THE BED?
YEAH!

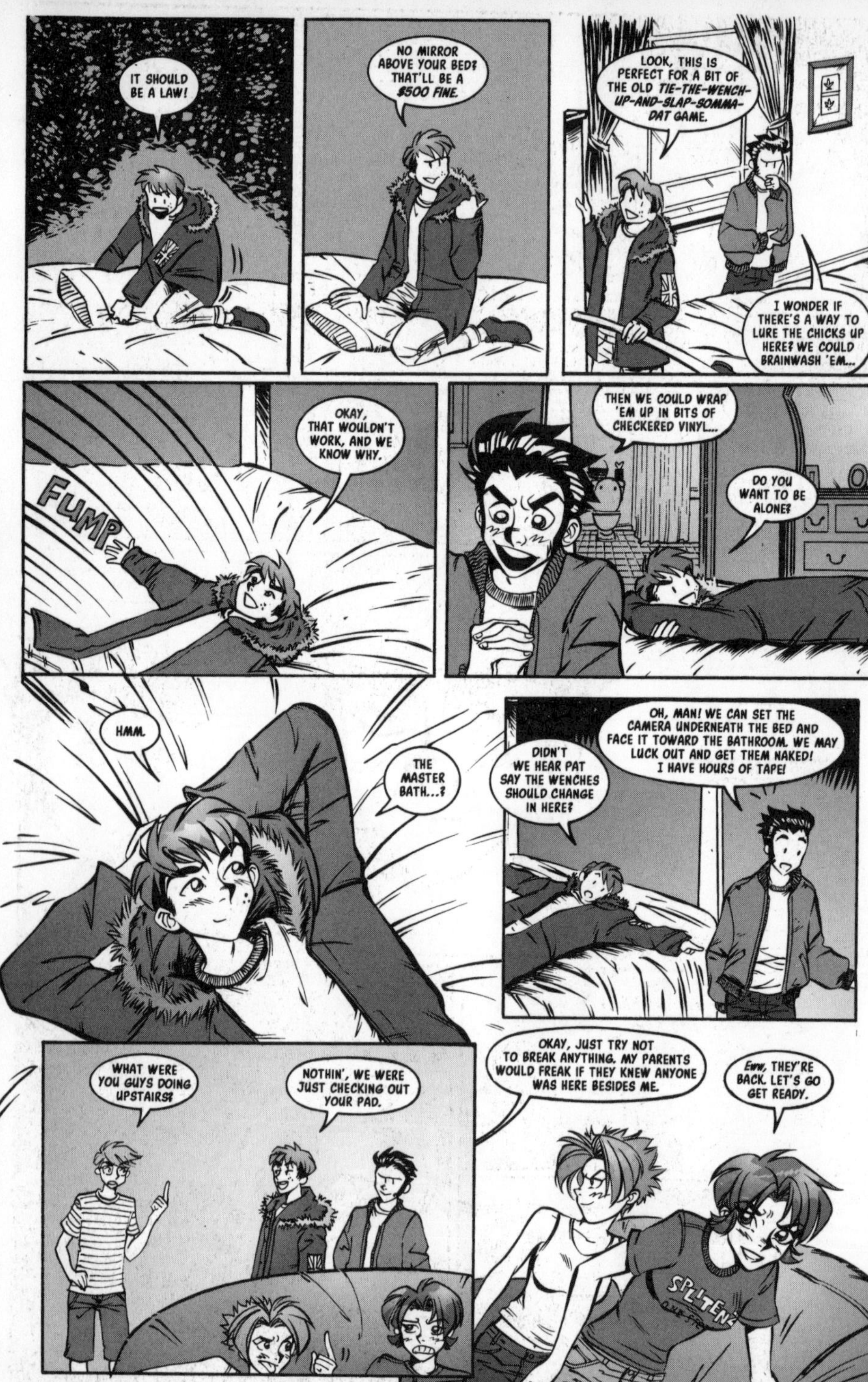
IT SHOULD BE A LAW!
NO MIRROR ABOVE YOUR BED? THAT'LL BE A $500 FINE.
LOOK, THIS IS PERFECT FOR A BIT OF THE OLD TIE-THE-WENCH-UP-AND-SLAP-SOMMA-DAT GAME.
I WONDER IF THERE'S A WAY TO LURE THE CHICKS UP HERE? WE COULD BRAINWASH 'EM...
FUMP
OKAY, THAT WOULDN'T WORK, AND WE KNOW WHY.
THEN WE COULD WRAP 'EM UP IN BITS OF CHECKERED VINYL...
DO YOU WANT TO BE ALONE?
HMM.
THE MASTER BATH...?
DIDN'T WE HEAR PAT SAY THE WENCHES SHOULD CHANGE IN HERE?
OH, MAN! WE CAN SET THE CAMERA UNDERNEATH THE BED AND FACE IT TOWARD THE BATHROOM. WE MAY LUCK OUT AND GET THEM NAKED! I HAVE HOURS OF TAPE!
WHAT WERE YOU GUYS DOING UPSTAIRS?
NOTHIN', WE WERE JUST CHECKING OUT YOUR PAD.
OKAY, JUST TRY NOT TO BREAK ANYTHING. MY PARENTS WOULD FREAK IF THEY KNEW ANYONE WAS HERE BESIDES ME.
Eww, THEY'RE BACK. LET'S GO GET READY.

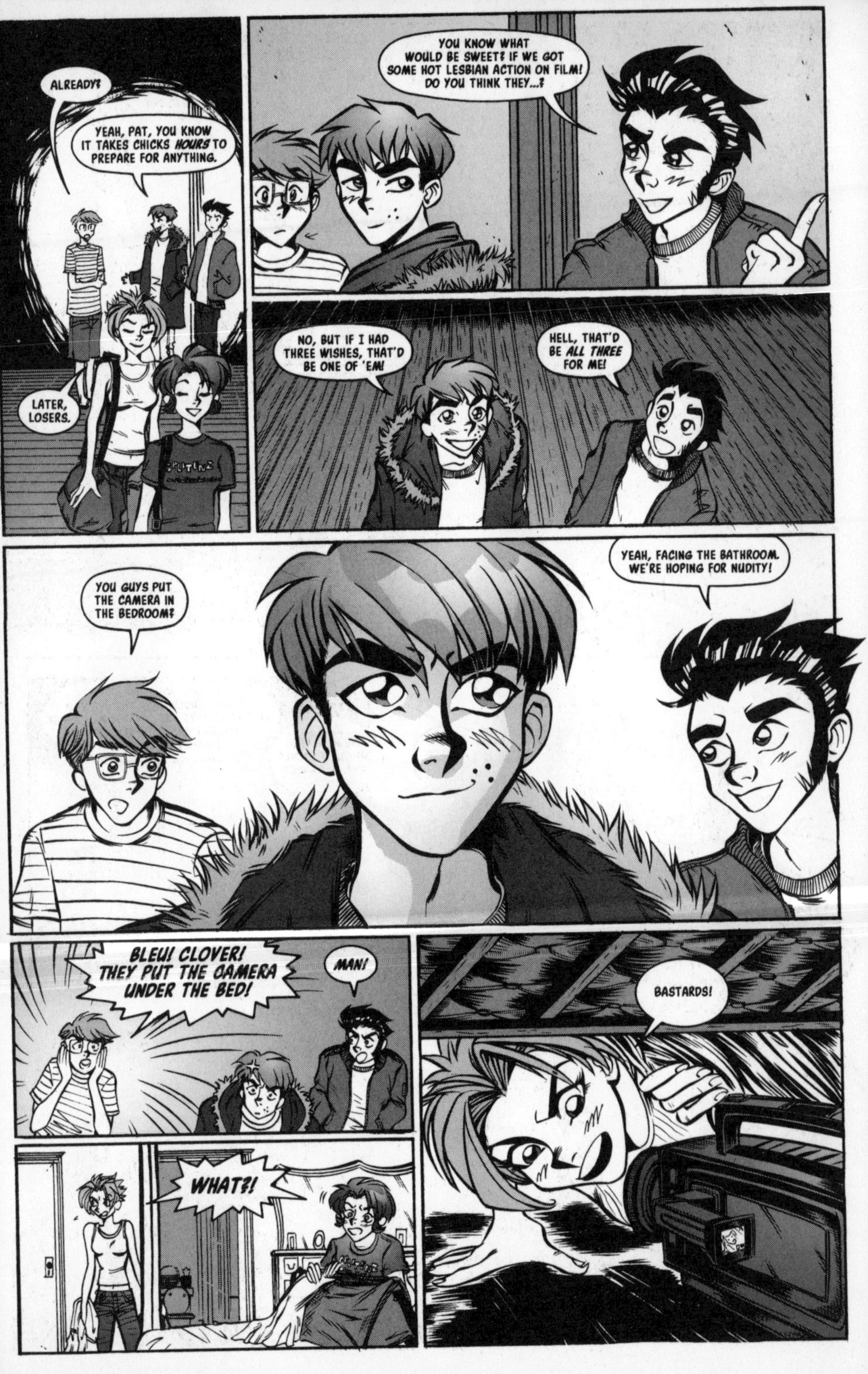
ALREADY?
YEAH, PAT, YOU KNOW IT TAKES CHICKS HOURS TO PREPARE FOR ANYTHING.
LATER, LOSERS.
YOU KNOW WHAT WOULD BE SWEET? IF WE GOT SOME HOT LESBIAN ACTION ON FILM! DO YOU THINK THEY...?
NO, BUT IF I HAD THREE WISHES, THAT'D BE ONE OF 'EM!
HELL, THAT'D BE ALL THREE FOR ME!
YOU GUYS PUT THE CAMERA IN THE BEDROOM?
YEAH, FACING THE BATHROOM. WE'RE HOPING FOR NUDITY!
BLEU! CLOVER! THEY PUT THE CAMERA UNDER THE BED!
MAN!
WHAT?!
BASTARDS!

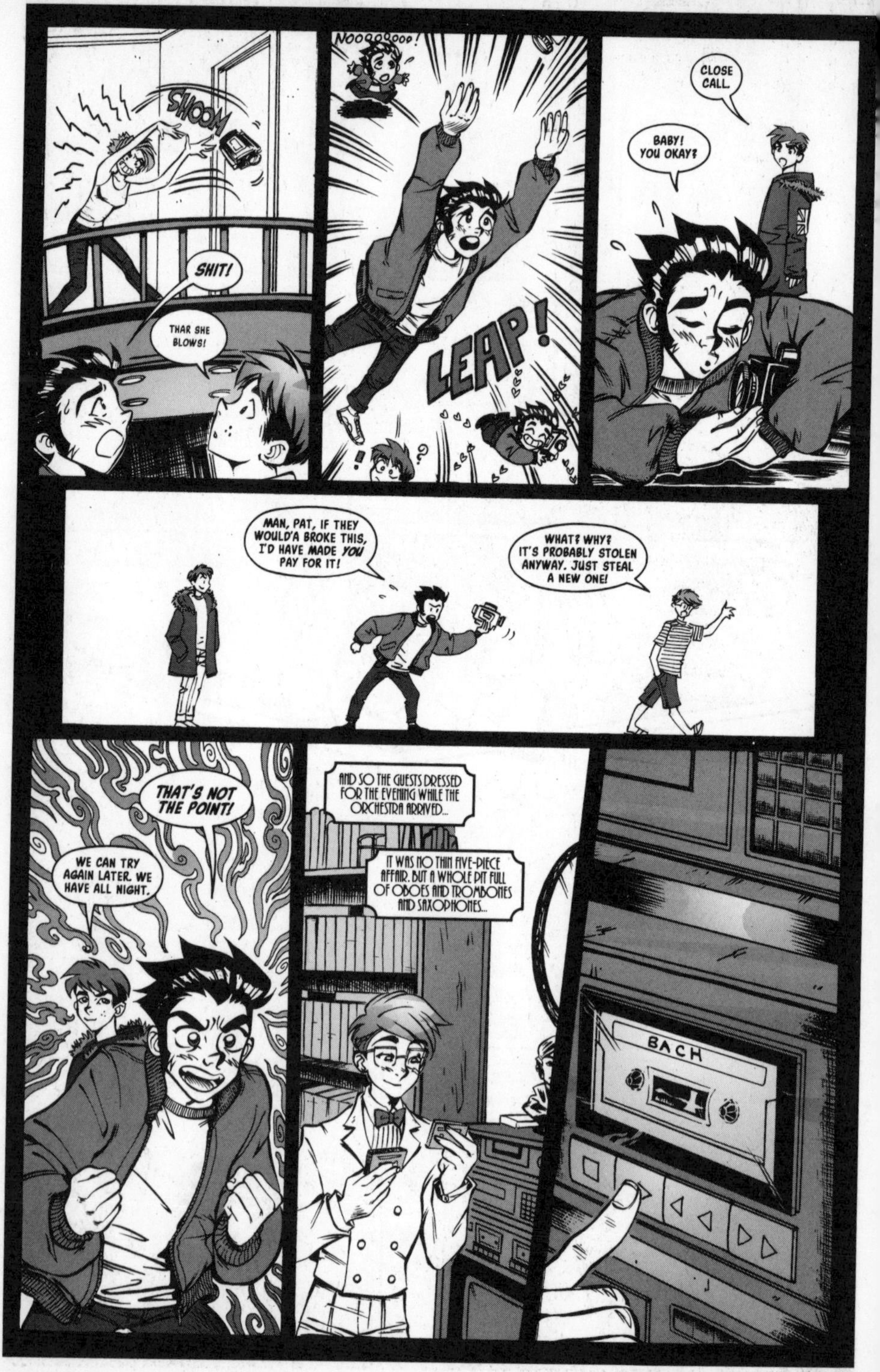
SHOOM
SHIT!
THAR SHE BLOWS!
NOOOOOOOO!
LEAP!
CLOSE CALL.
BABY! YOU OKAY?
MAN, PAT, IF THEY WOULD'A BROKE THIS, I'D HAVE MADE *YOU* PAY FOR IT!
WHAT? WHY? IT'S PROBABLY STOLEN ANYWAY. JUST STEAL A NEW ONE!
THAT'S NOT THE POINT!
WE CAN TRY AGAIN LATER. WE HAVE ALL NIGHT.
AND SO THE GUESTS DRESSED FOR THE EVENING WHILE THE ORCHESTRA ARRIVED...
IT WAS NO THIN FIVE-PIECE AFFAIR. BUT A WHOLE PIT FULL OF OBOES AND TROMBONES AND SAXOPHONES...
BACH

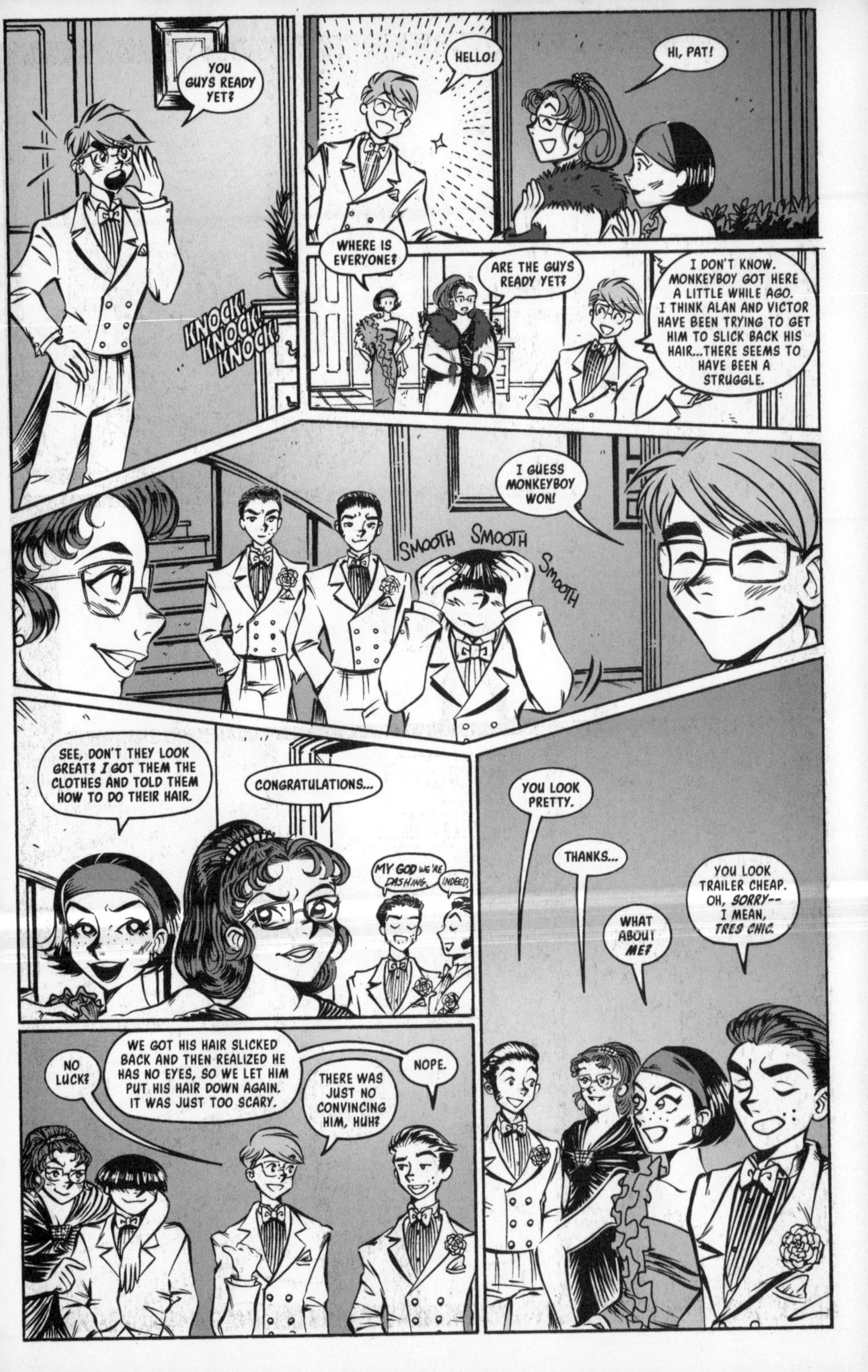
YOU GUYS READY YET?
KNOCK! KNOCK! KNOCK!
HELLO!
HI, PAT!
WHERE IS EVERYONE?
ARE THE GUYS READY YET?
I DON'T KNOW. MONKEYBOY GOT HERE A LITTLE WHILE AGO. I THINK ALAN AND VICTOR HAVE BEEN TRYING TO GET HIM TO SLICK BACK HIS HAIR...THERE SEEMS TO HAVE BEEN A STRUGGLE.
I GUESS MONKEYBOY WON!
SMOOTH SMOOTH SMOOTH
SEE, DON'T THEY LOOK GREAT? I GOT THEM THE CLOTHES AND TOLD THEM HOW TO DO THEIR HAIR.
CONGRATULATIONS...
MY GOD WE'RE DASHING.
INDEED.
YOU LOOK PRETTY.
THANKS...
WHAT ABOUT ME?
YOU LOOK TRAILER CHEAP. OH, SORRY-- I MEAN, TRES CHIC.
NO LUCK?
WE GOT HIS HAIR SLICKED BACK AND THEN REALIZED HE HAS NO EYES, SO WE LET HIM PUT HIS HAIR DOWN AGAIN. IT WAS JUST TOO SCARY.
THERE WAS JUST NO CONVINCING HIM, HUH?
NOPE.

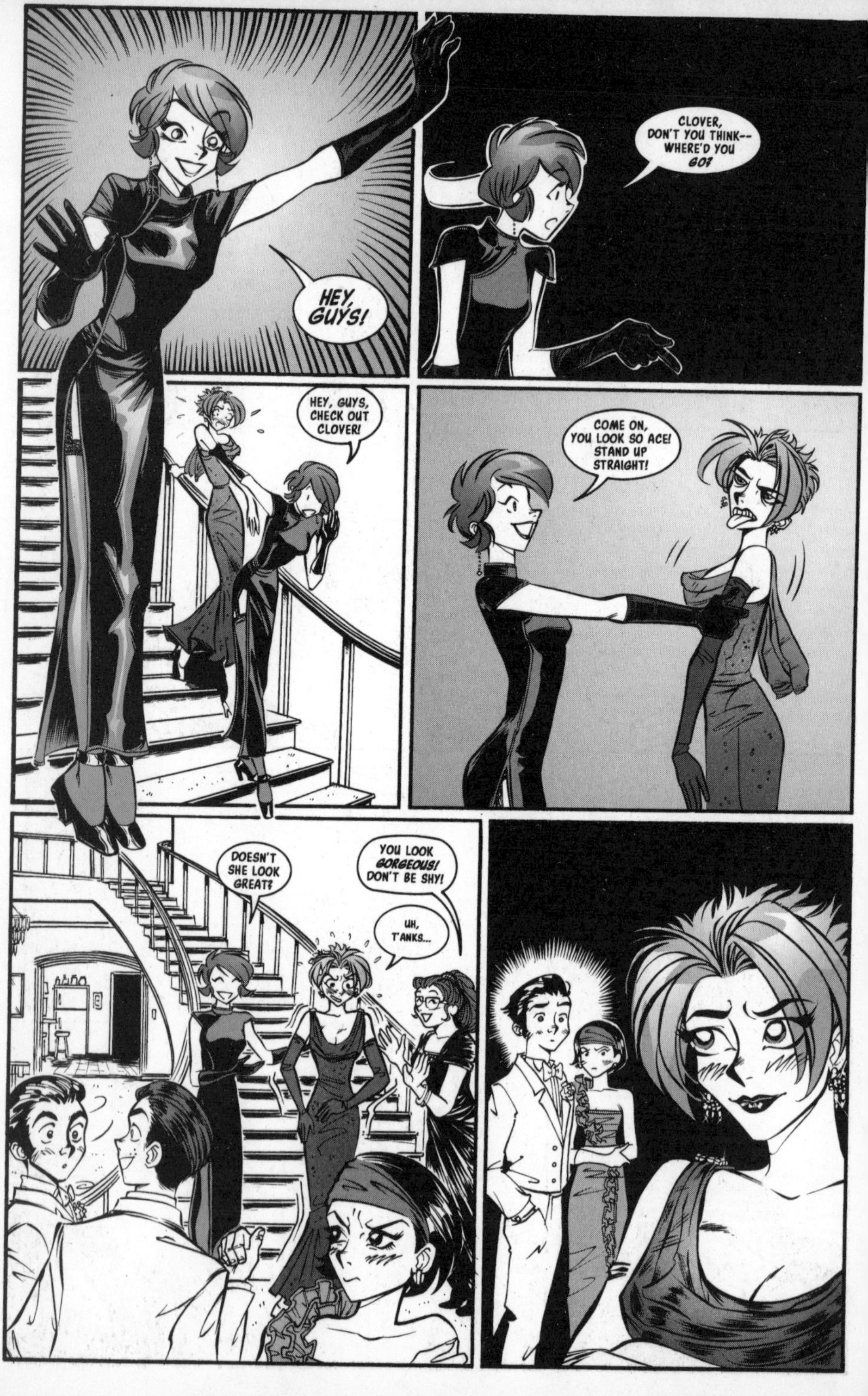
HEY, GUYS!
CLOVER, DON'T YOU THINK-- WHERE'D YOU GO?
HEY, GUYS, CHECK OUT CLOVER!
COME ON, YOU LOOK SO ACE! STAND UP STRAIGHT!
DOESN'T SHE LOOK GREAT?
YOU LOOK GORGEOUS! DON'T BE SHY!
UH, T'ANKS...

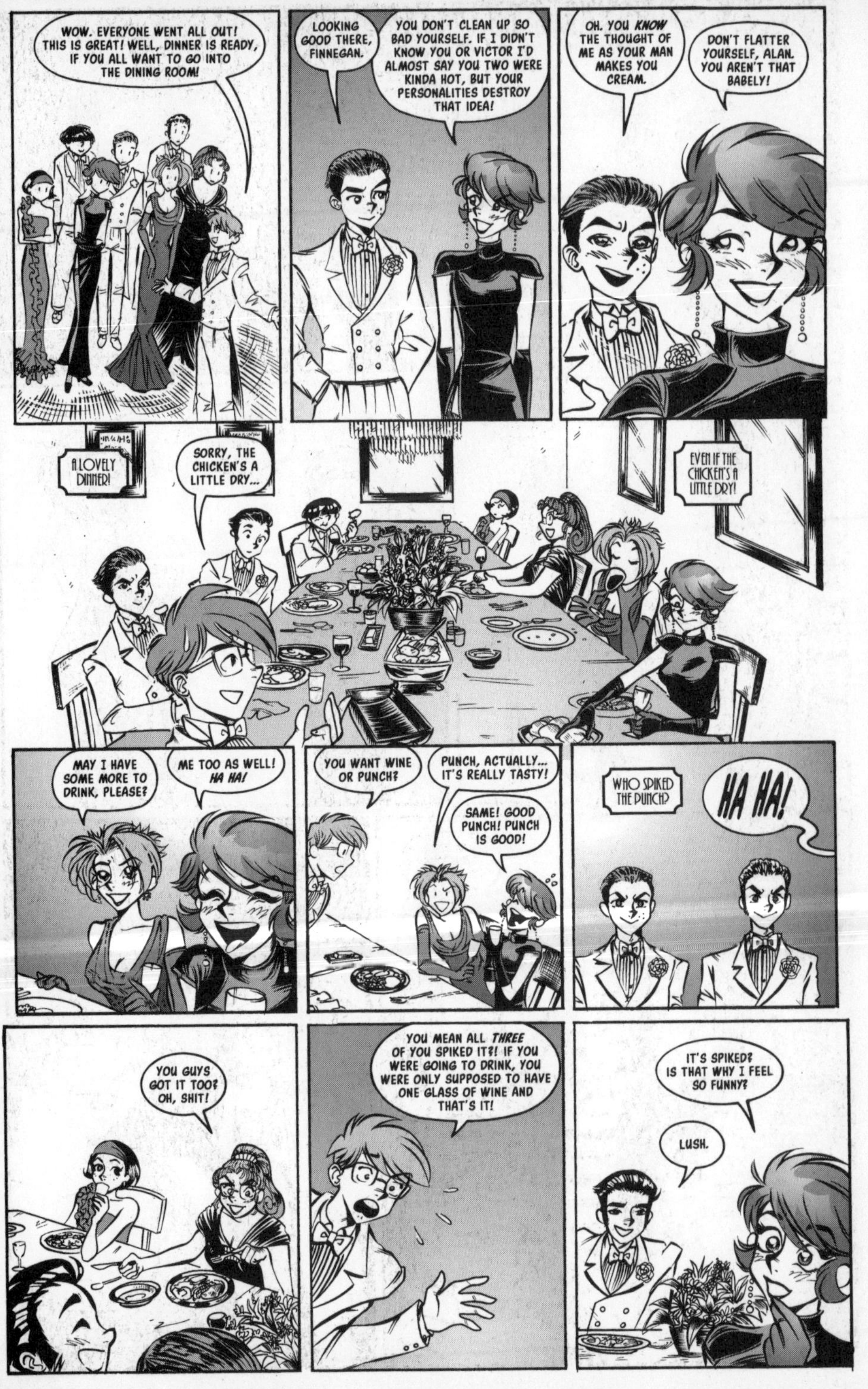
WOW. EVERYONE WENT ALL OUT! THIS IS GREAT! WELL, DINNER IS READY, IF YOU ALL WANT TO GO INTO THE DINING ROOM!
LOOKING GOOD THERE, FINNEGAN.
YOU DON'T CLEAN UP SO BAD YOURSELF. IF I DIDN'T KNOW YOU OR VICTOR I'D ALMOST SAY YOU TWO WERE KINDA HOT, BUT YOUR PERSONALITIES DESTROY THAT IDEA!
OH. YOU KNOW THE THOUGHT OF ME AS YOUR MAN MAKES YOU CREAM.
DON'T FLATTER YOURSELF, ALAN. YOU AREN'T THAT BABELY!
A LOVELY DINNER!
SORRY, THE CHICKEN'S A LITTLE DRY...
EVEN IF THE CHICKEN'S A LITTLE DRY!
MAY I HAVE SOME MORE TO DRINK, PLEASE?
ME TOO AS WELL! HA HA!
YOU WANT WINE OR PUNCH?
PUNCH, ACTUALLY... IT'S REALLY TASTY!
SAME! GOOD PUNCH! PUNCH IS GOOD!
WHO SPIKED THE PUNCH?
HA HA!
YOU GUYS GOT IT TOO? OH, SHIT!
YOU MEAN ALL THREE OF YOU SPIKED IT?! IF YOU WERE GOING TO DRINK, YOU WERE ONLY SUPPOSED TO HAVE ONE GLASS OF WINE AND THAT'S IT!
IT'S SPIKED? IS THAT WHY I FEEL SO FUNNY?
LUSH.

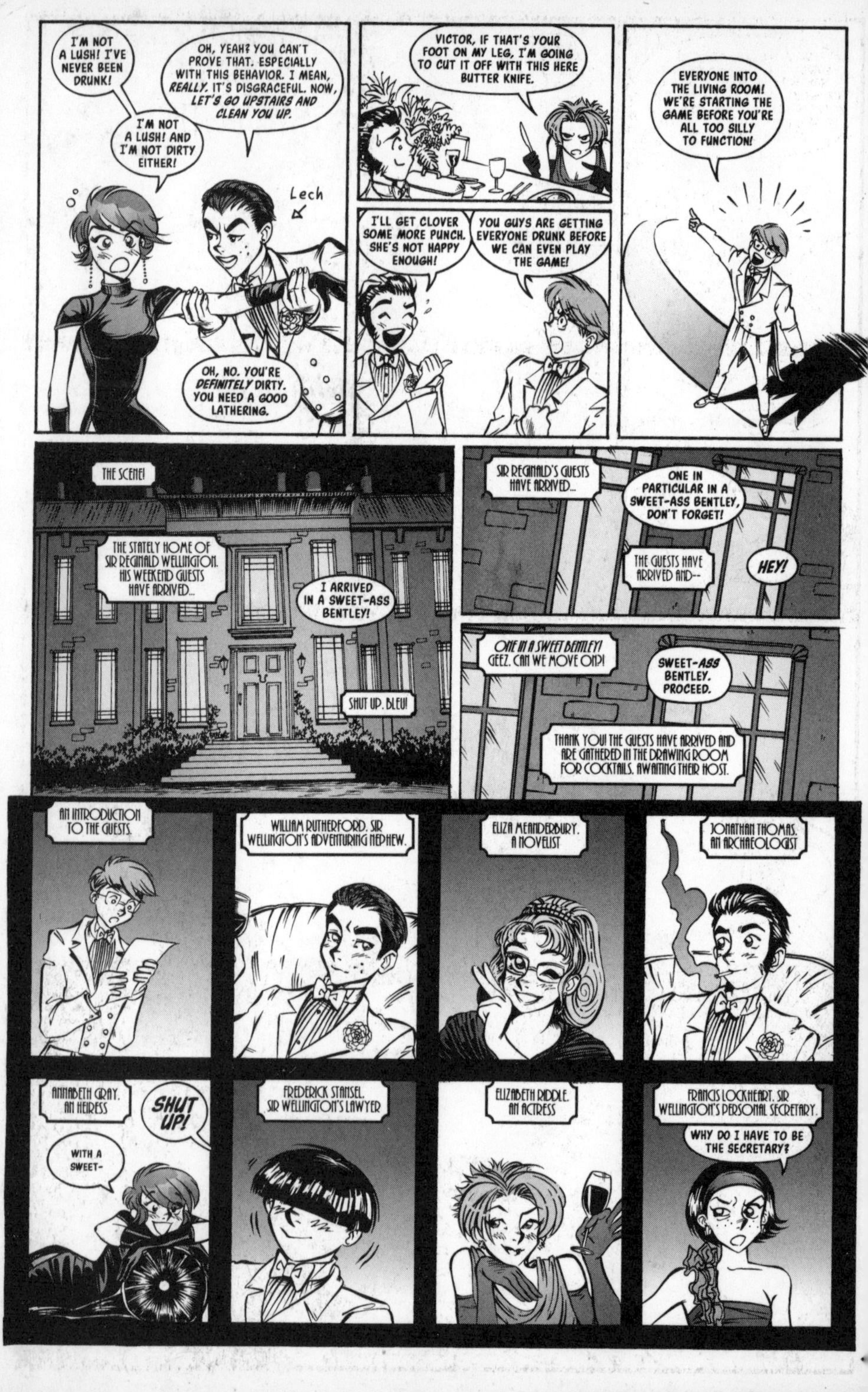
I'M NOT A LUSH! I'VE NEVER BEEN DRUNK!
OH, YEAH? YOU CAN'T PROVE THAT. ESPECIALLY WITH THIS BEHAVIOR. I MEAN, REALLY. IT'S DISGRACEFUL. NOW, LET'S GO UPSTAIRS AND CLEAN YOU UP.
I'M NOT A LUSH! AND I'M NOT DIRTY EITHER!
Lech
OH, NO. YOU'RE DEFINITELY DIRTY. YOU NEED A GOOD LATHERING.
VICTOR, IF THAT'S YOUR FOOT ON MY LEG, I'M GOING TO CUT IT OFF WITH THIS HERE BUTTER KNIFE.
I'LL GET CLOVER SOME MORE PUNCH. SHE'S NOT HAPPY ENOUGH!
YOU GUYS ARE GETTING EVERYONE DRUNK BEFORE WE CAN EVEN PLAY THE GAME!
EVERYONE INTO THE LIVING ROOM! WE'RE STARTING THE GAME BEFORE YOU'RE ALL TOO SILLY TO FUNCTION!
THE SCENE!
THE STATELY HOME OF SIR REGINALD WELLINGTON. HIS WEEKEND GUESTS HAVE ARRIVED...
I ARRIVED IN A SWEET-ASS BENTLEY!
SHUT UP, BLEU!
SIR REGINALD'S GUESTS HAVE ARRIVED...
ONE IN PARTICULAR IN A SWEET-ASS BENTLEY, DON'T FORGET!
THE GUESTS HAVE ARRIVED AND--
HEY!
ONE IN A SWEET BENTLEY! GEEZ. CAN WE MOVE ON?!
SWEET-ASS BENTLEY. PROCEED.
THANK YOU! THE GUESTS HAVE ARRIVED AND ARE GATHERED IN THE DRAWING ROOM FOR COCKTAILS, AWAITING THEIR HOST.
AN INTRODUCTION TO THE GUESTS.
WILLIAM RUTHERFORD, SIR WELLINGTON'S ADVENTURING NEPHEW.
ELIZA MEANDERBURY, A NOVELIST
JONATHAN THOMAS, AN ARCHAEOLOGIST
ANNABETH GRAY, AN HEIRESS
SHUT UP!
WITH A SWEET-
FREDERICK STANSEL, SIR WELLINGTON'S LAWYER
ELIZABETH RIDDLE, AN ACTRESS
FRANCIS LOCKHEART, SIR WELLINGTON'S PERSONAL SECRETARY.
WHY DO I HAVE TO BE THE SECRETARY?

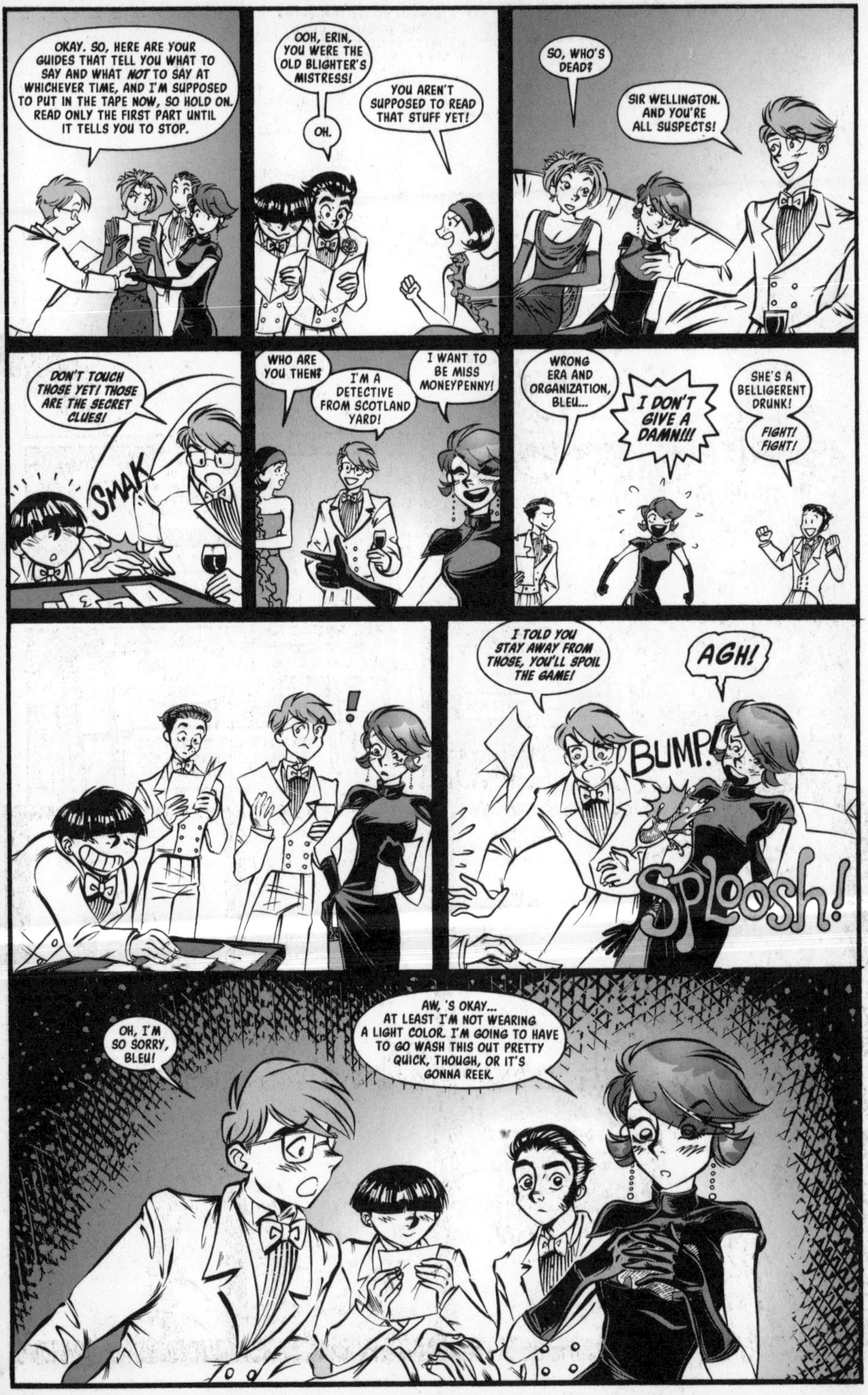
OKAY. SO, HERE ARE YOUR GUIDES THAT TELL YOU WHAT TO SAY AND WHAT *NOT* TO SAY AT WHICHEVER TIME, AND I'M SUPPOSED TO PUT IN THE TAPE NOW, SO HOLD ON. READ ONLY THE FIRST PART UNTIL IT TELLS YOU TO STOP.
OOH, ERIN, YOU WERE THE OLD BLIGHTER'S MISTRESS!
OH.
YOU AREN'T SUPPOSED TO READ THAT STUFF YET!
SO, WHO'S DEAD?
SIR WELLINGTON. AND YOU'RE ALL SUSPECTS!
DON'T TOUCH THOSE YET! THOSE ARE THE SECRET CLUES!
SMAK
WHO ARE YOU THEN?
I'M A DETECTIVE FROM SCOTLAND YARD!
I WANT TO BE MISS MONEYPENNY!
WRONG ERA AND ORGANIZATION, BLEU...
I DON'T GIVE A DAMN!!!
SHE'S A BELLIGERENT DRUNK!
FIGHT! FIGHT!
!
I TOLD YOU STAY AWAY FROM THOSE, YOU'LL SPOIL THE GAME!
AGH!
BUMP!
SPLOOSH!
OH, I'M SO SORRY, BLEU!
AW, 'S OKAY... AT LEAST I'M NOT WEARING A LIGHT COLOR. I'M GOING TO HAVE TO GO WASH THIS OUT PRETTY QUICK, THOUGH, OR IT'S GONNA REEK.

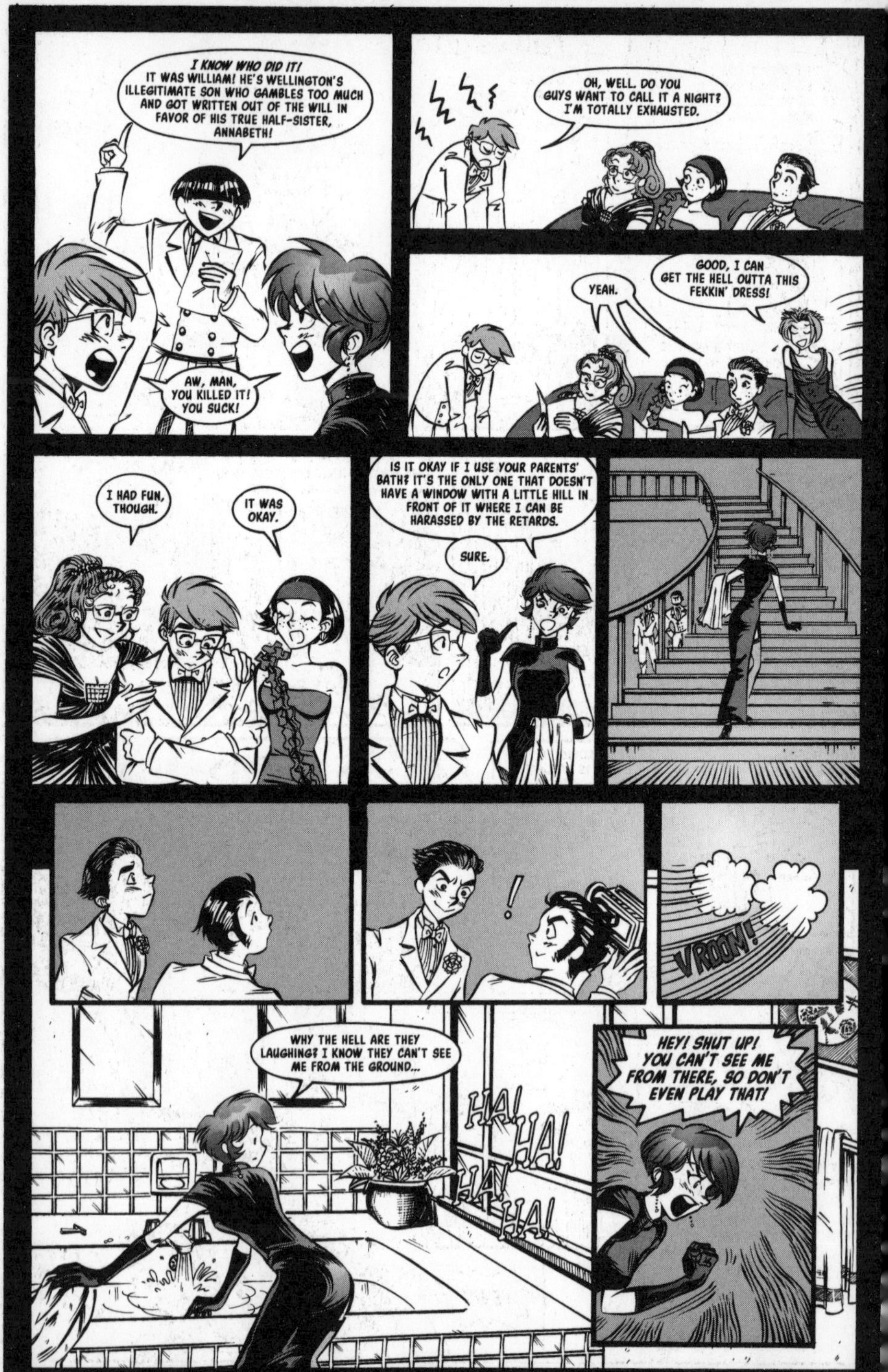
I KNOW WHO DID IT! IT WAS WILLIAM! HE'S WELLINGTON'S ILLEGITIMATE SON WHO GAMBLES TOO MUCH AND GOT WRITTEN OUT OF THE WILL IN FAVOR OF HIS TRUE HALF-SISTER, ANNABETH!
AW, MAN, YOU KILLED IT! YOU SUCK!
OH, WELL. DO YOU GUYS WANT TO CALL IT A NIGHT? I'M TOTALLY EXHAUSTED.
YEAH.
GOOD, I CAN GET THE HELL OUTTA THIS FEKKIN' DRESS!
I HAD FUN, THOUGH.
IT WAS OKAY.
IS IT OKAY IF I USE YOUR PARENTS' BATH? IT'S THE ONLY ONE THAT DOESN'T HAVE A WINDOW WITH A LITTLE HILL IN FRONT OF IT WHERE I CAN BE HARASSED BY THE RETARDS.
SURE.
!
VROOM!
WHY THE HELL ARE THEY LAUGHING? I KNOW THEY CAN'T SEE ME FROM THE GROUND...
HA! HA! HA! HA!
HEY! SHUT UP! YOU CAN'T SEE ME FROM THERE, SO DON'T EVEN PLAY THAT!

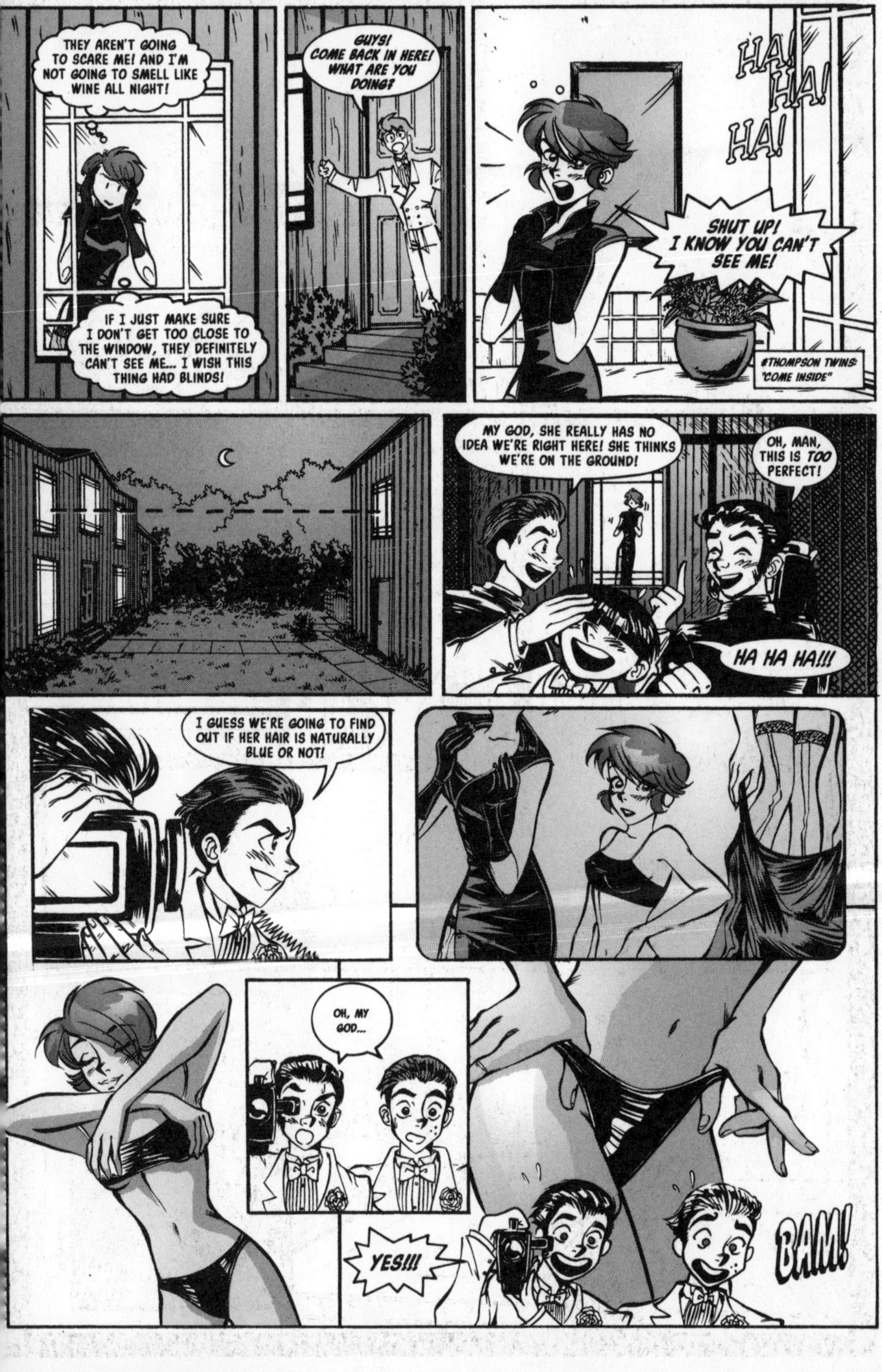

THEY AREN'T GOING TO SCARE ME! AND I'M NOT GOING TO SMELL LIKE WINE ALL NIGHT!
IF I JUST MAKE SURE I DON'T GET TOO CLOSE TO THE WINDOW, THEY DEFINITELY CAN'T SEE ME... I WISH THIS THING HAD BLINDS!
GUYS! COME BACK IN HERE! WHAT ARE YOU DOING?
HA! HA! HA!
SHUT UP! I KNOW YOU CAN'T SEE ME!
#THOMPSON TWINS: "COME INSIDE"
MY GOD, SHE REALLY HAS NO IDEA WE'RE RIGHT HERE! SHE THINKS WE'RE ON THE GROUND!
OH, MAN, THIS IS TOO PERFECT!
HA HA HA!!!
I GUESS WE'RE GOING TO FIND OUT IF HER HAIR IS NATURALLY BLUE OR NOT!
OH, MY GOD...
YES!!!
BAM!

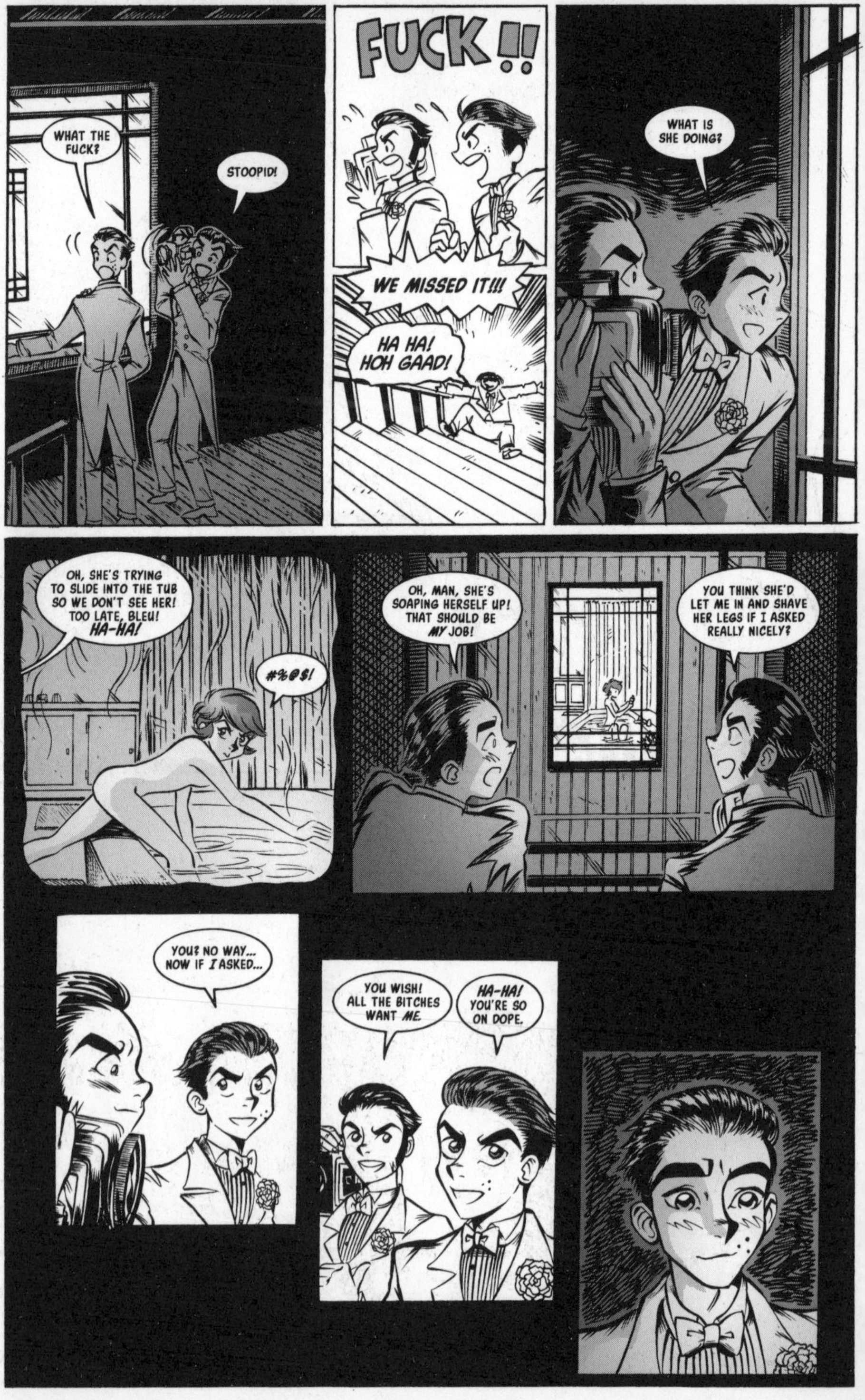
WHAT THE FUCK?
STOOPID!
FUCK !!
WE MISSED IT!!!
HA HA! HOH GAAD!
WHAT IS SHE DOING?
OH, SHE'S TRYING TO SLIDE INTO THE TUB SO WE DON'T SEE HER! TOO LATE, BLEU! HA-HA!
#%@$!
OH, MAN, SHE'S SOAPING HERSELF UP! THAT SHOULD BE MY JOB!
YOU THINK SHE'D LET ME IN AND SHAVE HER LEGS IF I ASKED REALLY NICELY?
YOU? NO WAY... NOW IF I ASKED...
YOU WISH! ALL THE BITCHES WANT ME.
HA-HA! YOU'RE SO ON DOPE.

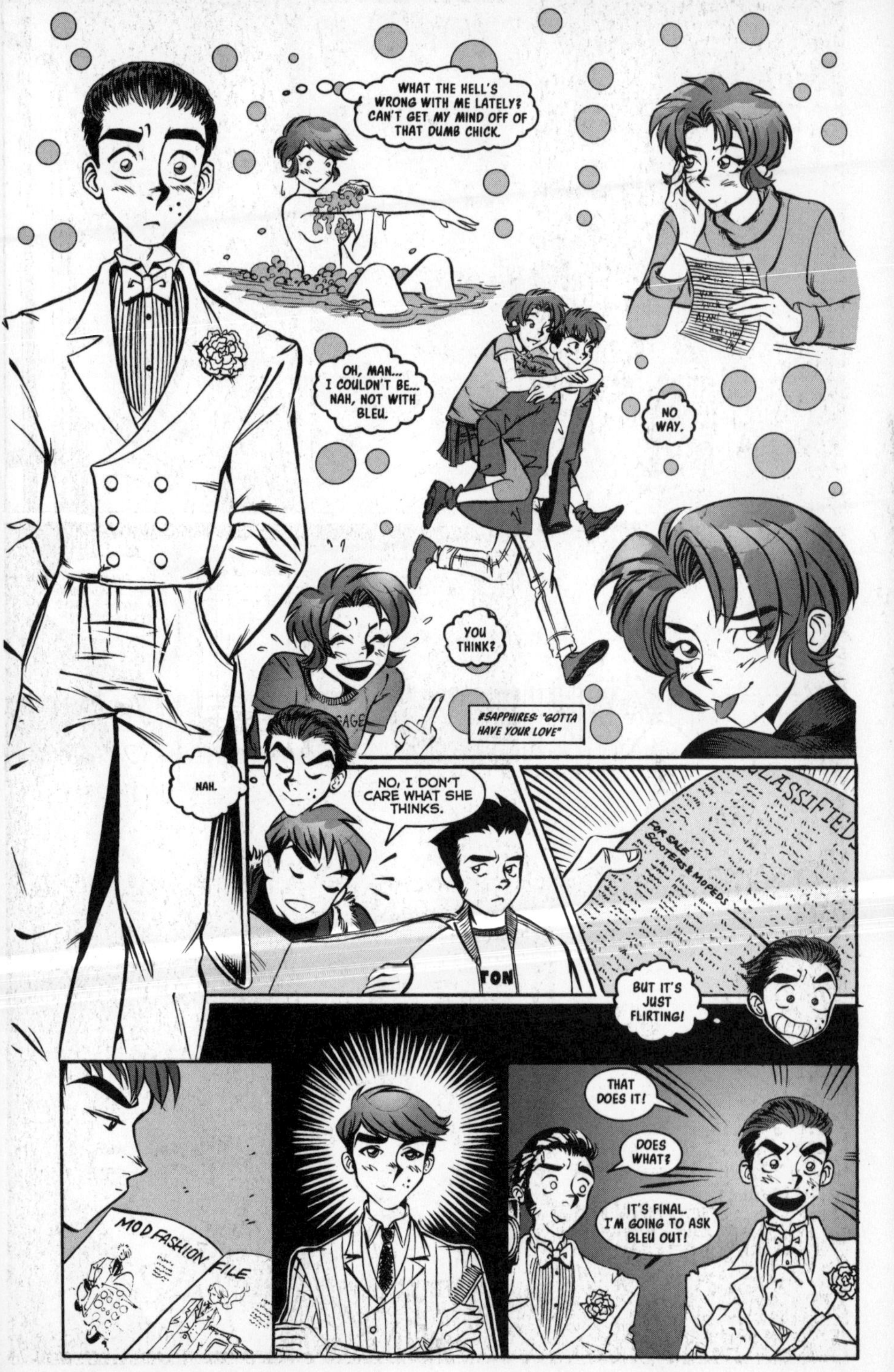
WHAT THE HELL'S WRONG WITH ME LATELY? CAN'T GET MY MIND OFF OF THAT DUMB CHICK.
OH, MAN... I COULDN'T BE... NAH, NOT WITH BLEU.
NO WAY.
YOU THINK?
#SAPPHIRES: "GOTTA HAVE YOUR LOVE"
NAH.
NO, I DON'T CARE WHAT SHE THINKS.
CLASSIFIED
FOR SALE SCOOTERS & MOPEDS
BUT IT'S JUST FLIRTING!
MOD FASHION FILE
THAT DOES IT!
DOES WHAT?
IT'S FINAL. I'M GOING TO ASK BLEU OUT!

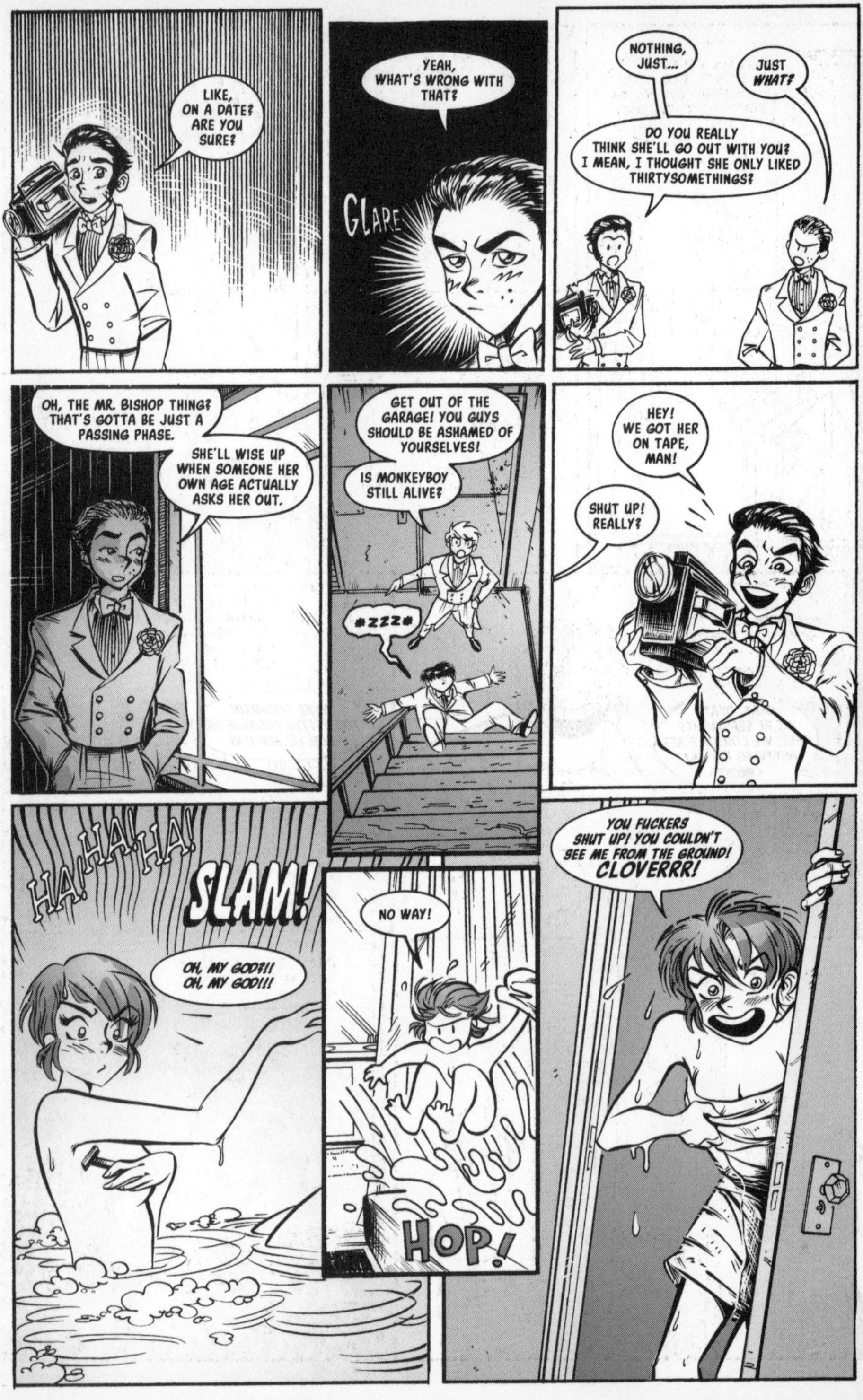
LIKE, ON A DATE? ARE YOU SURE?
YEAH, WHAT'S WRONG WITH THAT?
GLARE
NOTHING, JUST...
JUST WHAT?
DO YOU REALLY THINK SHE'LL GO OUT WITH YOU? I MEAN, I THOUGHT SHE ONLY LIKED THIRTYSOMETHINGS?
OH, THE MR. BISHOP THING? THAT'S GOTTA BE JUST A PASSING PHASE.
SHE'LL WISE UP WHEN SOMEONE HER OWN AGE ACTUALLY ASKS HER OUT.
GET OUT OF THE GARAGE! YOU GUYS SHOULD BE ASHAMED OF YOURSELVES!
IS MONKEYBOY STILL ALIVE?
#ZZZ#
HEY! WE GOT HER ON TAPE, MAN!
SHUT UP! REALLY?
HA! HA! HA! HA!
SLAM!
OH, MY GOD?!! OH, MY GOD!!!
NO WAY!
HOP!
YOU FUCKERS SHUT UP! YOU COULDN'T SEE ME FROM THE GROUND! CLOVERRR!

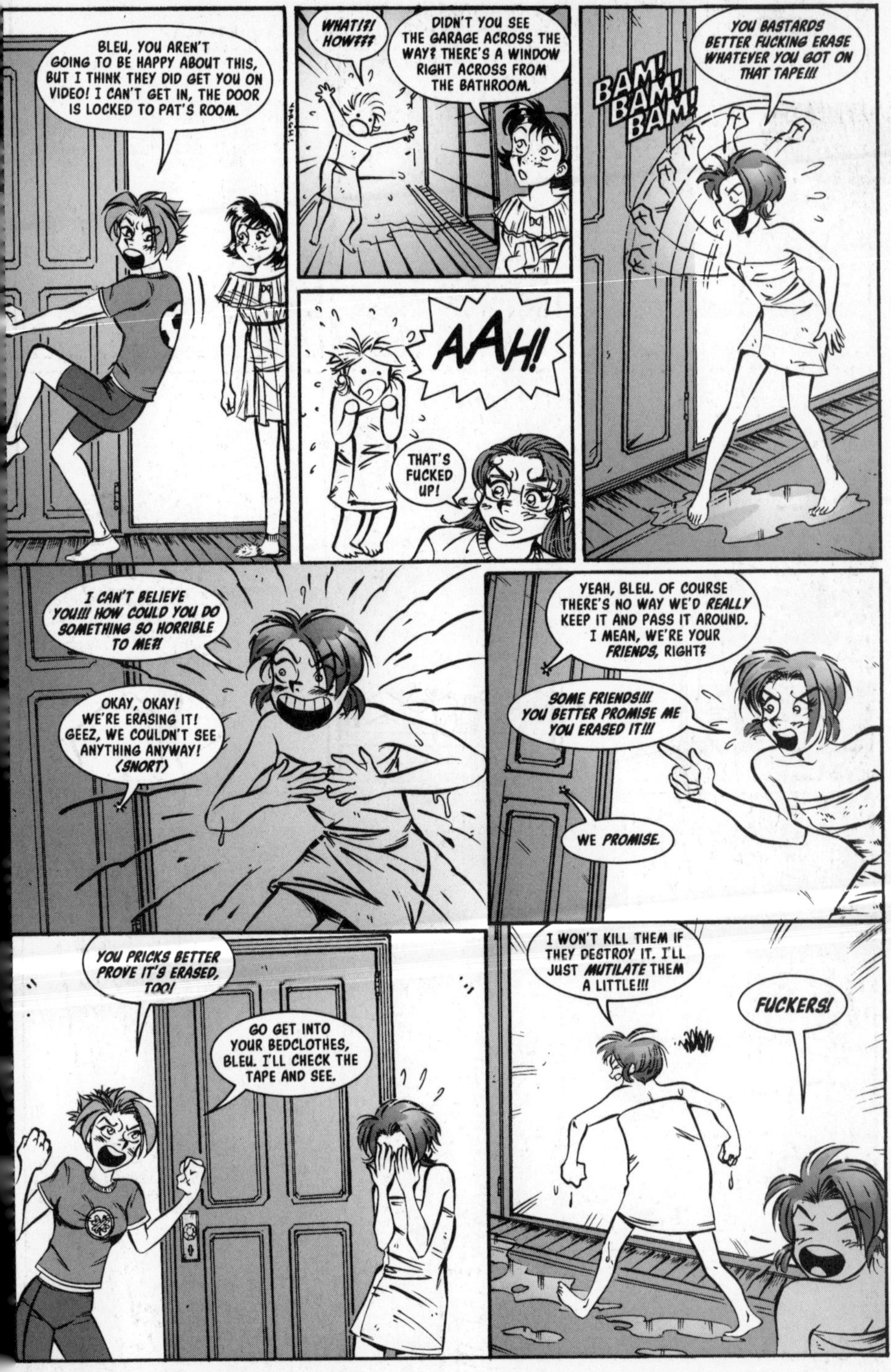
BLEU, YOU AREN'T GOING TO BE HAPPY ABOUT THIS, BUT I THINK THEY DID GET YOU ON VIDEO! I CAN'T GET IN, THE DOOR IS LOCKED TO PAT'S ROOM.
WHAT!?! HOW???
DIDN'T YOU SEE THE GARAGE ACROSS THE WAY? THERE'S A WINDOW RIGHT ACROSS FROM THE BATHROOM.
AAH!
THAT'S FUCKED UP!
BAM! BAM! BAM!
YOU BASTARDS BETTER FUCKING ERASE WHATEVER YOU GOT ON THAT TAPE!!!
I CAN'T BELIEVE YOU!!! HOW COULD YOU DO SOMETHING SO HORRIBLE TO ME?!
OKAY, OKAY! WE'RE ERASING IT! GEEZ, WE COULDN'T SEE ANYTHING ANYWAY! <SNORT>
YEAH, BLEU. OF COURSE THERE'S NO WAY WE'D REALLY KEEP IT AND PASS IT AROUND. I MEAN, WE'RE YOUR FRIENDS, RIGHT?
SOME FRIENDS!!! YOU BETTER PROMISE ME YOU ERASED IT!!!
WE PROMISE.
YOU PRICKS BETTER PROVE IT'S ERASED, TOO!
GO GET INTO YOUR BEDCLOTHES, BLEU. I'LL CHECK THE TAPE AND SEE.
I WON'T KILL THEM IF THEY DESTROY IT. I'LL JUST MUTILATE THEM A LITTLE!!!
FUCKERS!

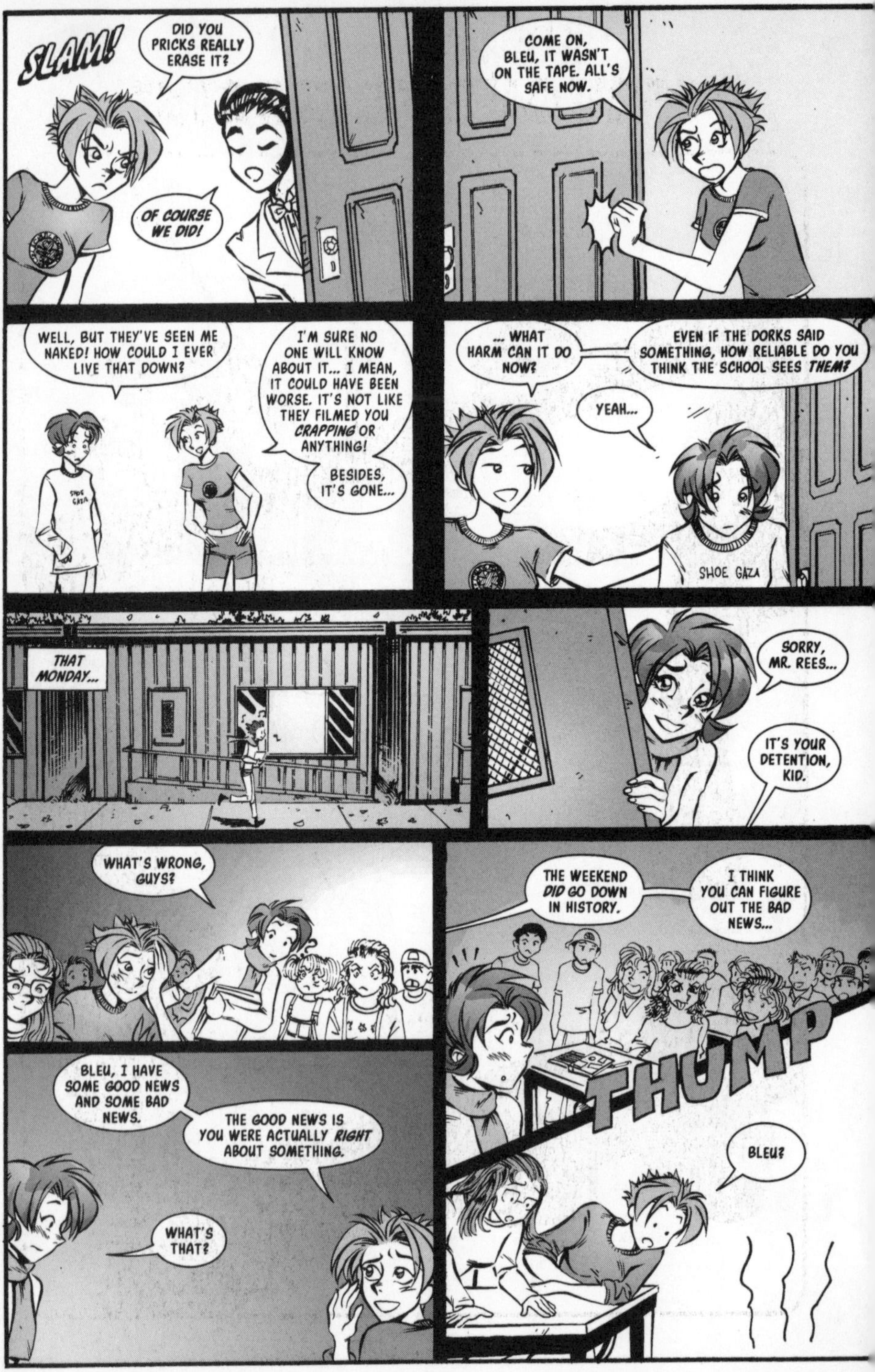
SLAM!
DID YOU PRICKS REALLY ERASE IT?
OF COURSE WE DID!
COME ON, BLEU, IT WASN'T ON THE TAPE. ALL'S SAFE NOW.
WELL, BUT THEY'VE SEEN ME NAKED! HOW COULD I EVER LIVE THAT DOWN?
I'M SURE NO ONE WILL KNOW ABOUT IT... I MEAN, IT COULD HAVE BEEN WORSE. IT'S NOT LIKE THEY FILMED YOU CRAPPING OR ANYTHING!
BESIDES, IT'S GONE...
SHOE GAZA
... WHAT HARM CAN IT DO NOW?
EVEN IF THE DORKS SAID SOMETHING, HOW RELIABLE DO YOU THINK THE SCHOOL SEES THEM?
YEAH...
SHOE GAZA
THAT MONDAY...
SORRY, MR. REES...
IT'S YOUR DETENTION, KID.
WHAT'S WRONG, GUYS?
BLEU, I HAVE SOME GOOD NEWS AND SOME BAD NEWS.
THE GOOD NEWS IS YOU WERE ACTUALLY RIGHT ABOUT SOMETHING.
WHAT'S THAT?
THE WEEKEND DID GO DOWN IN HISTORY.
I THINK YOU CAN FIGURE OUT THE BAD NEWS...
THUMP
BLEU?

chapter two:
“FAVOURITE SHIRTS”

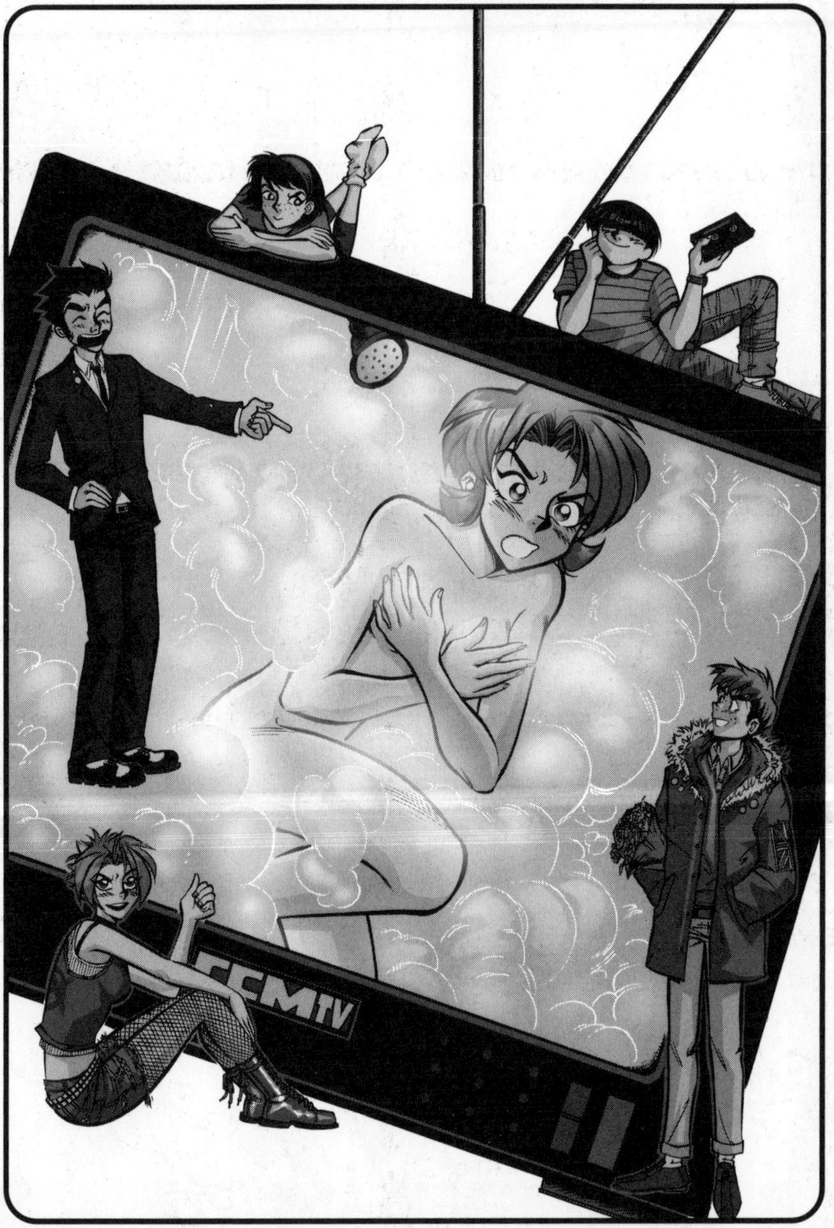

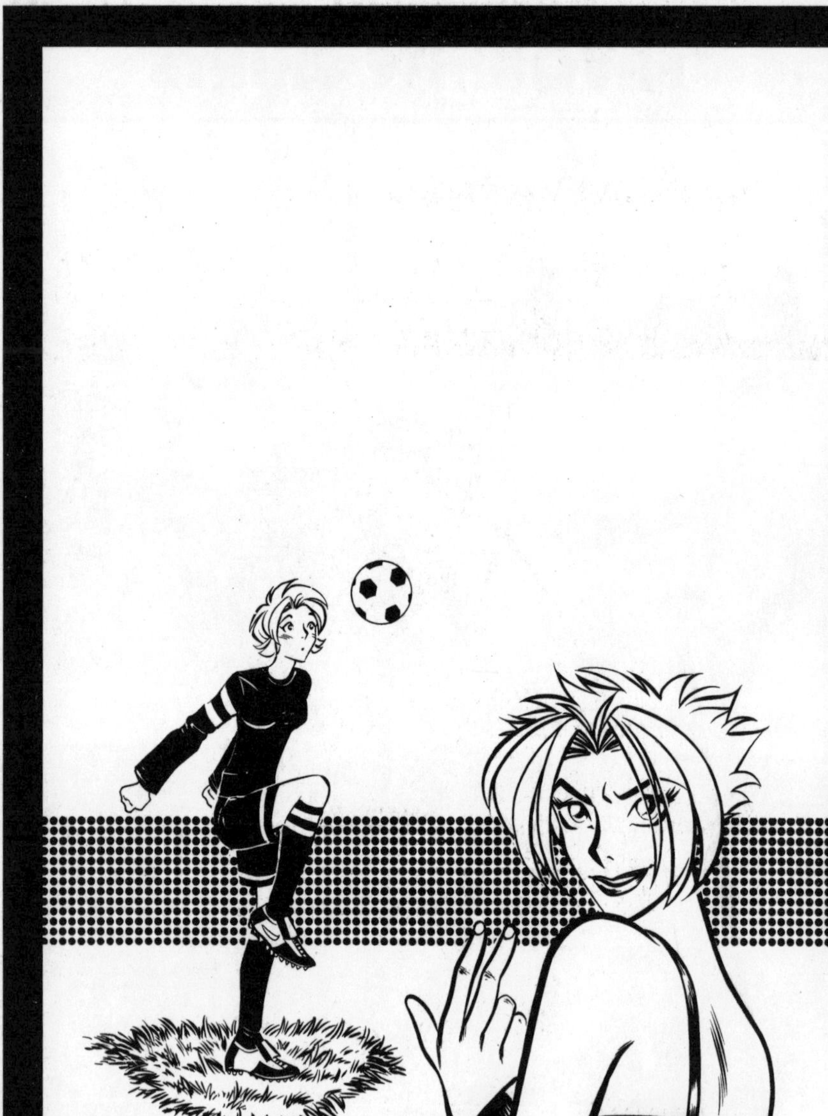

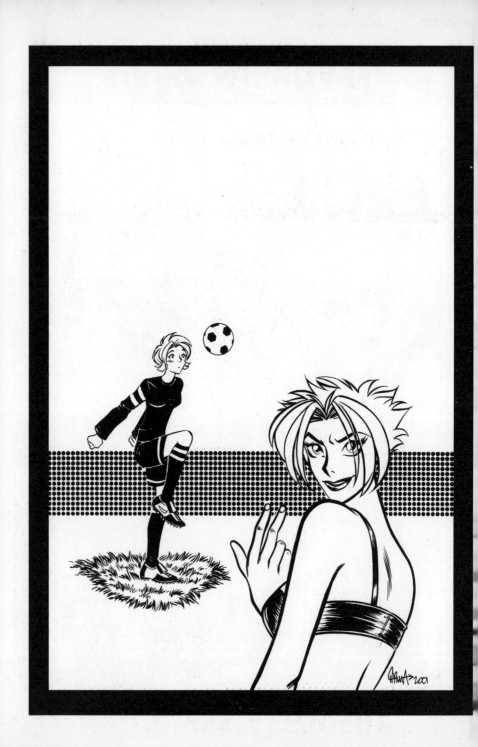

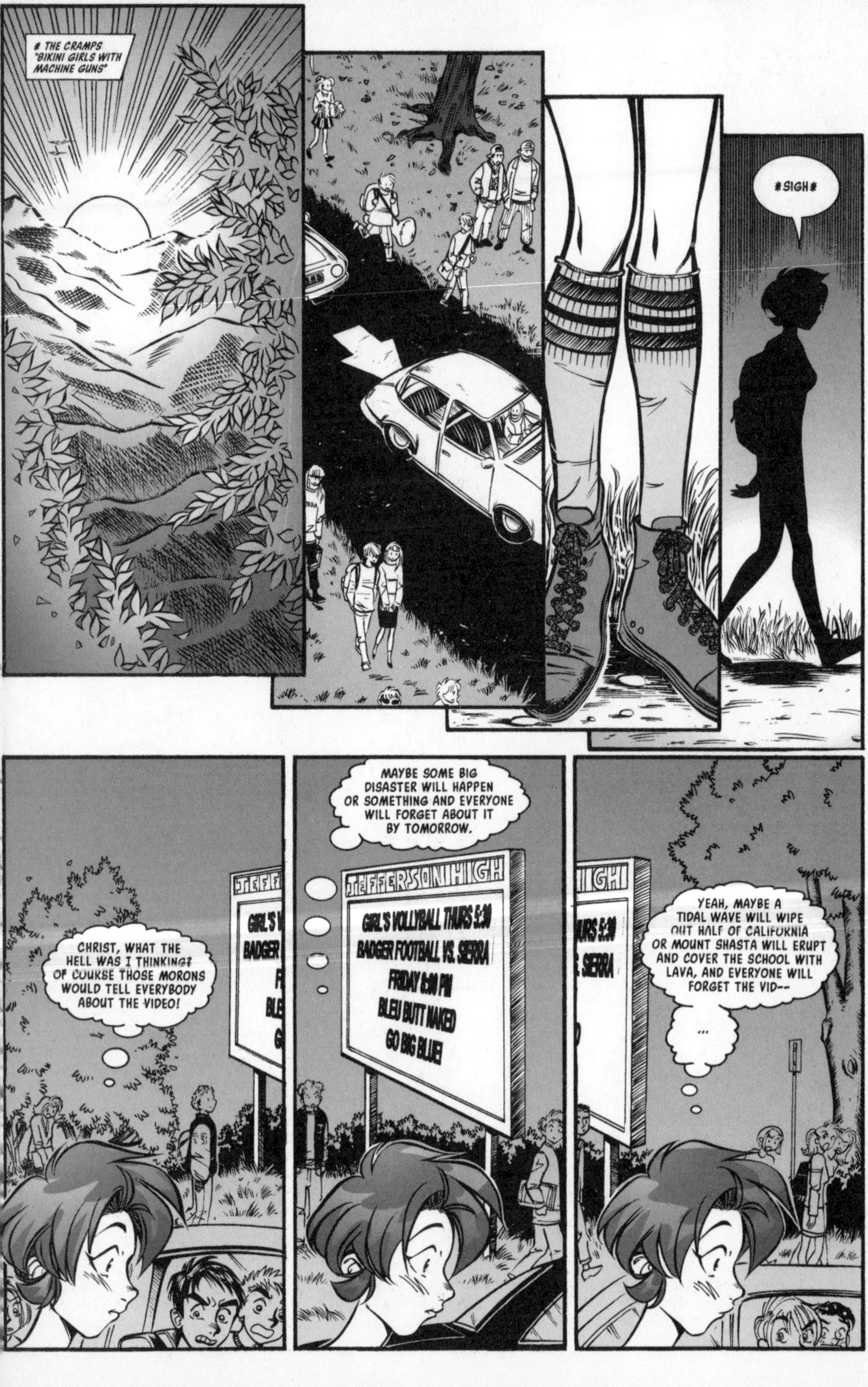
♯ THE CRAMPS "BIKINI GIRLS WITH MACHINE GUNS"
♯SIGH♯
CHRIST, WHAT THE HELL WAS I THINKING? OF COURSE THOSE MORONS WOULD TELL EVERYBODY ABOUT THE VIDEO!
MAYBE SOME BIG DISASTER WILL HAPPEN OR SOMETHING AND EVERYONE WILL FORGET ABOUT IT BY TOMORROW.
JEFFERSON HIGH
GIRL'S VOLLYBALL THURS 5:30
BADGER FOOTBALL VS. SIERRA
FRIDAY 6:30 PM
BLEU BUTT NAKED
GO BIG BLUE!
YEAH, MAYBE A TIDAL WAVE WILL WIPE OUT HALF OF CALIFORNIA OR MOUNT SHASTA WILL ERUPT AND COVER THE SCHOOL WITH LAVA, AND EVERYONE WILL FORGET THE VID--
...

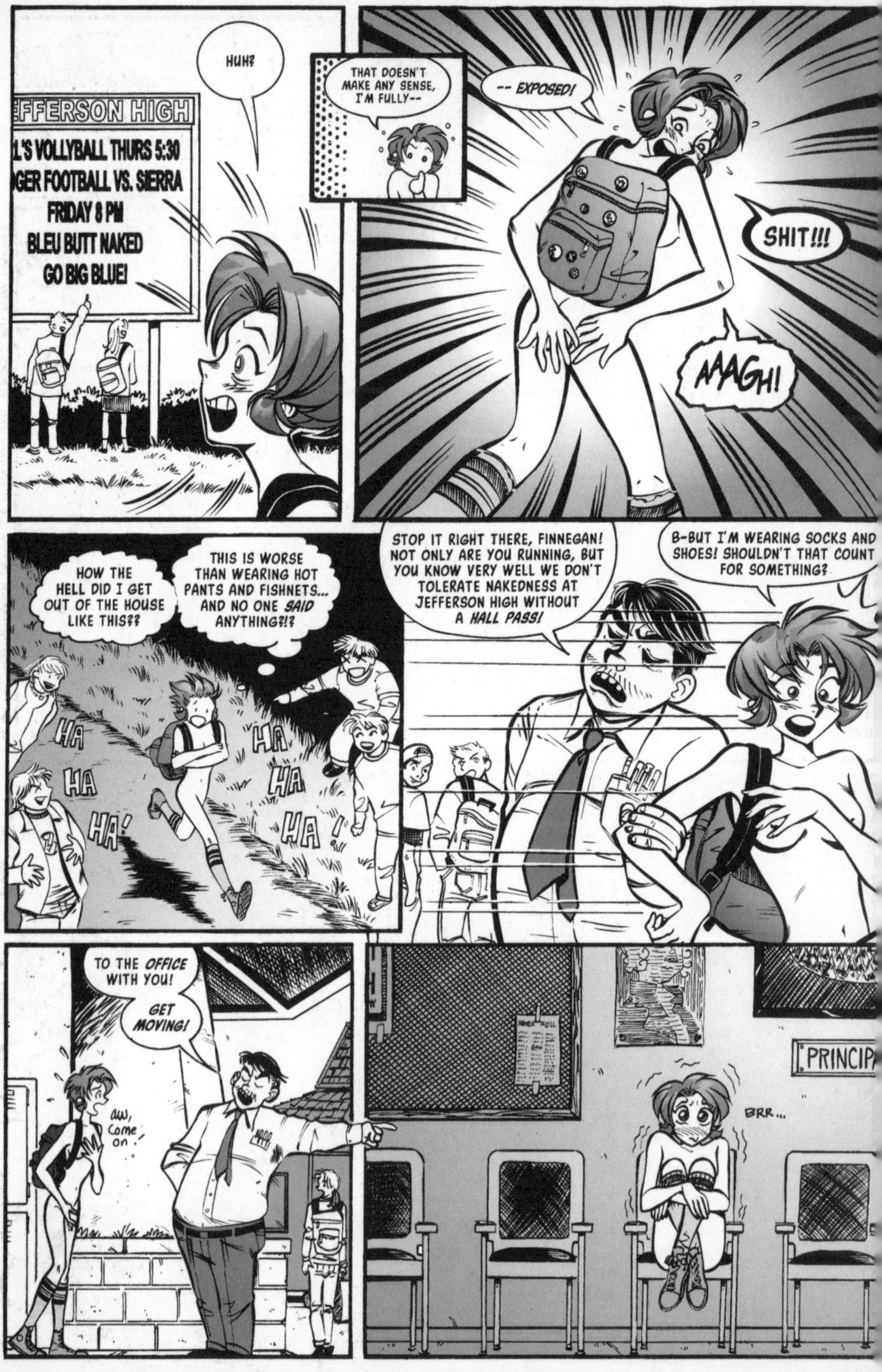

EFFERSON HIGH
L'S VOLLYBALL THURS 5:30
GER FOOTBALL VS. SIERRA
FRIDAY 8 PM
BLEU BUTT NAKED
GO BIG BLUE!
HUH?
THAT DOESN'T MAKE ANY SENSE, I'M FULLY--
-- EXPOSED!
SHIT!!!
AAAGH!
HOW THE HELL DID I GET OUT OF THE HOUSE LIKE THIS??
THIS IS WORSE THAN WEARING HOT PANTS AND FISHNETS... AND NO ONE SAID ANYTHING?!?
HA
HA
HA!
HA
HA
HA!
STOP IT RIGHT THERE, FINNEGAN! NOT ONLY ARE YOU RUNNING, BUT YOU KNOW VERY WELL WE DON'T TOLERATE NAKEDNESS AT JEFFERSON HIGH WITHOUT A HALL PASS!
B-BUT I'M WEARING SOCKS AND SHOES! SHOULDN'T THAT COUNT FOR SOMETHING?
TO THE OFFICE WITH YOU!
GET MOVING!
aw, come on!
PRINCIP
BRR...

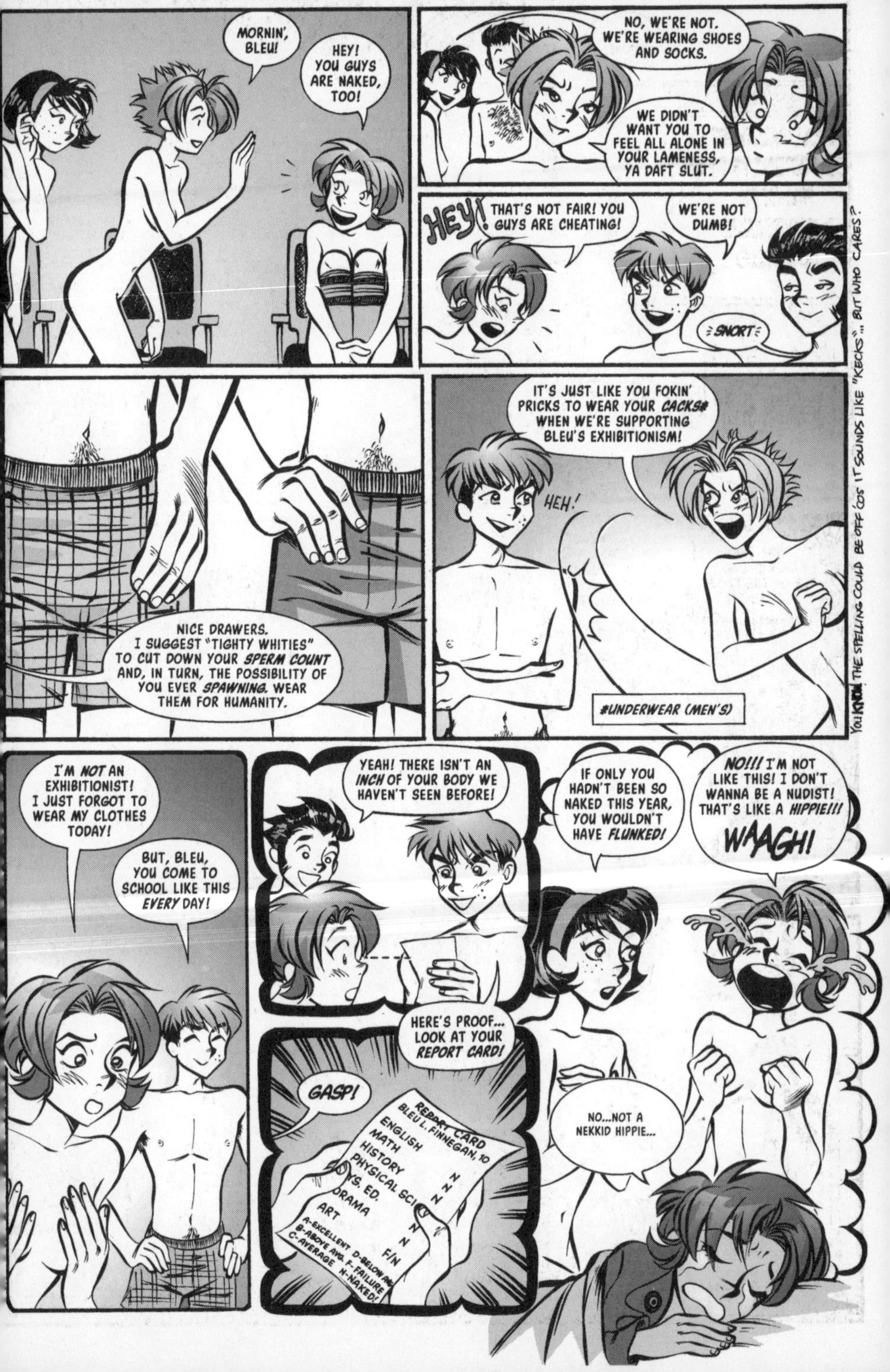
MORNIN', BLEU!
HEY! YOU GUYS ARE NAKED, TOO!
NO, WE'RE NOT. WE'RE WEARING SHOES AND SOCKS.
WE DIDN'T WANT YOU TO FEEL ALL ALONE IN YOUR LAMENESS, YA DAFT SLUT.
HEY!
THAT'S NOT FAIR! YOU GUYS ARE CHEATING!
WE'RE NOT DUMB!
SNORT
NICE DRAWERS. I SUGGEST "TIGHTY WHITIES" TO CUT DOWN YOUR SPERM COUNT AND, IN TURN, THE POSSIBILITY OF YOU EVER SPAWNING. WEAR THEM FOR HUMANITY.
IT'S JUST LIKE YOU FOKIN' PRICKS TO WEAR YOUR CACKS# WHEN WE'RE SUPPORTING BLEU'S EXHIBITIONISM!
HEH!
#UNDERWEAR (MEN'S)
YOU KNOW THE SPELLING COULD BE OFF 'COS IT SOUNDS LIKE "KECKS"... BUT WHO CARES?
I'M NOT AN EXHIBITIONIST! I JUST FORGOT TO WEAR MY CLOTHES TODAY!
BUT, BLEU, YOU COME TO SCHOOL LIKE THIS EVERY DAY!
YEAH! THERE ISN'T AN INCH OF YOUR BODY WE HAVEN'T SEEN BEFORE!
HERE'S PROOF... LOOK AT YOUR REPORT CARD!
GASP!
REPORT CARD
BLEU L. FINNEGAN, 10
ENGLISH N
MATH N
HISTORY N
PHYSICAL SCI
YS. ED. N
RAMA N
ART F/N
A-EXCELLENT D-BELOW AVG.
B-ABOVE AVG. F-FAILURE
C-AVERAGE N-NAKED!
IF ONLY YOU HADN'T BEEN SO NAKED THIS YEAR, YOU WOULDN'T HAVE FLUNKED!
NO!!! I'M NOT LIKE THIS! I DON'T WANNA BE A NUDIST! THAT'S LIKE A HIPPIE!!!
WAAGH!
NO...NOT A NEKKID HIPPIE...

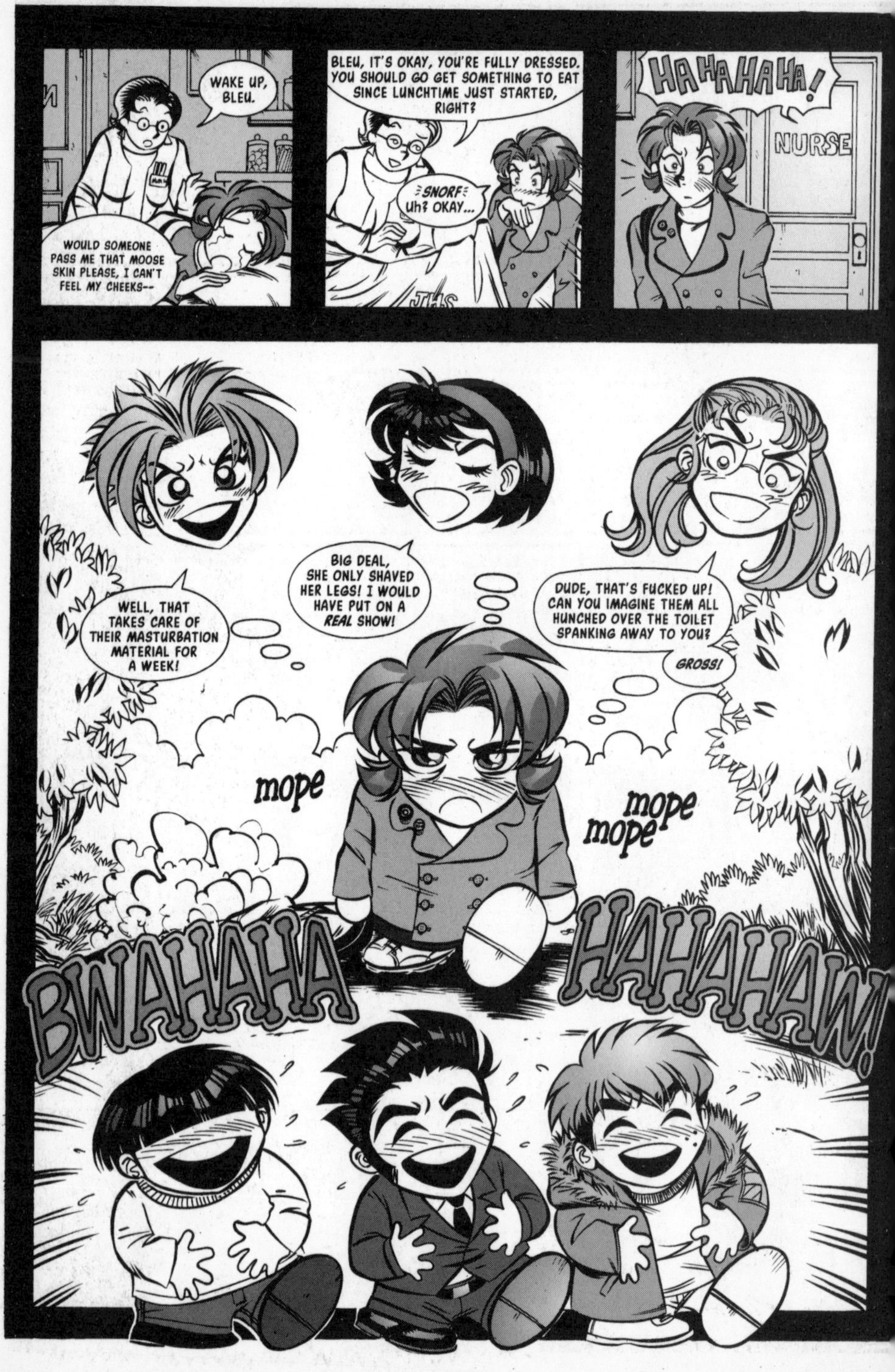
WAKE UP, BLEU.
WOULD SOMEONE PASS ME THAT MOOSE SKIN PLEASE, I CAN'T FEEL MY CHEEKS--
BLEU, IT'S OKAY, YOU'RE FULLY DRESSED. YOU SHOULD GO GET SOMETHING TO EAT SINCE LUNCHTIME JUST STARTED, RIGHT?
SNORF uh? OKAY...
JHS
HAHAHAHAHA!
NURSE
WELL, THAT TAKES CARE OF THEIR MASTURBATION MATERIAL FOR A WEEK!
BIG DEAL, SHE ONLY SHAVED HER LEGS! I WOULD HAVE PUT ON A REAL SHOW!
DUDE, THAT'S FUCKED UP! CAN YOU IMAGINE THEM ALL HUNCHED OVER THE TOILET SPANKING AWAY TO YOU?
GROSS!
mope
mope mope
BWAHAHA
HAHAHAW!

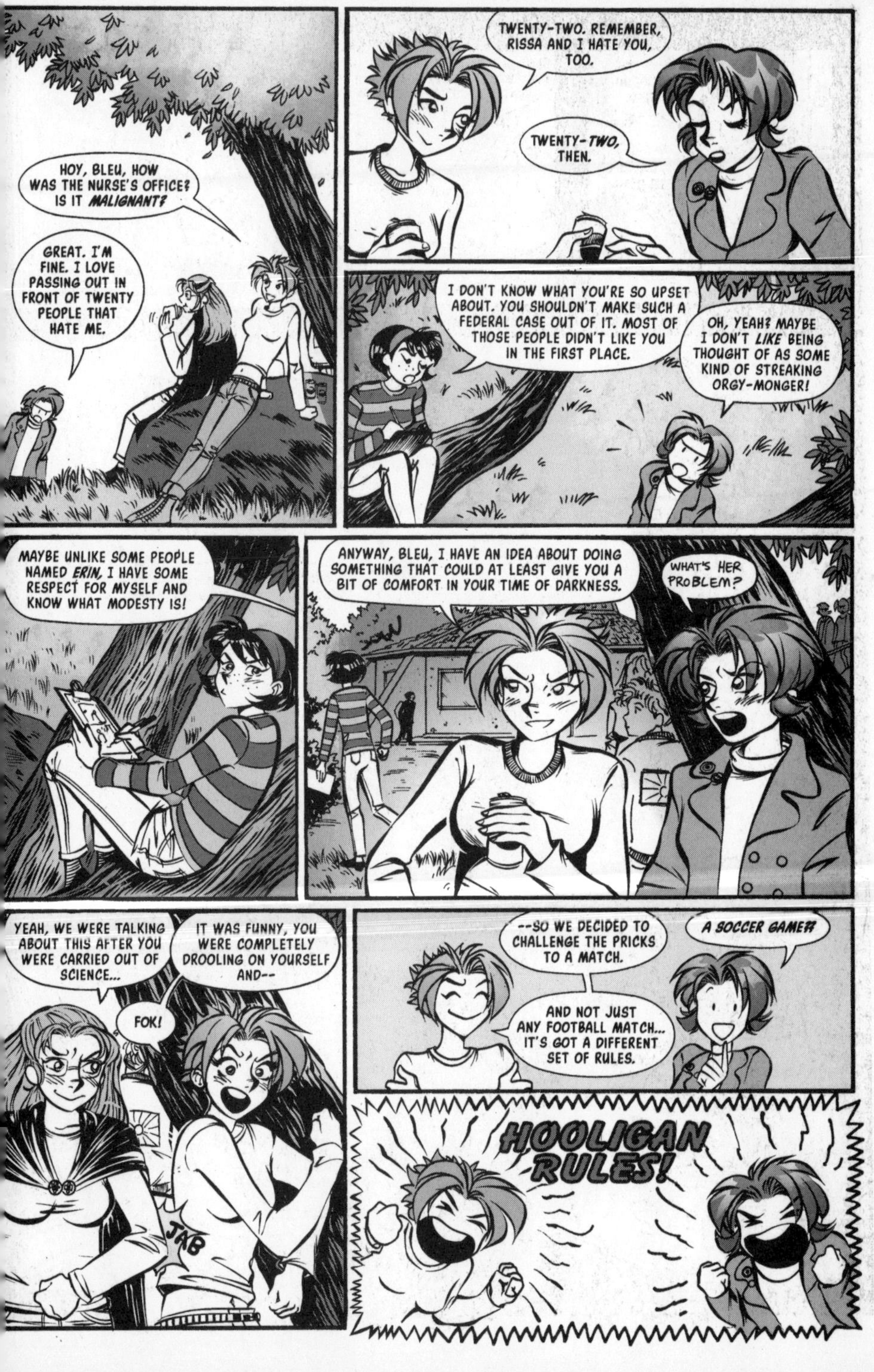

HOY, BLEU, HOW WAS THE NURSE'S OFFICE? IS IT MALIGNANT?
GREAT. I'M FINE. I LOVE PASSING OUT IN FRONT OF TWENTY PEOPLE THAT HATE ME.
TWENTY-TWO. REMEMBER, RISSA AND I HATE YOU, TOO.
TWENTY-TWO, THEN.
I DON'T KNOW WHAT YOU'RE SO UPSET ABOUT. YOU SHOULDN'T MAKE SUCH A FEDERAL CASE OUT OF IT. MOST OF THOSE PEOPLE DIDN'T LIKE YOU IN THE FIRST PLACE.
OH, YEAH? MAYBE I DON'T LIKE BEING THOUGHT OF AS SOME KIND OF STREAKING ORGY-MONGER!
MAYBE UNLIKE SOME PEOPLE NAMED ERIN, I HAVE SOME RESPECT FOR MYSELF AND KNOW WHAT MODESTY IS!
ANYWAY, BLEU, I HAVE AN IDEA ABOUT DOING SOMETHING THAT COULD AT LEAST GIVE YOU A BIT OF COMFORT IN YOUR TIME OF DARKNESS.
WHAT'S HER PROBLEM?
YEAH, WE WERE TALKING ABOUT THIS AFTER YOU WERE CARRIED OUT OF SCIENCE...
IT WAS FUNNY, YOU WERE COMPLETELY DROOLING ON YOURSELF AND--
FOK!
JAB
--SO WE DECIDED TO CHALLENGE THE PRICKS TO A MATCH.
A SOCCER GAME??
AND NOT JUST ANY FOOTBALL MATCH... IT'S GOT A DIFFERENT SET OF RULES.
HOOLIGAN RULES!

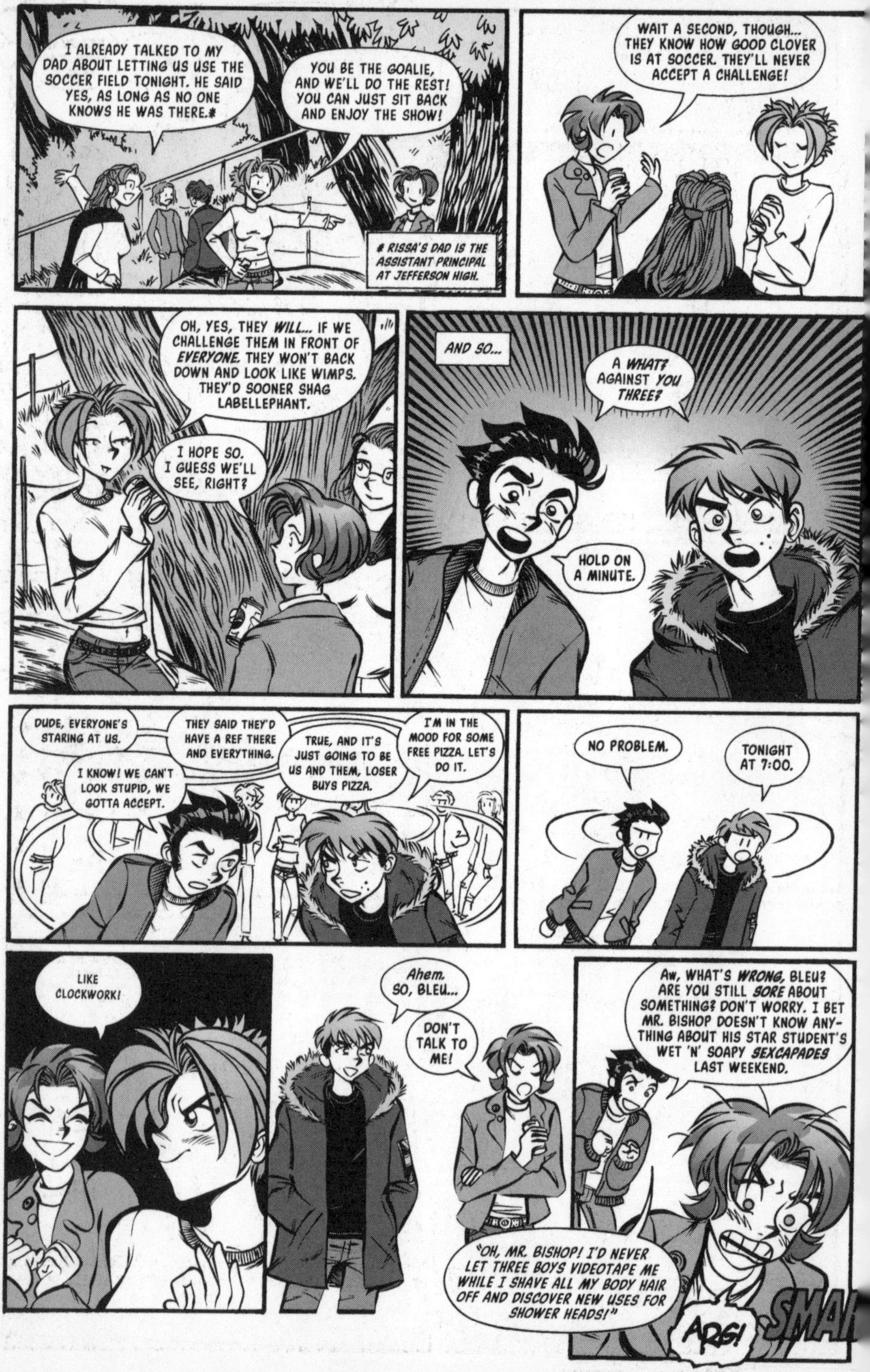
I ALREADY TALKED TO MY DAD ABOUT LETTING US USE THE SOCCER FIELD TONIGHT. HE SAID YES, AS LONG AS NO ONE KNOWS HE WAS THERE.*
YOU BE THE GOALIE, AND WE'LL DO THE REST! YOU CAN JUST SIT BACK AND ENJOY THE SHOW!
* RISSA'S DAD IS THE ASSISTANT PRINCIPAL AT JEFFERSON HIGH.
WAIT A SECOND, THOUGH... THEY KNOW HOW GOOD CLOVER IS AT SOCCER. THEY'LL NEVER ACCEPT A CHALLENGE!
OH, YES, THEY WILL... IF WE CHALLENGE THEM IN FRONT OF EVERYONE. THEY WON'T BACK DOWN AND LOOK LIKE WIMPS. THEY'D SOONER SHAG LABELLEPHANT.
I HOPE SO. I GUESS WE'LL SEE, RIGHT?
AND SO...
A WHAT? AGAINST YOU THREE?
HOLD ON A MINUTE.
DUDE, EVERYONE'S STARING AT US.
THEY SAID THEY'D HAVE A REF THERE AND EVERYTHING.
I KNOW! WE CAN'T LOOK STUPID, WE GOTTA ACCEPT.
TRUE, AND IT'S JUST GOING TO BE US AND THEM, LOSER BUYS PIZZA.
I'M IN THE MOOD FOR SOME FREE PIZZA. LET'S DO IT.
NO PROBLEM.
TONIGHT AT 7:00.
LIKE CLOCKWORK!
Ahem. SO, BLEU...
DON'T TALK TO ME!
Aw, WHAT'S WRONG, BLEU? ARE YOU STILL SORE ABOUT SOMETHING? DON'T WORRY. I BET MR. BISHOP DOESN'T KNOW ANYTHING ABOUT HIS STAR STUDENT'S WET 'N' SOAPY SEXCAPADES LAST WEEKEND.
"OH, MR. BISHOP! I'D NEVER LET THREE BOYS VIDEOTAPE ME WHILE I SHAVE ALL MY BODY HAIR OFF AND DISCOVER NEW USES FOR SHOWER HEADS!"
ARG!
SMA

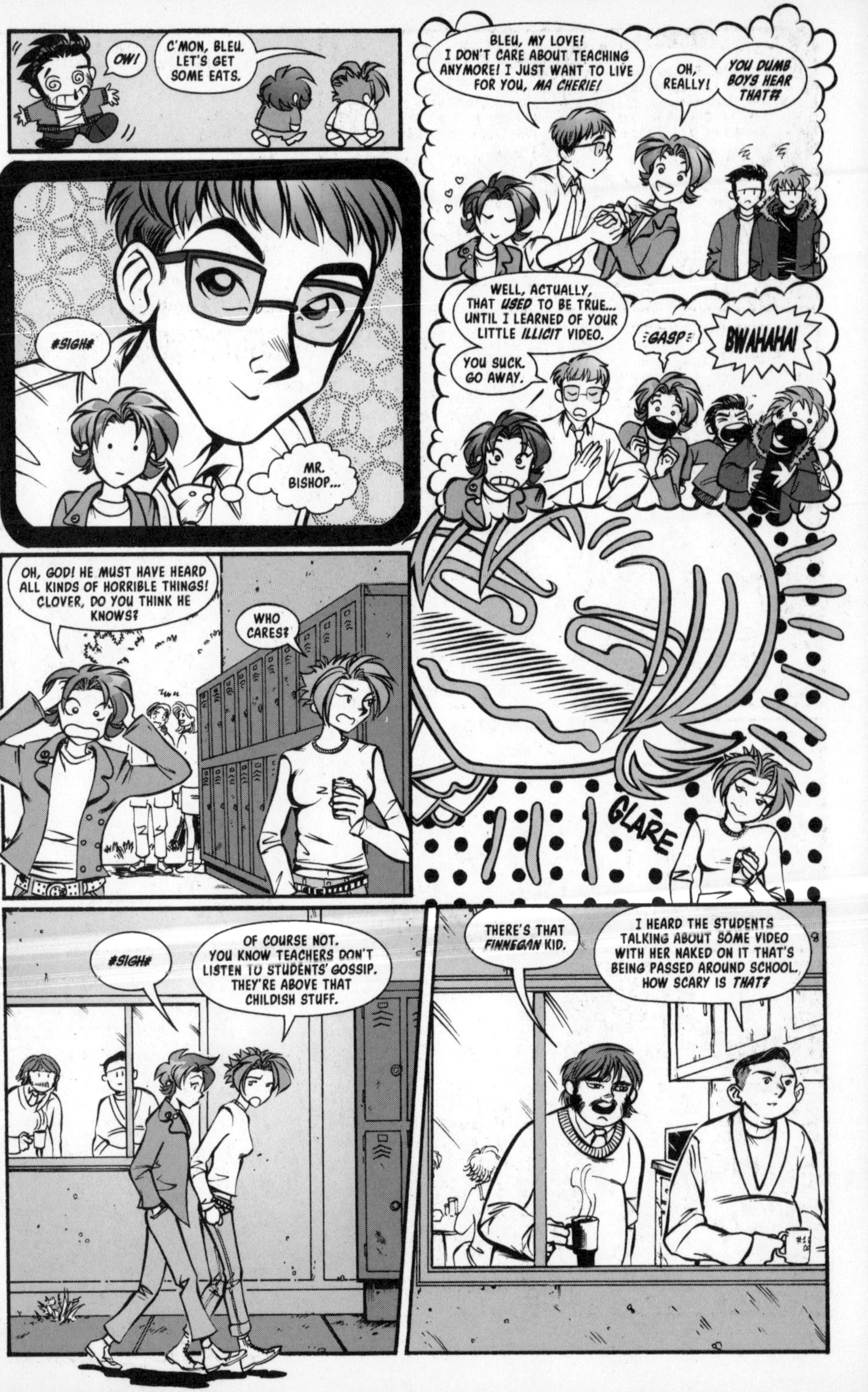

OW!
C'MON, BLEU. LET'S GET SOME EATS.
#SIGH#
MR. BISHOP...
BLEU, MY LOVE! I DON'T CARE ABOUT TEACHING ANYMORE! I JUST WANT TO LIVE FOR YOU, MA CHERIE!
OH, REALLY!
YOU DUMB BOYS HEAR THAT??
WELL, ACTUALLY, THAT USED TO BE TRUE... UNTIL I LEARNED OF YOUR LITTLE ILLICIT VIDEO.
GASP
BWAHAHA!
YOU SUCK. GO AWAY.
OH, GOD! HE MUST HAVE HEARD ALL KINDS OF HORRIBLE THINGS! CLOVER, DO YOU THINK HE KNOWS?
WHO CARES?
GLARE
#SIGH#
OF COURSE NOT. YOU KNOW TEACHERS DON'T LISTEN TO STUDENTS' GOSSIP. THEY'RE ABOVE THAT CHILDISH STUFF.
THERE'S THAT FINNEGAN KID.
I HEARD THE STUDENTS TALKING ABOUT SOME VIDEO WITH HER NAKED ON IT THAT'S BEING PASSED AROUND SCHOOL. HOW SCARY IS THAT?

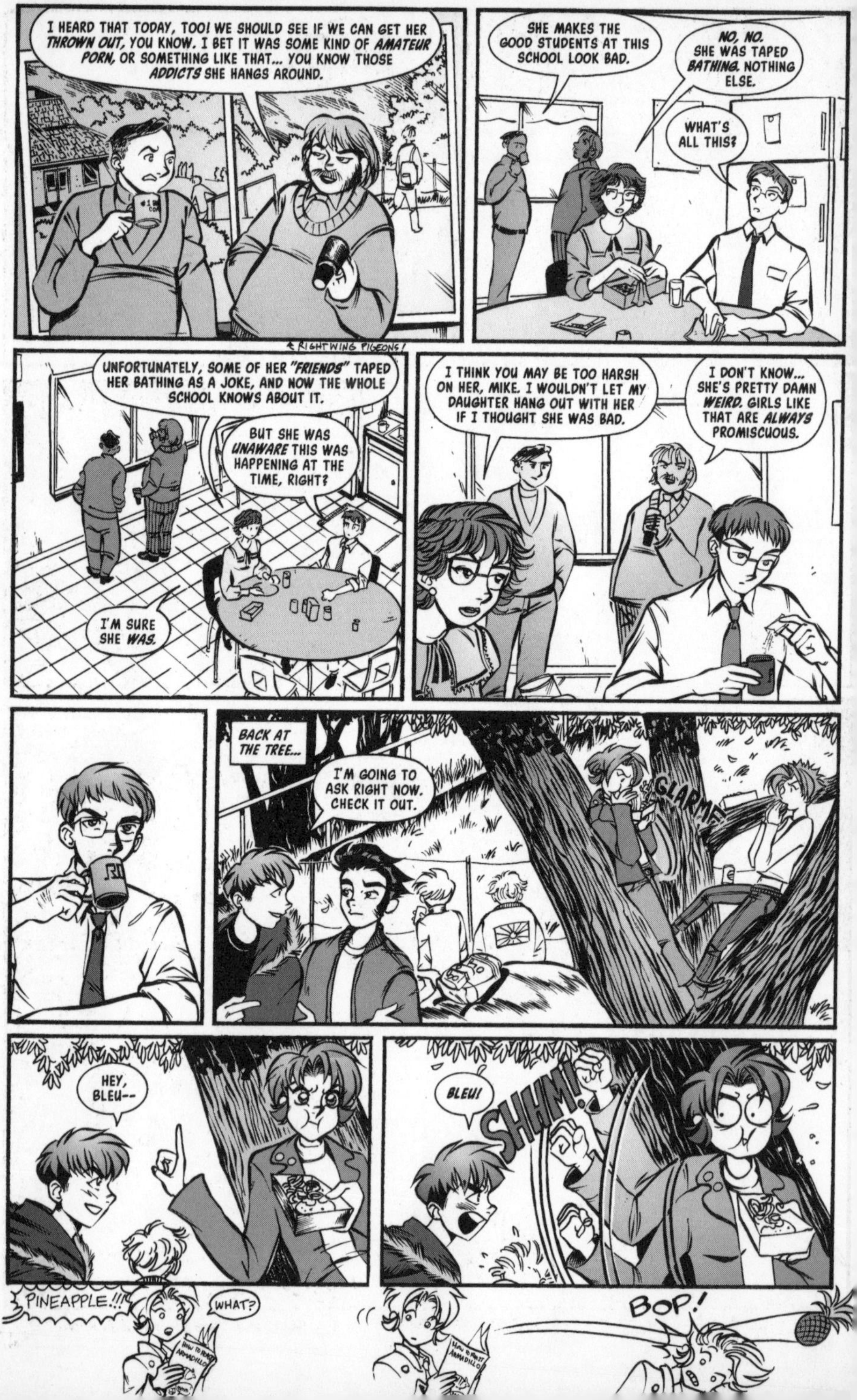
I HEARD THAT TODAY, TOO! WE SHOULD SEE IF WE CAN GET HER THROWN OUT, YOU KNOW. I BET IT WAS SOME KIND OF AMATEUR PORN, OR SOMETHING LIKE THAT... YOU KNOW THOSE ADDICTS SHE HANGS AROUND.
SHE MAKES THE GOOD STUDENTS AT THIS SCHOOL LOOK BAD.
NO, NO. SHE WAS TAPED BATHING. NOTHING ELSE.
WHAT'S ALL THIS?
← RIGHTWING PIGEONS!
UNFORTUNATELY, SOME OF HER "FRIENDS" TAPED HER BATHING AS A JOKE, AND NOW THE WHOLE SCHOOL KNOWS ABOUT IT.
BUT SHE WAS UNAWARE THIS WAS HAPPENING AT THE TIME, RIGHT?
I'M SURE SHE WAS.
I THINK YOU MAY BE TOO HARSH ON HER, MIKE. I WOULDN'T LET MY DAUGHTER HANG OUT WITH HER IF I THOUGHT SHE WAS BAD.
I DON'T KNOW... SHE'S PRETTY DAMN WEIRD. GIRLS LIKE THAT ARE ALWAYS PROMISCUOUS.
BACK AT THE TREE...
I'M GOING TO ASK RIGHT NOW. CHECK IT OUT.
GLARME
HEY, BLEU--
BLEU!
SHHM!
PINEAPPLE!!!
WHAT?
HOW TO ROAST ARMADILLO
BOP!

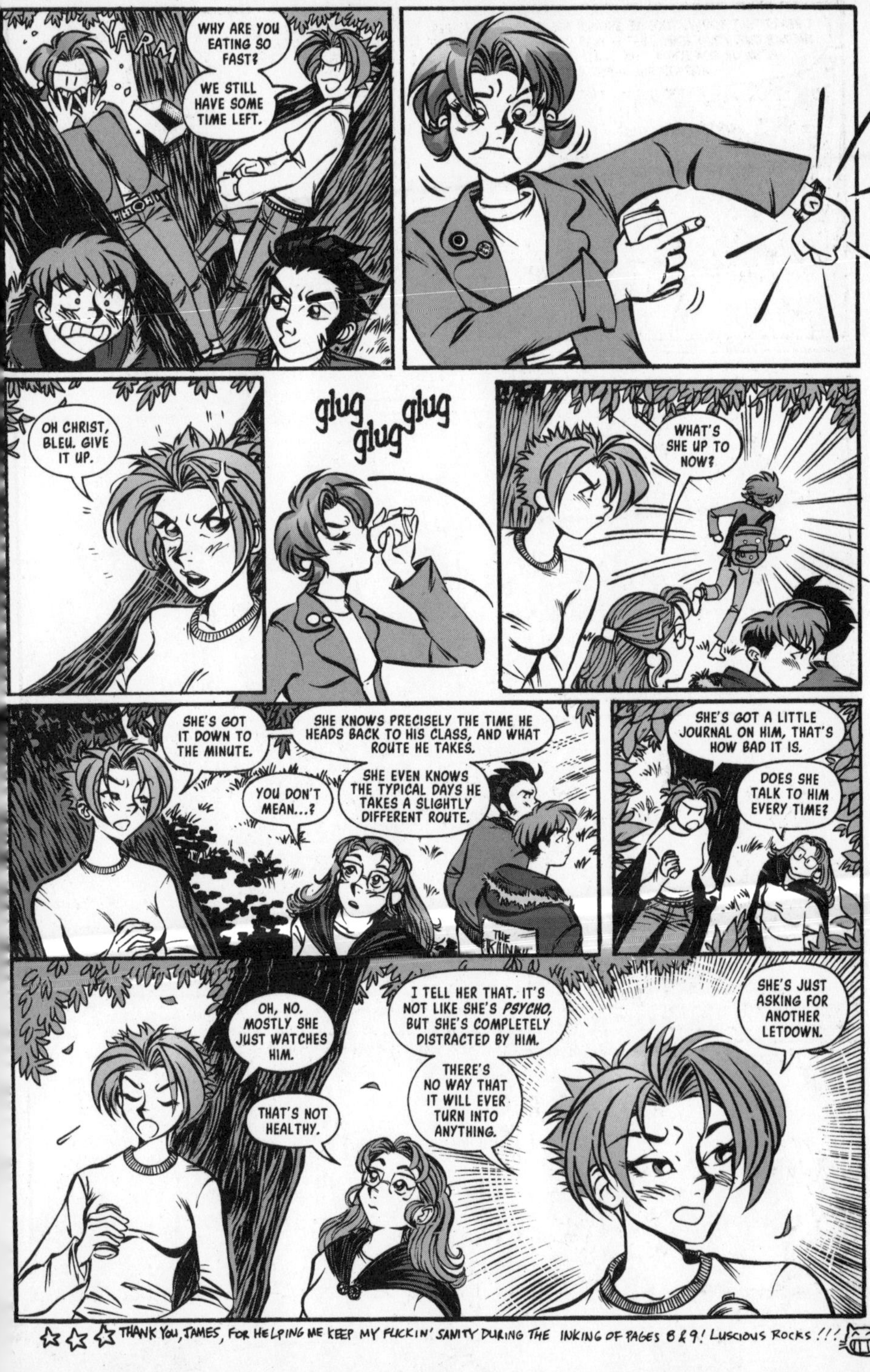
YARM
WHY ARE YOU EATING SO FAST?
WE STILL HAVE SOME TIME LEFT.
OH CHRIST, BLEU. GIVE IT UP.
glug glug glug
WHAT'S SHE UP TO NOW?
SHE'S GOT IT DOWN TO THE MINUTE.
SHE KNOWS PRECISELY THE TIME HE HEADS BACK TO HIS CLASS, AND WHAT ROUTE HE TAKES.
YOU DON'T MEAN...?
SHE EVEN KNOWS THE TYPICAL DAYS HE TAKES A SLIGHTLY DIFFERENT ROUTE.
SHE'S GOT A LITTLE JOURNAL ON HIM, THAT'S HOW BAD IT IS.
DOES SHE TALK TO HIM EVERY TIME?
OH, NO. MOSTLY SHE JUST WATCHES HIM.
THAT'S NOT HEALTHY.
I TELL HER THAT. IT'S NOT LIKE SHE'S *PSYCHO,* BUT SHE'S COMPLETELY DISTRACTED BY HIM.
THERE'S NO WAY THAT IT WILL EVER TURN INTO ANYTHING.
SHE'S JUST ASKING FOR ANOTHER LETDOWN.

☆☆☆ THANK YOU, JAMES, FOR HELPING ME KEEP MY FUCKIN' SANITY DURING THE INKING OF PAGES 8 & 9! LUSCIOUS ROCKS!!!

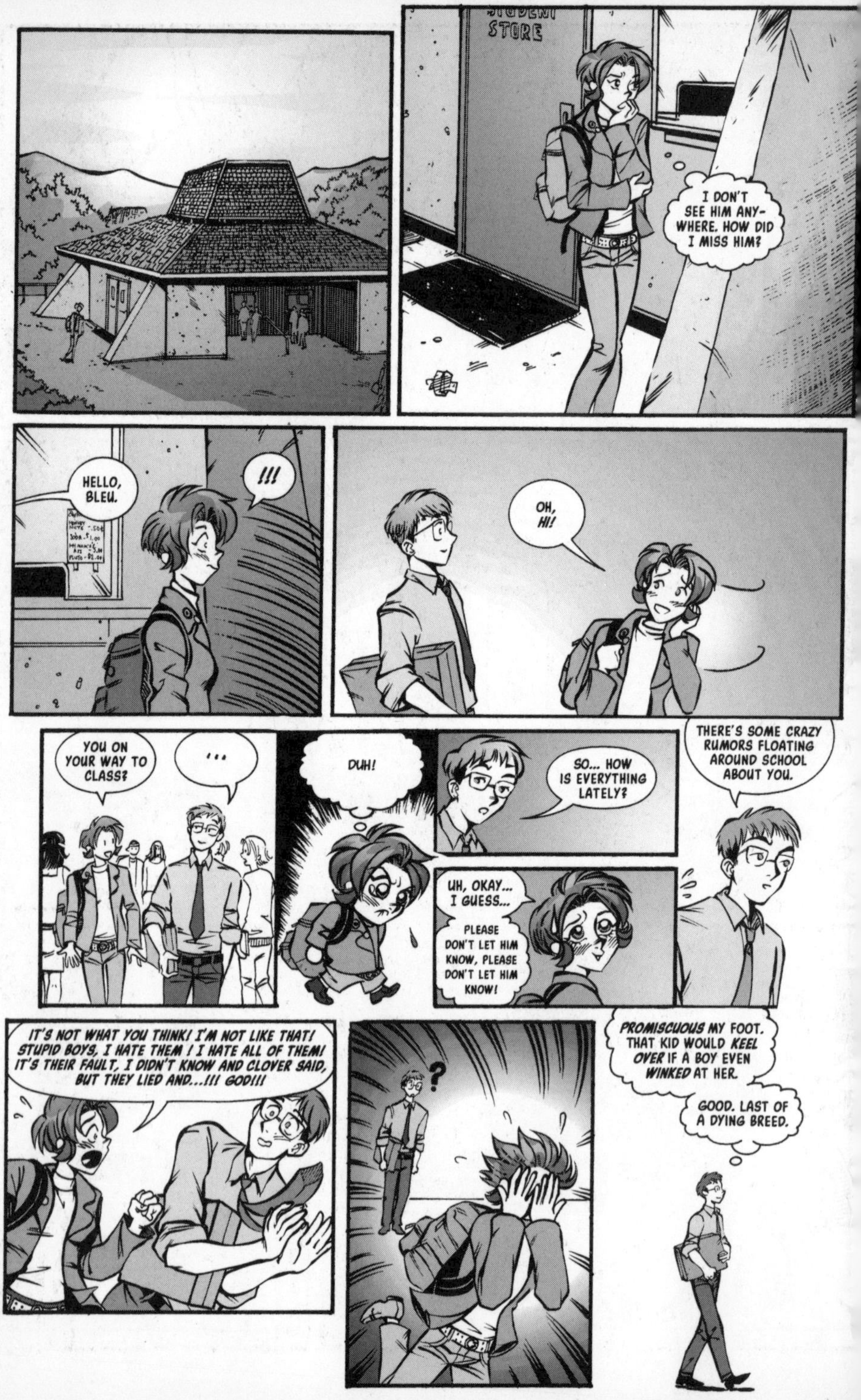

STUDENT STORE
I DON'T SEE HIM ANYWHERE. HOW DID I MISS HIM?
HELLO, BLEU.
!!!
OH, HI!
YOU ON YOUR WAY TO CLASS?
...
DUH!
SO... HOW IS EVERYTHING LATELY?
UH, OKAY... I GUESS...
PLEASE DON'T LET HIM KNOW, PLEASE DON'T LET HIM KNOW!
THERE'S SOME CRAZY RUMORS FLOATING AROUND SCHOOL ABOUT YOU.
IT'S NOT WHAT YOU THINK! I'M NOT LIKE THAT! STUPID BOYS, I HATE THEM ! I HATE ALL OF THEM! IT'S THEIR FAULT, I DIDN'T KNOW AND CLOVER SAID, BUT THEY LIED AND...!!! GOD!!!
?
PROMISCUOUS MY FOOT. THAT KID WOULD KEEL OVER IF A BOY EVEN WINKED AT HER.
GOOD. LAST OF A DYING BREED.

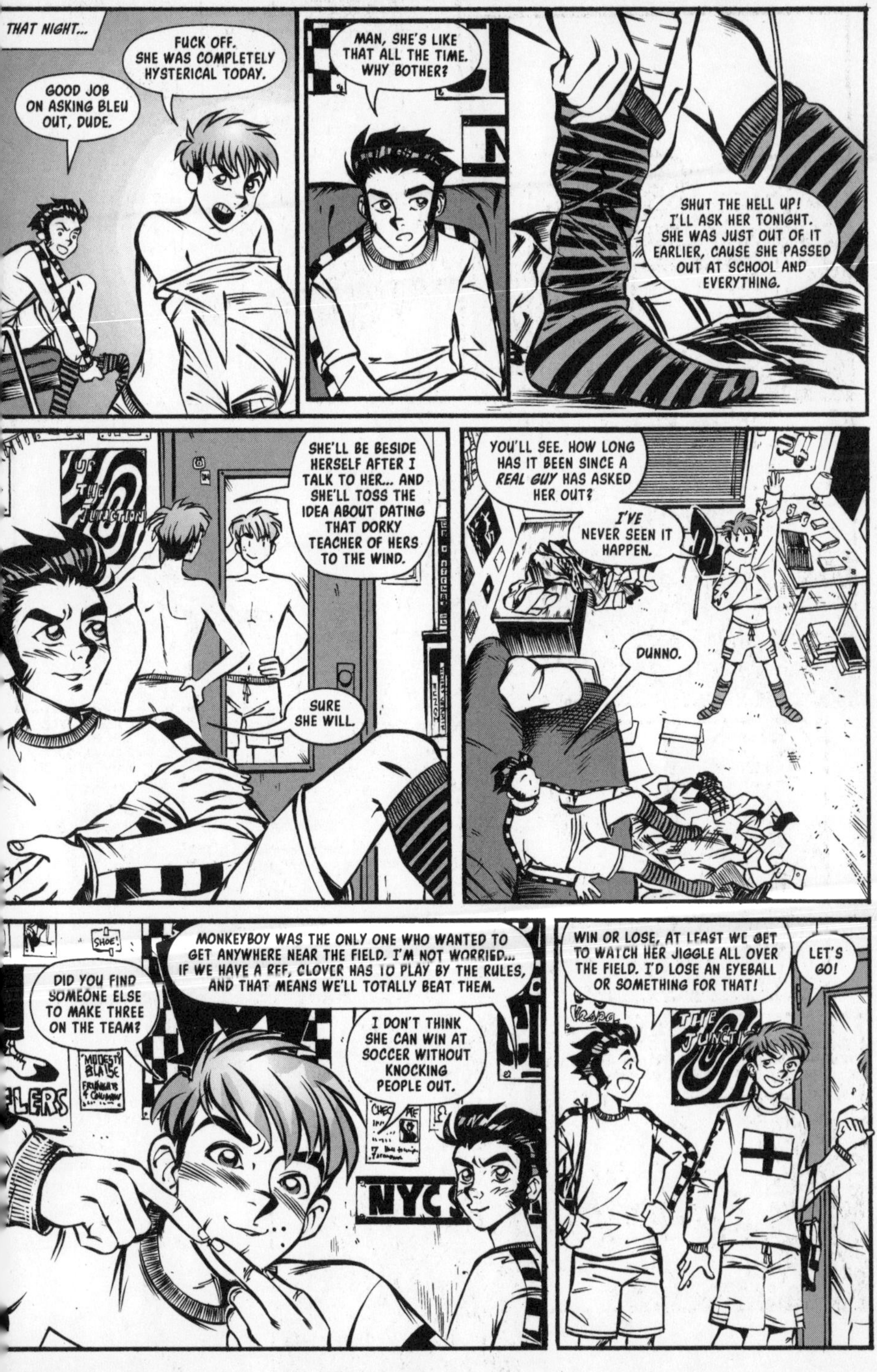

THAT NIGHT...
GOOD JOB ON ASKING BLEU OUT, DUDE.
FUCK OFF. SHE WAS COMPLETELY HYSTERICAL TODAY.
MAN, SHE'S LIKE THAT ALL THE TIME. WHY BOTHER?
SHUT THE HELL UP! I'LL ASK HER TONIGHT. SHE WAS JUST OUT OF IT EARLIER, CAUSE SHE PASSED OUT AT SCHOOL AND EVERYTHING.
SHE'LL BE BESIDE HERSELF AFTER I TALK TO HER... AND SHE'LL TOSS THE IDEA ABOUT DATING THAT DORKY TEACHER OF HERS TO THE WIND.
SURE SHE WILL.
YOU'LL SEE. HOW LONG HAS IT BEEN SINCE A REAL GUY HAS ASKED HER OUT?
I'VE NEVER SEEN IT HAPPEN.
DUNNO.
DID YOU FIND SOMEONE ELSE TO MAKE THREE ON THE TEAM?
MONKEYBOY WAS THE ONLY ONE WHO WANTED TO GET ANYWHERE NEAR THE FIELD. I'M NOT WORRIED... IF WE HAVE A REF, CLOVER HAS TO PLAY BY THE RULES, AND THAT MEANS WE'LL TOTALLY BEAT THEM.
I DON'T THINK SHE CAN WIN AT SOCCER WITHOUT KNOCKING PEOPLE OUT.
WIN OR LOSE, AT LEAST WE GET TO WATCH HER JIGGLE ALL OVER THE FIELD. I'D LOSE AN EYEBALL OR SOMETHING FOR THAT!
LET'S GO!

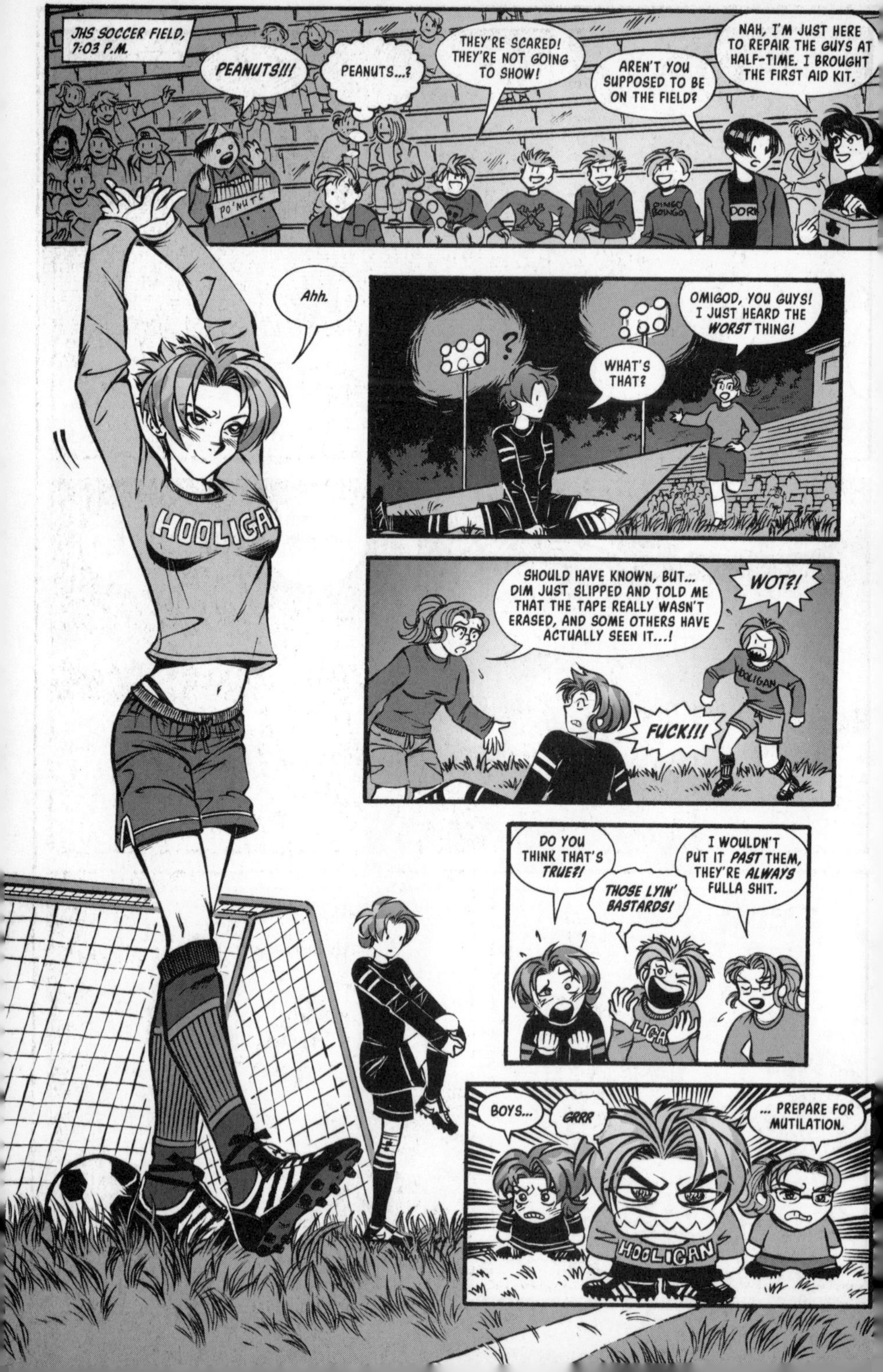

JHS SOCCER FIELD, 7:03 P.M.
PEANUTS!!!
PEANUTS...?
THEY'RE SCARED! THEY'RE NOT GOING TO SHOW!
AREN'T YOU SUPPOSED TO BE ON THE FIELD?
NAH, I'M JUST HERE TO REPAIR THE GUYS AT HALF-TIME. I BROUGHT THE FIRST AID KIT.
PO'NUTS
DORK
HOOLIGAN
Ahh.
OMIGOD, YOU GUYS! I JUST HEARD THE WORST THING!
WHAT'S THAT?
SHOULD HAVE KNOWN, BUT... DIM JUST SLIPPED AND TOLD ME THAT THE TAPE REALLY WASN'T ERASED, AND SOME OTHERS HAVE ACTUALLY SEEN IT...!
WOT?!
FUCK!!!
HOOLIGAN
DO YOU THINK THAT'S TRUE?!
THOSE LYIN' BASTARDS!
I WOULDN'T PUT IT PAST THEM, THEY'RE ALWAYS FULLA SHIT.
BOYS...
GRRR
... PREPARE FOR MUTILATION.
HOOLIGAN

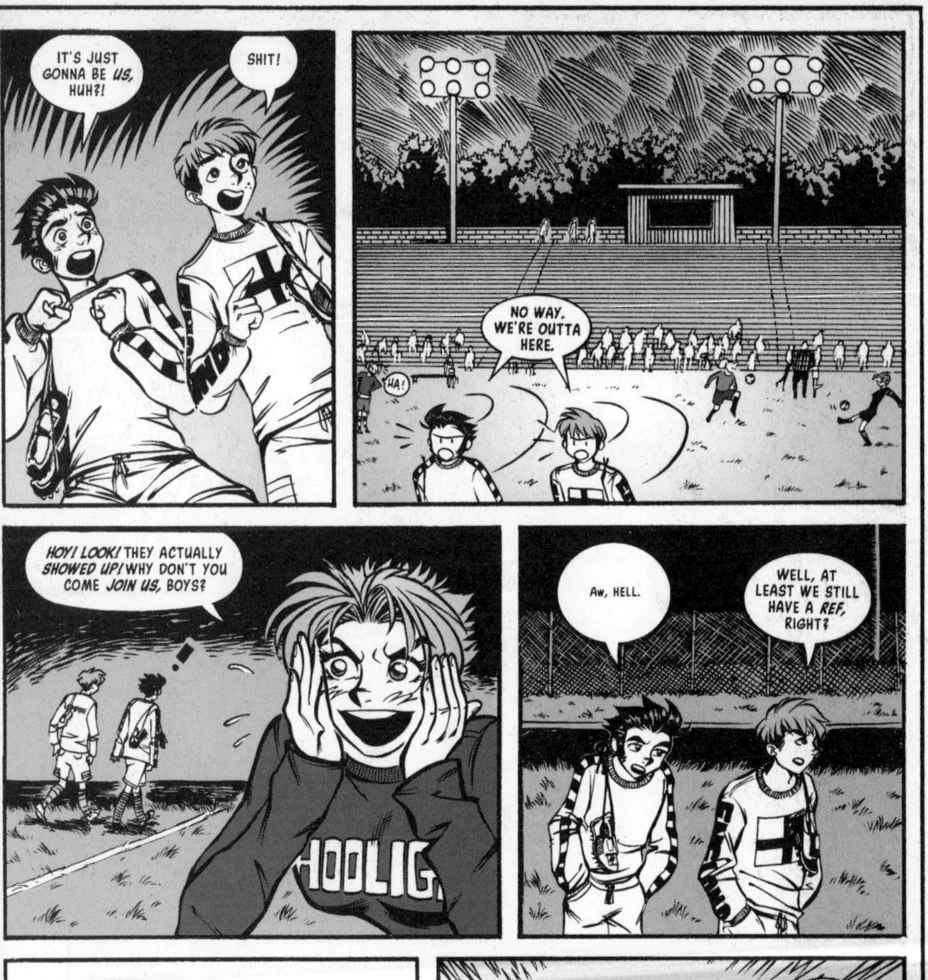
IT'S JUST GONNA BE US, HUH?!
SHIT!
NO WAY. WE'RE OUTTA HERE.
HA!
HOY! LOOK! THEY ACTUALLY SHOWED UP! WHY DON'T YOU COME JOIN US, BOYS?
HOOLIG
Aw, HELL.
WELL, AT LEAST WE STILL HAVE A REF, RIGHT?
NO FUCKING WAY. ISN'T THAT TRAVIS?
DIDN'T YOU ASK ANYTHING AT ALL ABOUT HAVING A LEGITIMATE REFEREE?!
Heh.

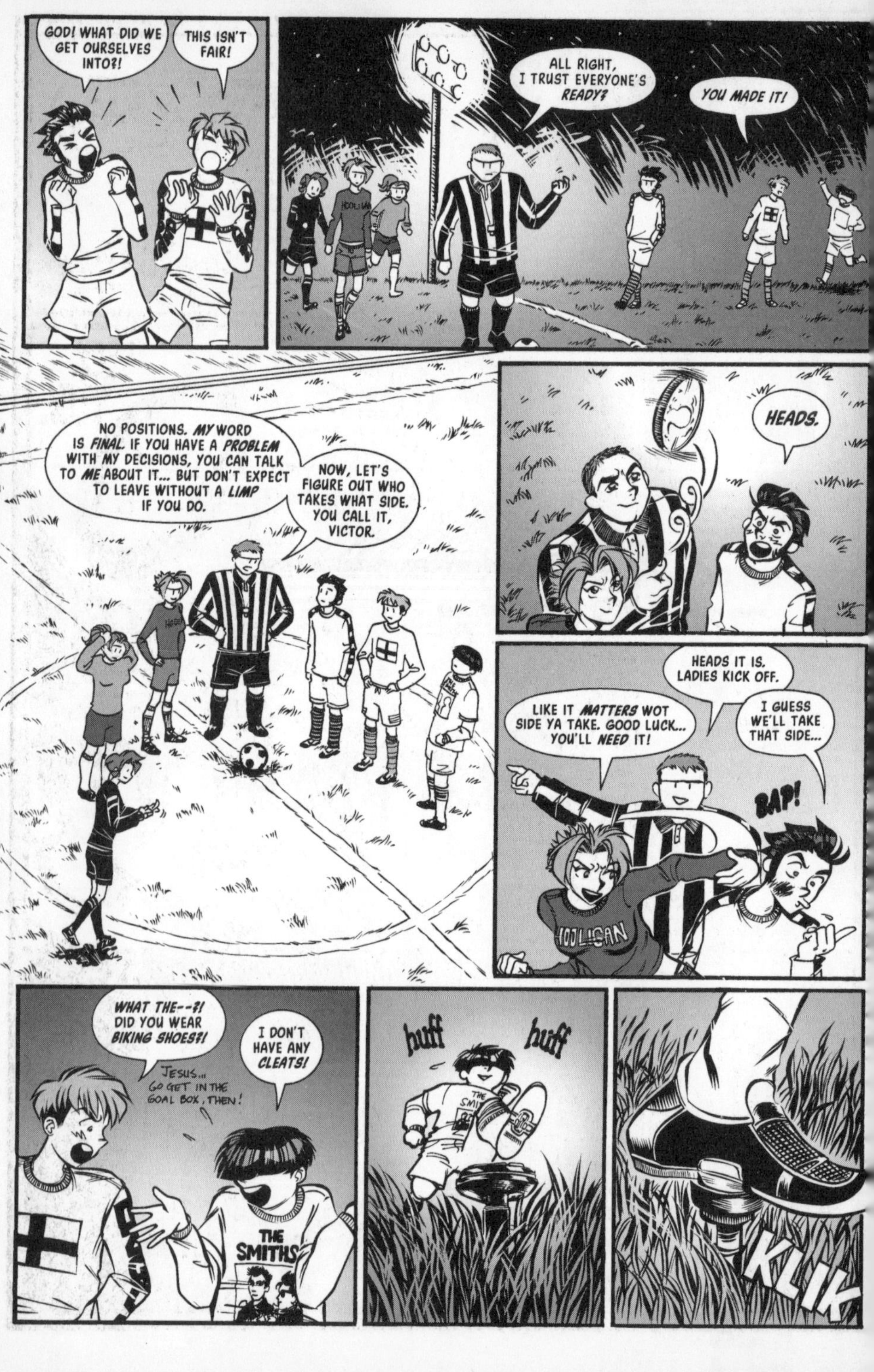
GOD! WHAT DID WE GET OURSELVES INTO?!
THIS ISN'T FAIR!
ALL RIGHT, I TRUST EVERYONE'S *READY?*
YOU MADE IT!
HOOLIGAN
NO POSITIONS. *MY* WORD IS *FINAL.* IF YOU HAVE A *PROBLEM* WITH MY DECISIONS, YOU CAN TALK TO *ME* ABOUT IT... BUT DON'T EXPECT TO LEAVE WITHOUT A *LIMP* IF YOU DO.
NOW, LET'S FIGURE OUT WHO TAKES WHAT SIDE. YOU CALL IT, VICTOR.
HEADS.
HEADS IT IS. LADIES KICK OFF.
LIKE IT *MATTERS* WOT SIDE YA TAKE. GOOD LUCK... YOU'LL *NEED* IT!
I GUESS WE'LL TAKE THAT SIDE...
BAP!
HOOLIGAN
WHAT THE--?! DID YOU WEAR BIKING SHOES?!
JESUS... GO GET IN THE GOAL BOX, THEN!
I DON'T HAVE ANY *CLEATS!*
THE SMITHS
huff
huff
KLIK

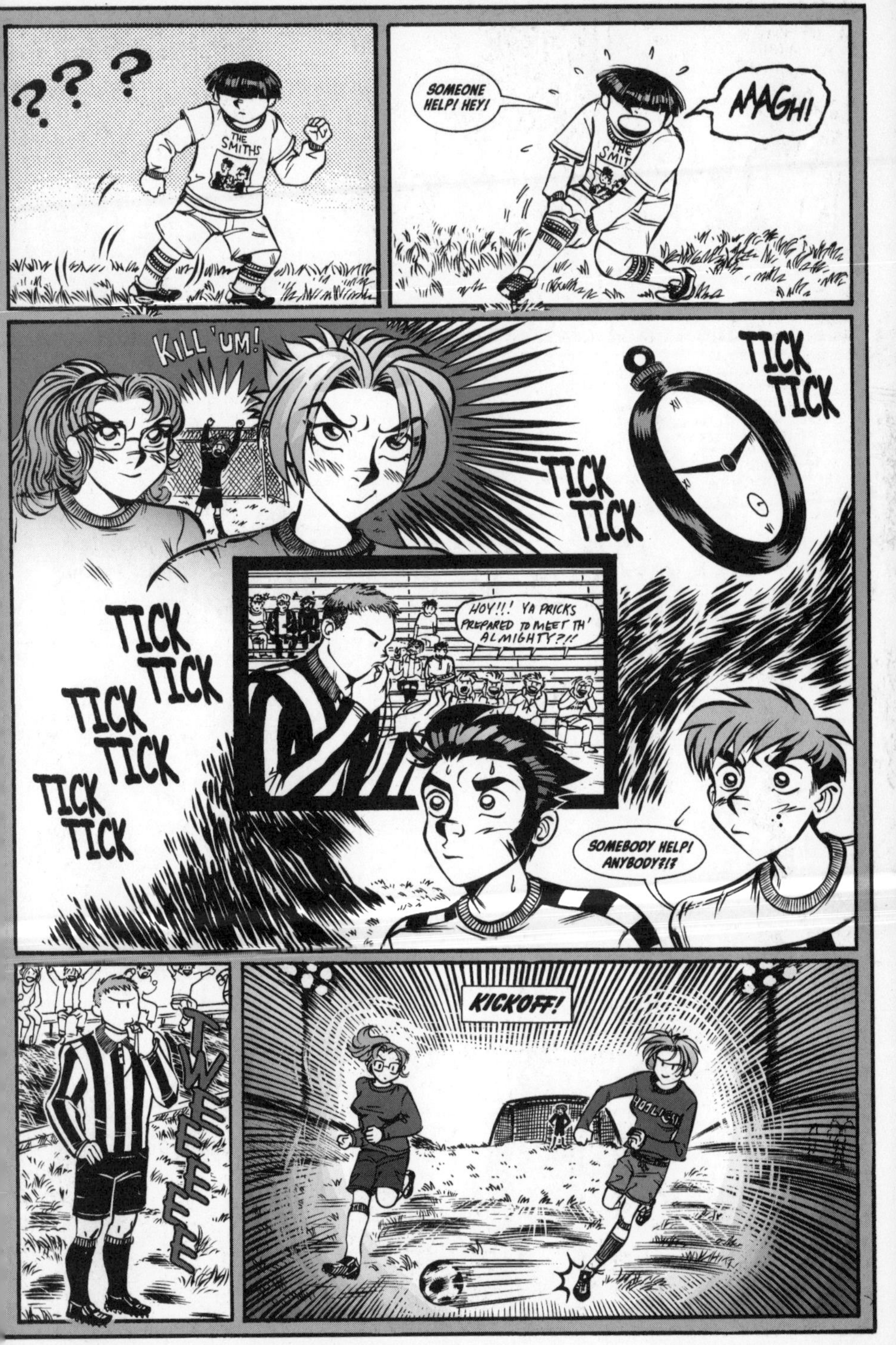
???
THE SMITHS
SOMEONE HELP! HEY!
AAAGH!
KILL 'UM!
TICK TICK
TICK TICK
HOY!!! YA PRICKS PREPARED TO MEET TH' ALMIGHTY?!!
TICK TICK
TICK TICK
TICK TICK
SOMEBODY HELP! ANYBODY?!?
TWEEEEE
KICKOFF!

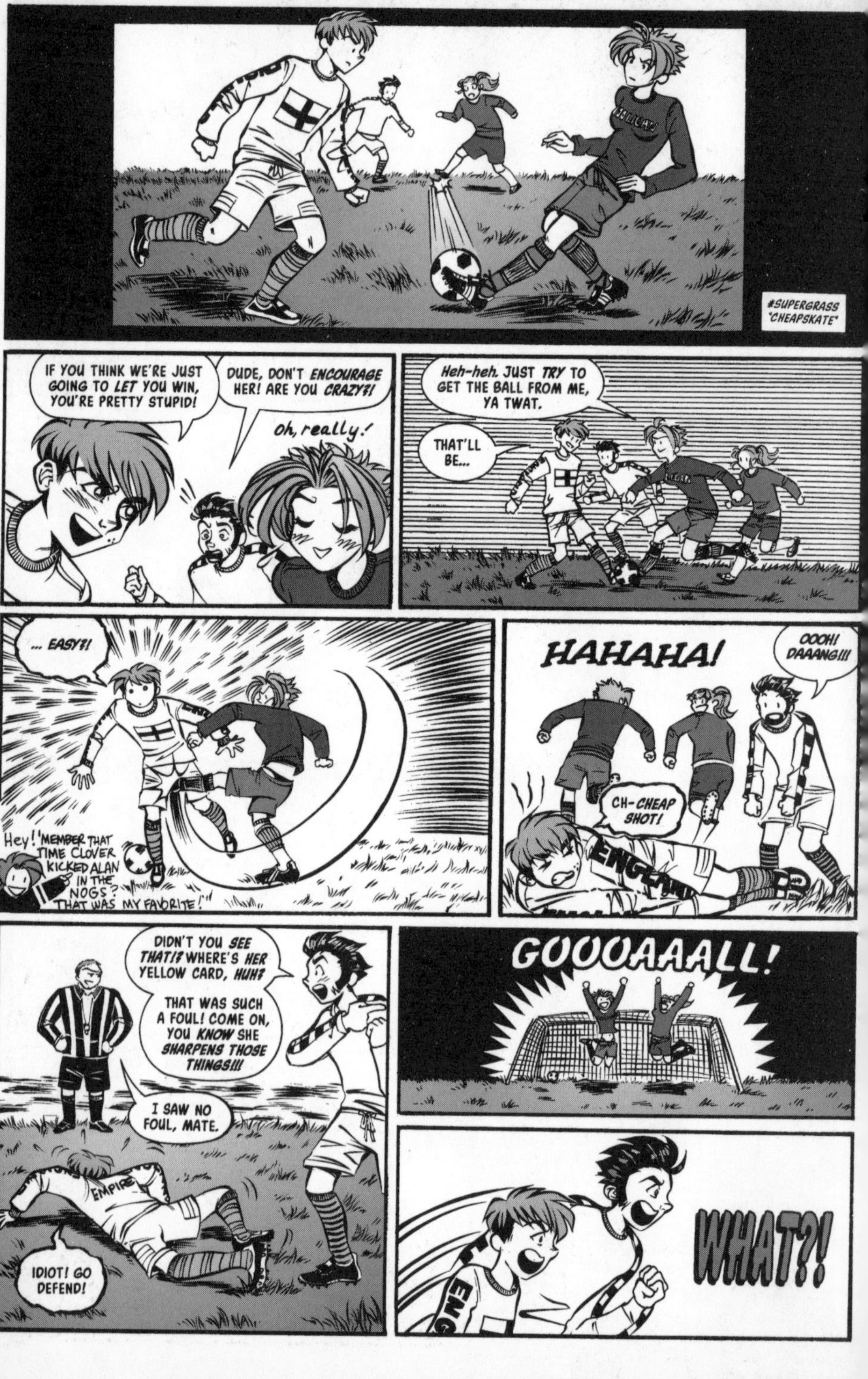
#SUPERGRASS
"CHEAPSKATE"
IF YOU THINK WE'RE JUST GOING TO LET YOU WIN, YOU'RE PRETTY STUPID!
DUDE, DON'T ENCOURAGE HER! ARE YOU CRAZY?!
Oh, really!
Heh-heh. JUST TRY TO GET THE BALL FROM ME, YA TWAT.
THAT'LL BE...
... EASY?!
Hey! 'MEMBER THAT TIME CLOVER KICKED ALAN IN THE NOGS? THAT WAS MY FAVORITE!
HAHAHA!
OOOH! DAAANG!!!
CH-CHEAP SHOT!
ENGLAND
DIDN'T YOU SEE THAT!? WHERE'S HER YELLOW CARD, HUH?
THAT WAS SUCH A FOUL! COME ON, YOU KNOW SHE SHARPENS THOSE THINGS!!!
I SAW NO FOUL, MATE.
EMPIRE
IDIOT! GO DEFEND!
GOOOAAALL!
WHAT?!

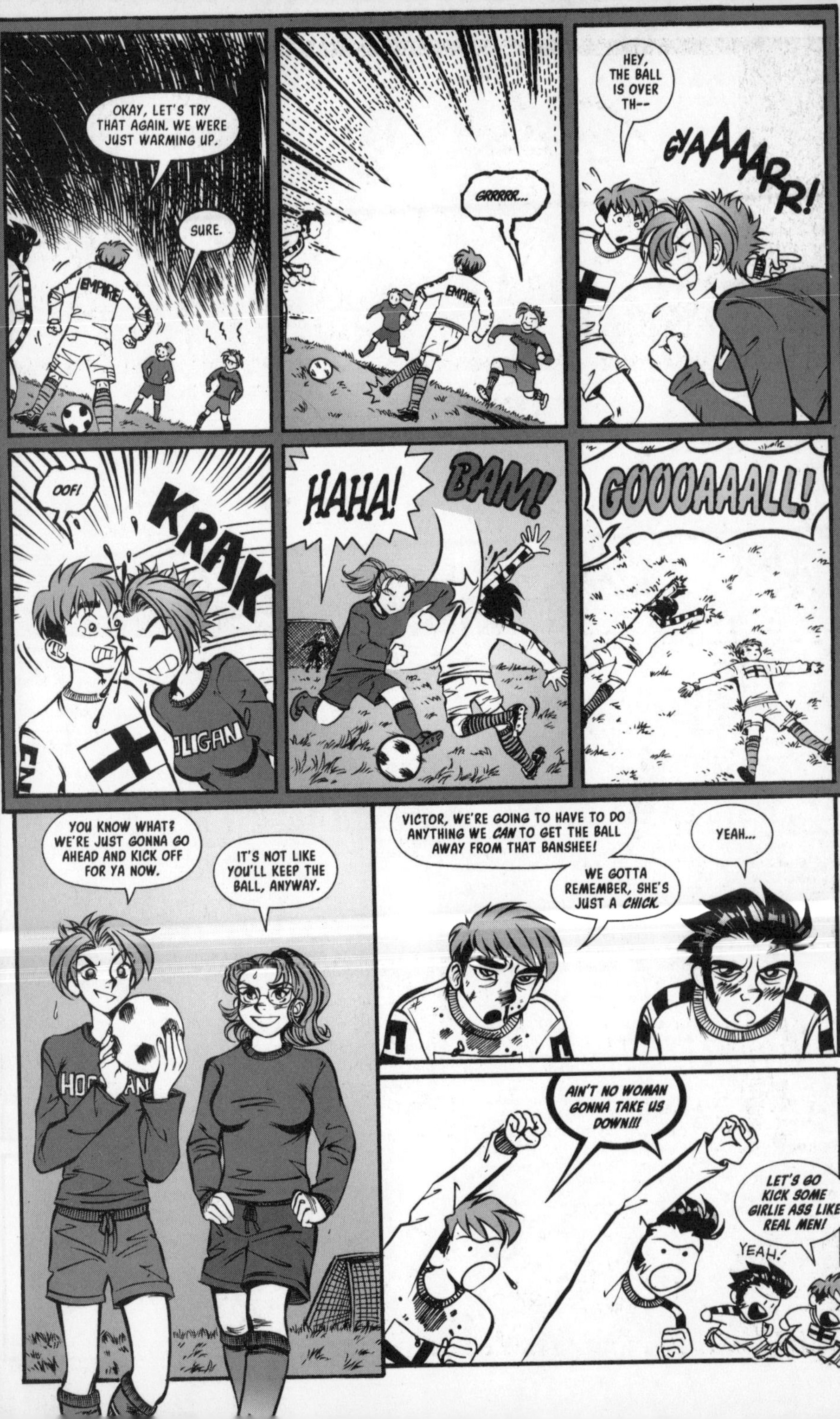

OKAY, LET'S TRY THAT AGAIN. WE WERE JUST WARMING UP.
SURE.
GRRRRR...
HEY, THE BALL IS OVER TH--
GYAAAAARRR!
OOF!
KRAK
HAHA!
BAM!
GOOOAAALL!
YOU KNOW WHAT? WE'RE JUST GONNA GO AHEAD AND KICK OFF FOR YA NOW.
IT'S NOT LIKE YOU'LL KEEP THE BALL, ANYWAY.
VICTOR, WE'RE GOING TO HAVE TO DO ANYTHING WE *CAN* TO GET THE BALL AWAY FROM THAT BANSHEE!
WE GOTTA REMEMBER, SHE'S JUST A *CHICK*.
YEAH...
AIN'T NO WOMAN GONNA TAKE US DOWN!!!
LET'S GO KICK SOME GIRLIE ASS LIKE REAL MEN!
YEAH!

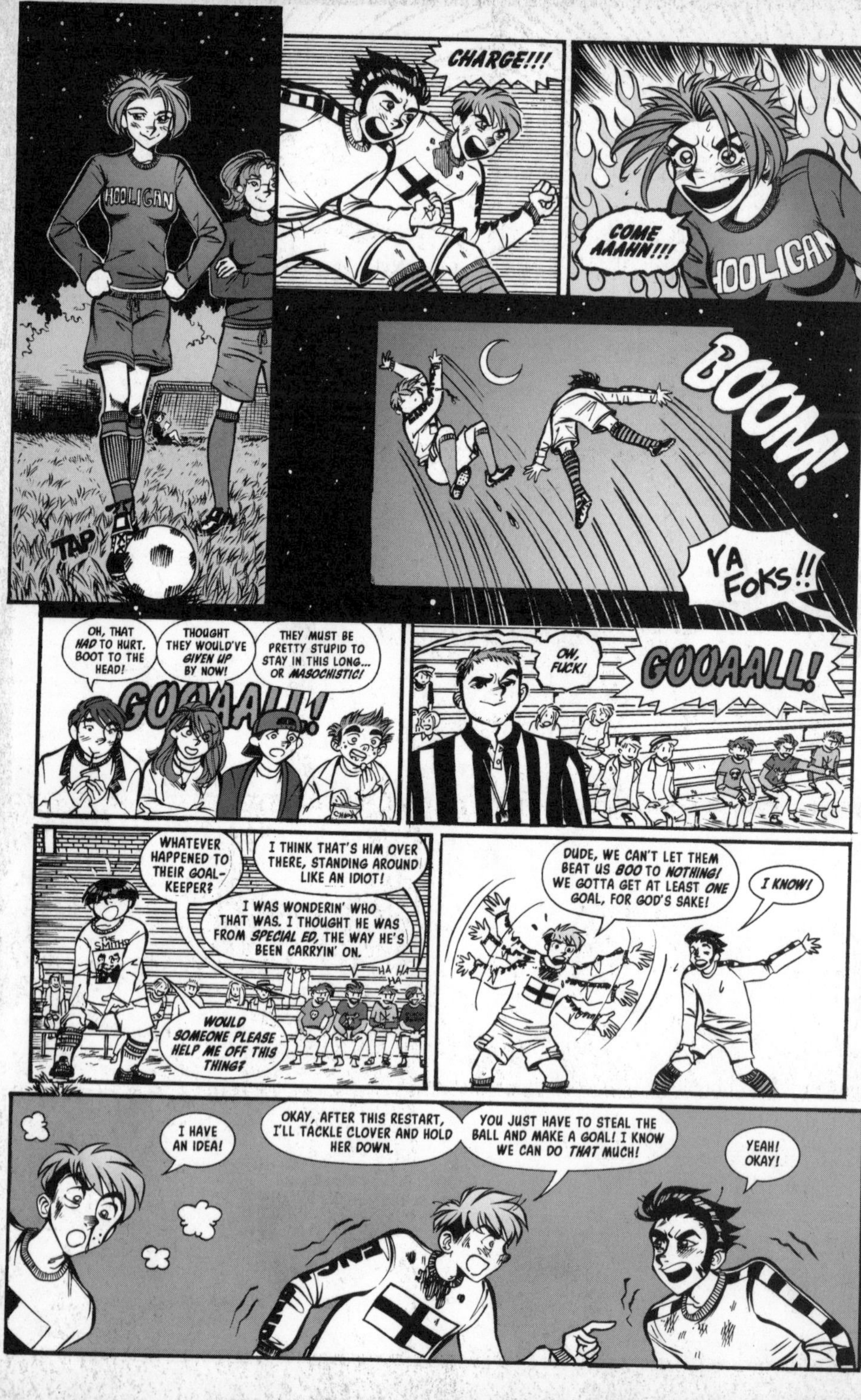
TAP
CHARGE!!!
COME AAAHN!!!
HOOLIGAN
BOOM!
YA FOKS!!
OH, THAT HAD TO HURT. BOOT TO THE HEAD!
THOUGHT THEY WOULD'VE GIVEN UP BY NOW!
THEY MUST BE PRETTY STUPID TO STAY IN THIS LONG... OR MASOCHISTIC!
OW, FUCK!
GOOAALL!
WHATEVER HAPPENED TO THEIR GOAL-KEEPER?
I THINK THAT'S HIM OVER THERE, STANDING AROUND LIKE AN IDIOT!
I WAS WONDERIN' WHO THAT WAS. I THOUGHT HE WAS FROM SPECIAL ED, THE WAY HE'S BEEN CARRYIN' ON.
HA HA HA
WOULD SOMEONE PLEASE HELP ME OFF THIS THING?
DUDE, WE CAN'T LET THEM BEAT US 800 TO NOTHING! WE GOTTA GET AT LEAST ONE GOAL, FOR GOD'S SAKE!
I KNOW!
I HAVE AN IDEA!
OKAY, AFTER THIS RESTART, I'LL TACKLE CLOVER AND HOLD HER DOWN.
YOU JUST HAVE TO STEAL THE BALL AND MAKE A GOAL! I KNOW WE CAN DO THAT MUCH!
YEAH! OKAY!

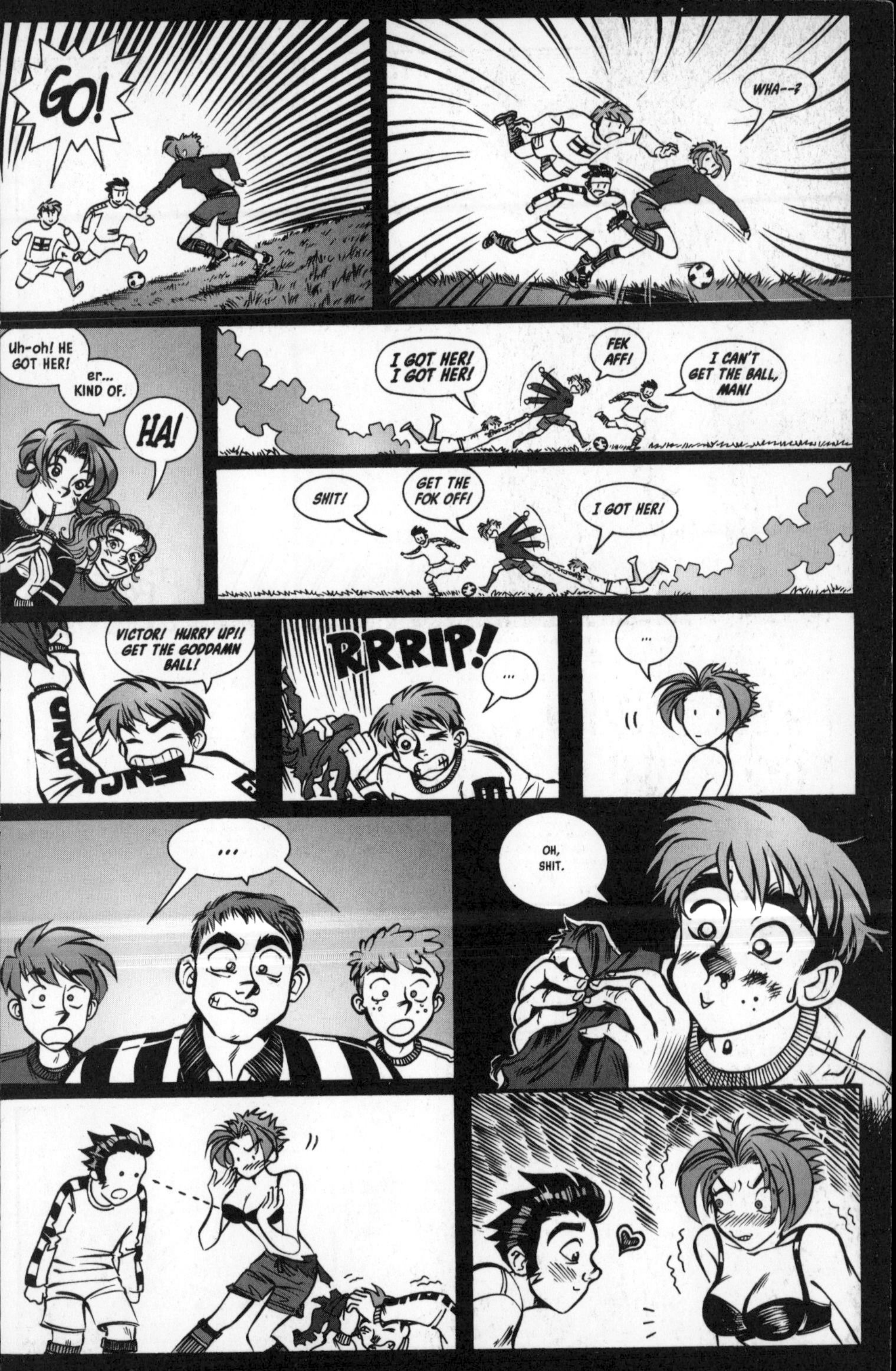
GO!
WHA--?
Uh-oh! HE GOT HER!
er... KIND OF.
HA!
I GOT HER! I GOT HER!
FEK AFF!
I CAN'T GET THE BALL, MAN!
SHIT!
GET THE FOK OFF!
I GOT HER!
VICTOR! HURRY UP!! GET THE GODDAMN BALL!
RRRIP!
...
...
...
OH, SHIT.

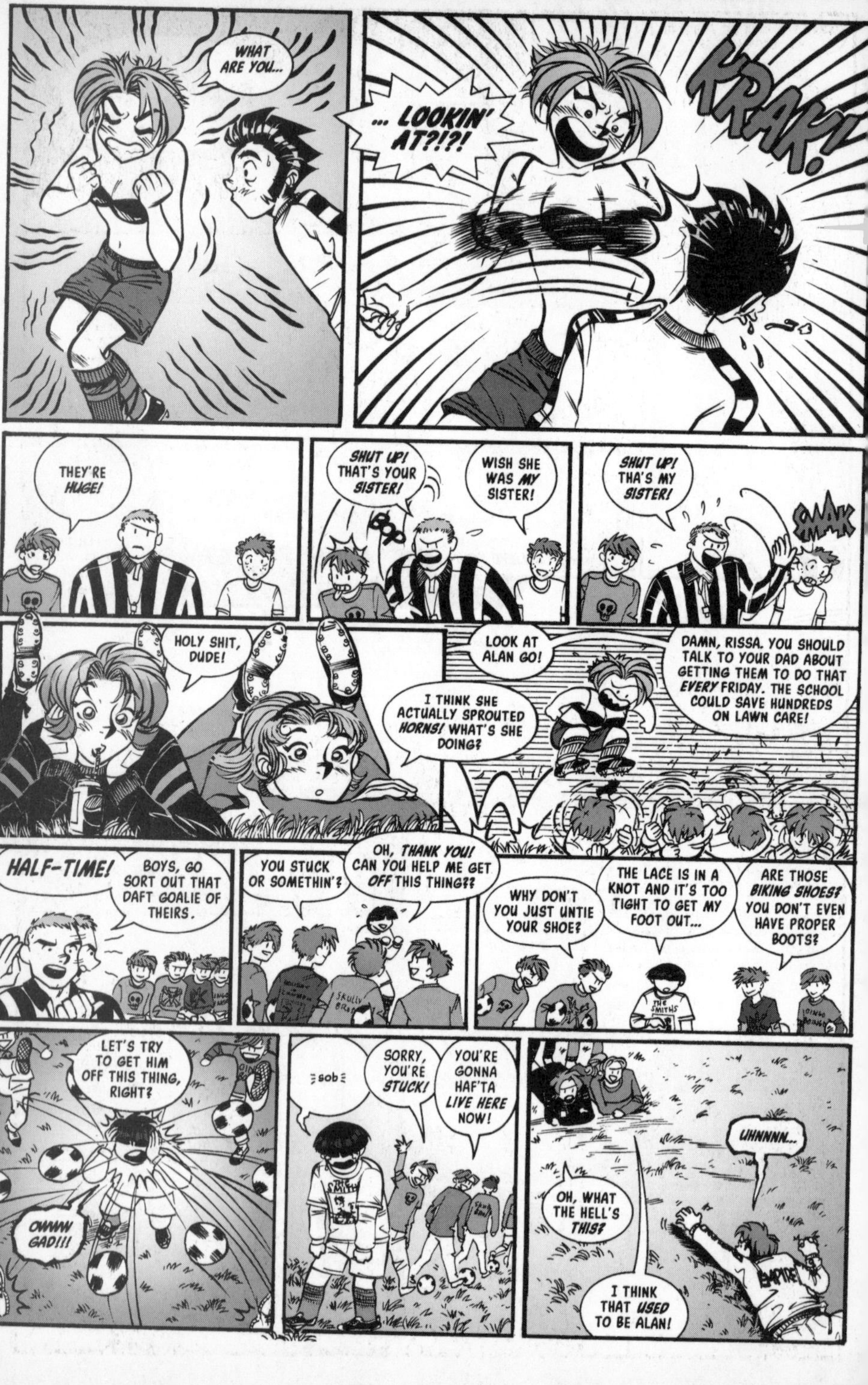
WHAT ARE YOU...
... LOOKIN' AT?!?!
KRAK!!
THEY'RE HUGE!
SHUT UP! THAT'S YOUR SISTER!
BOP
WISH SHE WAS MY SISTER!
SHUT UP! THA'S MY SISTER!
SMAK
HOLY SHIT, DUDE!
LOOK AT ALAN GO!
I THINK SHE ACTUALLY SPROUTED HORNS! WHAT'S SHE DOING?
DAMN, RISSA. YOU SHOULD TALK TO YOUR DAD ABOUT GETTING THEM TO DO THAT EVERY FRIDAY. THE SCHOOL COULD SAVE HUNDREDS ON LAWN CARE!
HALF-TIME!
BOYS, GO SORT OUT THAT DAFT GOALIE OF THEIRS.
YOU STUCK OR SOMETHIN'?
OH, THANK YOU! CAN YOU HELP ME GET OFF THIS THING??
WHY DON'T YOU JUST UNTIE YOUR SHOE?
THE LACE IS IN A KNOT AND IT'S TOO TIGHT TO GET MY FOOT OUT...
ARE THOSE BIKING SHOES? YOU DON'T EVEN HAVE PROPER BOOTS?
LET'S TRY TO GET HIM OFF THIS THING, RIGHT?
OWWW GAD!!!
sob
SORRY, YOU'RE STUCK!
YOU'RE GONNA HAF'TA LIVE HERE NOW!
UHNNNN...
OH, WHAT THE HELL'S THIS?
I THINK THAT USED TO BE ALAN!

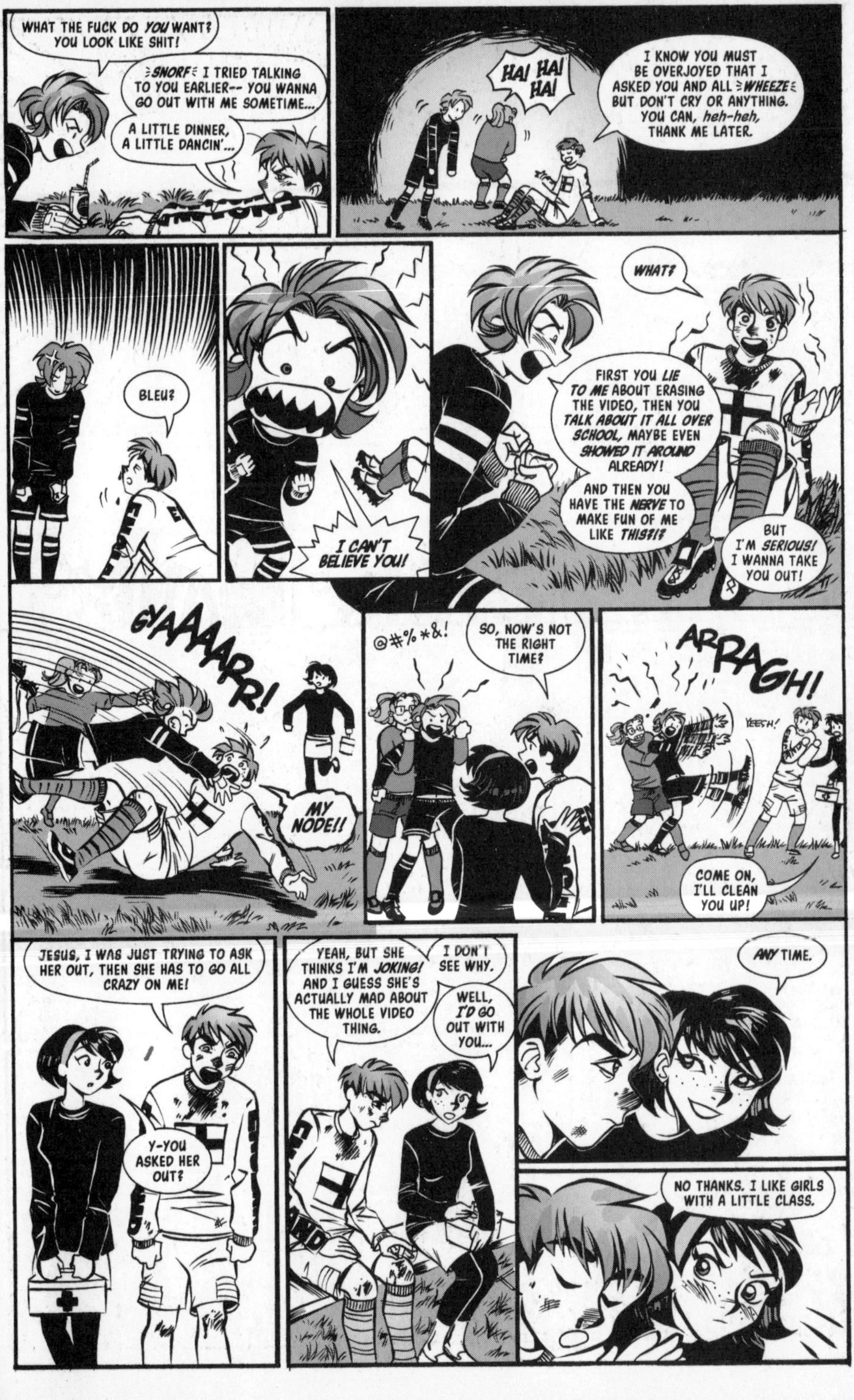
WHAT THE FUCK DO YOU WANT? YOU LOOK LIKE SHIT!
SNORF I TRIED TALKING TO YOU EARLIER-- YOU WANNA GO OUT WITH ME SOMETIME...
A LITTLE DINNER, A LITTLE DANCIN'...
HA! HA! HA!
I KNOW YOU MUST BE OVERJOYED THAT I ASKED YOU AND ALL WHEEZE BUT DON'T CRY OR ANYTHING. YOU CAN, heh-heh, THANK ME LATER.
BLEU?
I CAN'T BELIEVE YOU!
WHAT?
FIRST YOU LIE TO ME ABOUT ERASING THE VIDEO, THEN YOU TALK ABOUT IT ALL OVER SCHOOL, MAYBE EVEN SHOWED IT AROUND ALREADY!
AND THEN YOU HAVE THE NERVE TO MAKE FUN OF ME LIKE THIS?!?
BUT I'M SERIOUS! I WANNA TAKE YOU OUT!
GYAAAARR!
MY NODE!!
@#%*&!
SO, NOW'S NOT THE RIGHT TIME?
ARRAGH!
YEESH!
COME ON, I'LL CLEAN YOU UP!
JESUS, I WAS JUST TRYING TO ASK HER OUT, THEN SHE HAS TO GO ALL CRAZY ON ME!
Y-YOU ASKED HER OUT?
YEAH, BUT SHE THINKS I'M JOKING! AND I GUESS SHE'S ACTUALLY MAD ABOUT THE WHOLE VIDEO THING.
I DON'T SEE WHY.
WELL, I'D GO OUT WITH YOU...
ANY TIME.
NO THANKS. I LIKE GIRLS WITH A LITTLE CLASS.

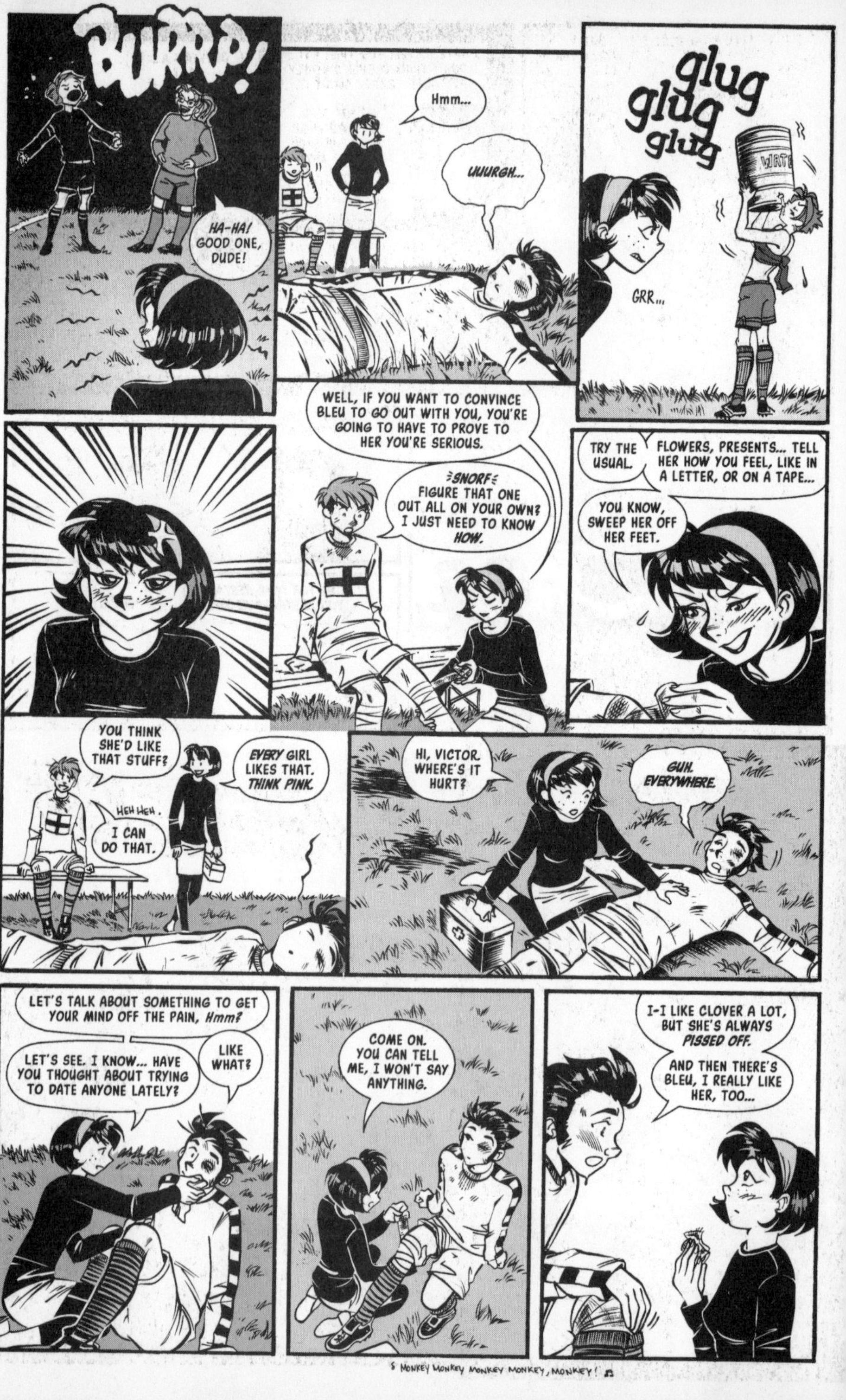
BURRP!
HA-HA! GOOD ONE, DUDE!
Hmm...
UUURGH...
glug glug glug
WATE
GRR...
WELL, IF YOU WANT TO CONVINCE BLEU TO GO OUT WITH YOU, YOU'RE GOING TO HAVE TO PROVE TO HER YOU'RE SERIOUS.
SNORF
FIGURE THAT ONE OUT ALL ON YOUR OWN? I JUST NEED TO KNOW HOW.
TRY THE USUAL.
FLOWERS, PRESENTS... TELL HER HOW YOU FEEL, LIKE IN A LETTER, OR ON A TAPE...
YOU KNOW, SWEEP HER OFF HER FEET.
YOU THINK SHE'D LIKE THAT STUFF?
EVERY GIRL LIKES THAT. THINK PINK.
HEH HEH. I CAN DO THAT.
HI, VICTOR. WHERE'S IT HURT?
GUH. EVERYWHERE.
LET'S TALK ABOUT SOMETHING TO GET YOUR MIND OFF THE PAIN, Hmm?
LET'S SEE. I KNOW... HAVE YOU THOUGHT ABOUT TRYING TO DATE ANYONE LATELY?
LIKE WHAT?
COME ON. YOU CAN TELL ME, I WON'T SAY ANYTHING.
I-I LIKE CLOVER A LOT, BUT SHE'S ALWAYS PISSED OFF.
AND THEN THERE'S BLEU, I REALLY LIKE HER, TOO...
MONKEY MONKEY MONKEY MONKEY, MONKEY!

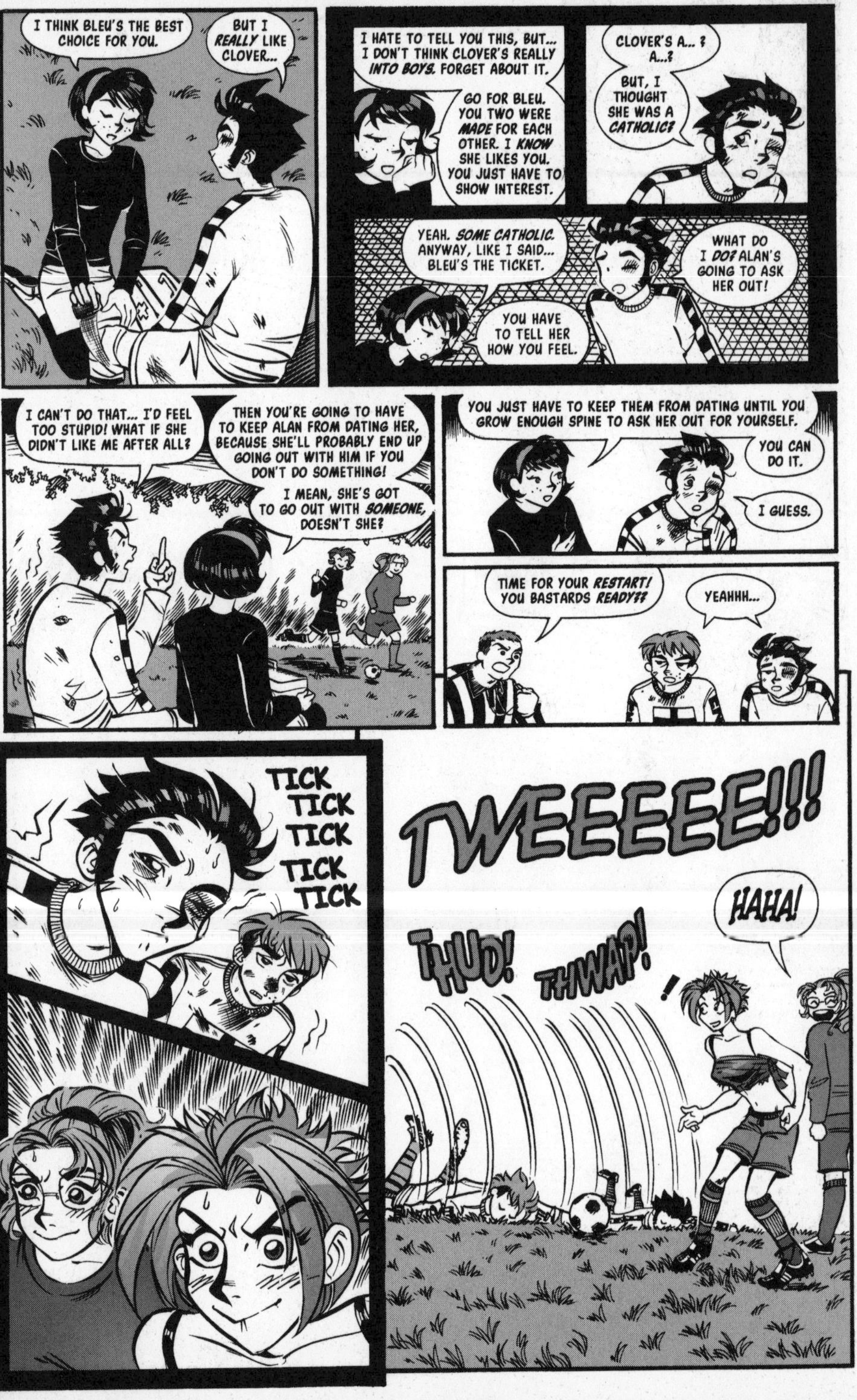

I THINK BLEU'S THE BEST CHOICE FOR YOU.
BUT I REALLY LIKE CLOVER...
I HATE TO TELL YOU THIS, BUT... I DON'T THINK CLOVER'S REALLY INTO BOYS. FORGET ABOUT IT.
GO FOR BLEU. YOU TWO WERE MADE FOR EACH OTHER. I KNOW SHE LIKES YOU. YOU JUST HAVE TO SHOW INTEREST.
CLOVER'S A...? A...?
BUT, I THOUGHT SHE WAS A CATHOLIC?
YEAH. SOME CATHOLIC. ANYWAY, LIKE I SAID... BLEU'S THE TICKET.
WHAT DO I DO? ALAN'S GOING TO ASK HER OUT!
YOU HAVE TO TELL HER HOW YOU FEEL.
I CAN'T DO THAT... I'D FEEL TOO STUPID! WHAT IF SHE DIDN'T LIKE ME AFTER ALL?
THEN YOU'RE GOING TO HAVE TO KEEP ALAN FROM DATING HER, BECAUSE SHE'LL PROBABLY END UP GOING OUT WITH HIM IF YOU DON'T DO SOMETHING!
I MEAN, SHE'S GOT TO GO OUT WITH SOMEONE, DOESN'T SHE?
YOU JUST HAVE TO KEEP THEM FROM DATING UNTIL YOU GROW ENOUGH SPINE TO ASK HER OUT FOR YOURSELF.
YOU CAN DO IT.
I GUESS.
TIME FOR YOUR RESTART! YOU BASTARDS READY??
YEAHHH...
TICK TICK TICK TICK TICK
TWEEEEE!!!
THUD! THWAP!
HAHA!
!

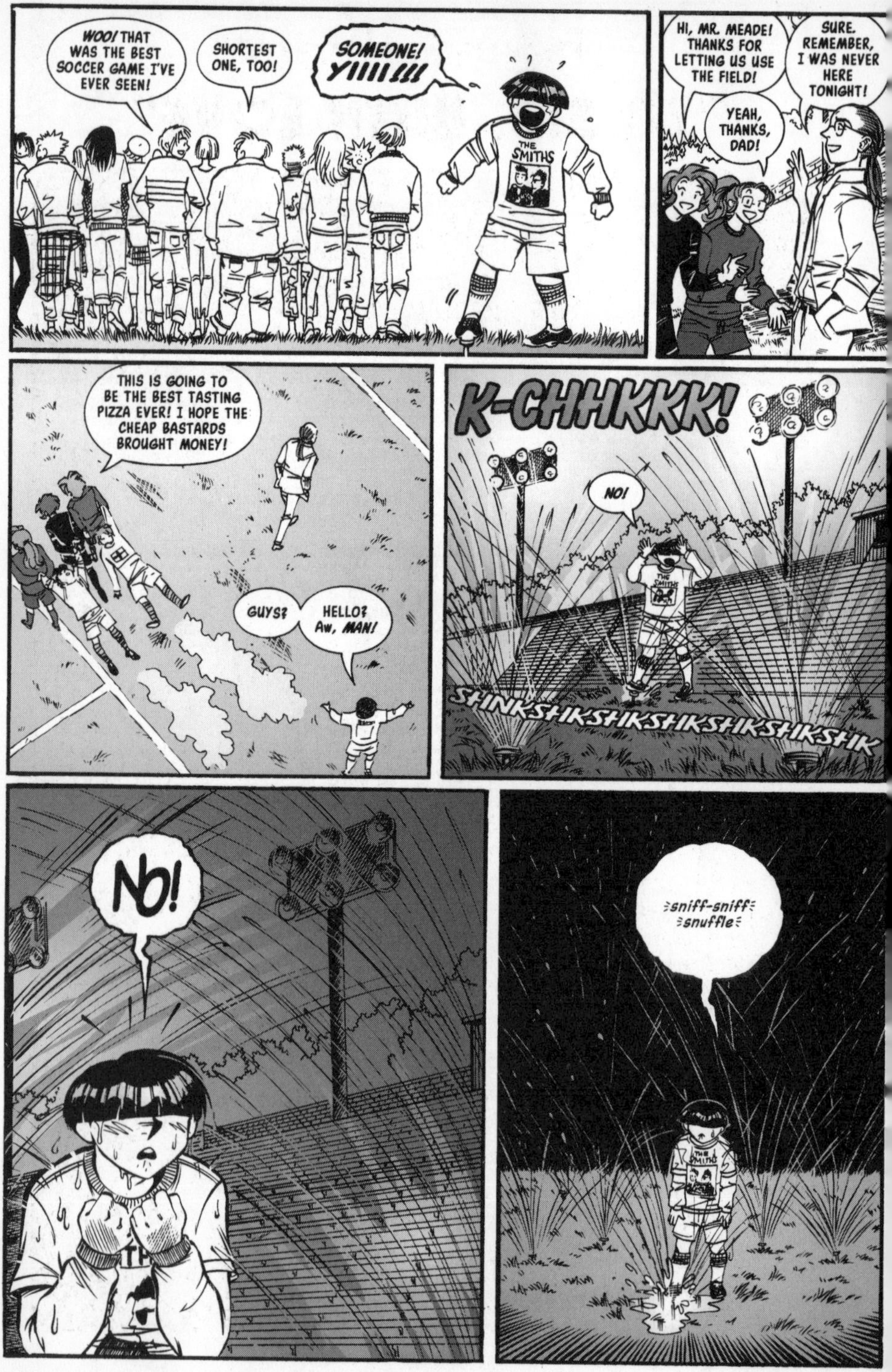
WOO! THAT WAS THE BEST SOCCER GAME I'VE EVER SEEN!
SHORTEST ONE, TOO!
SOMEONE! YIIII!!!
HI, MR. MEADE! THANKS FOR LETTING US USE THE FIELD!
YEAH, THANKS, DAD!
SURE. REMEMBER, I WAS NEVER HERE TONIGHT!
THIS IS GOING TO BE THE BEST TASTING PIZZA EVER! I HOPE THE CHEAP BASTARDS BROUGHT MONEY!
GUYS?
HELLO? Aw, MAN!
K-CHHKKK!
NO!
SHIKSHIKSHIKSHIKSHIKSHIKSHIKSHIK
NO!
sniff-sniff
snuffle

chapter three:

"TO SIR, WITH LOVE"

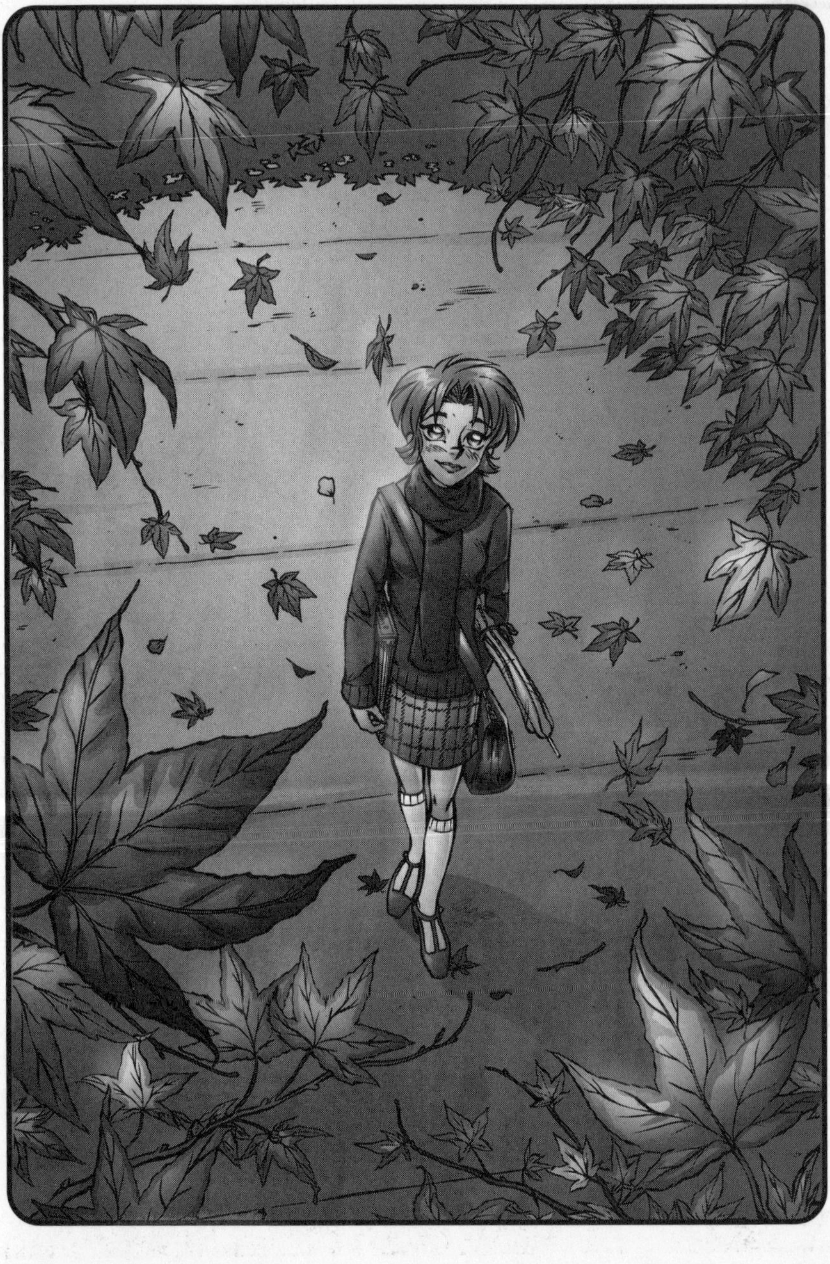

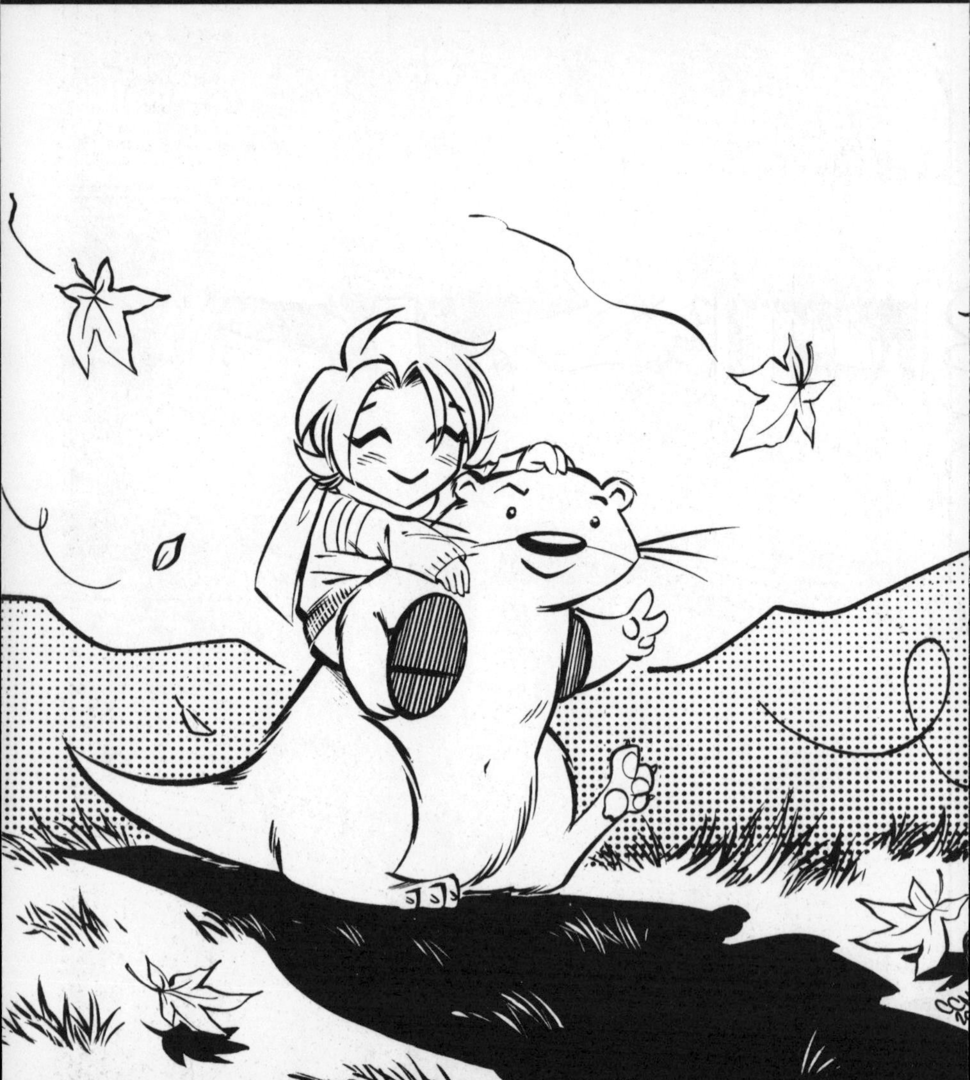

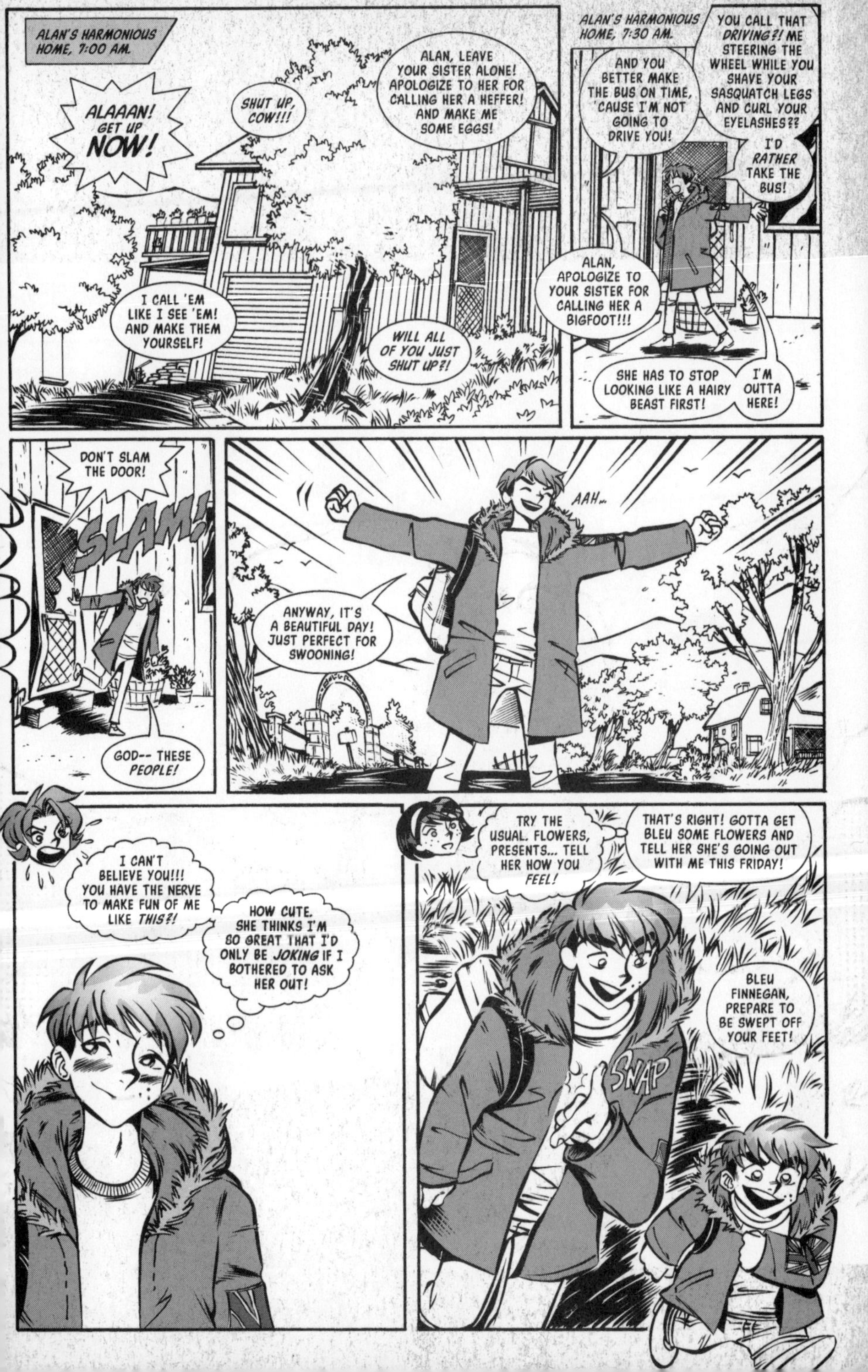
ALAN'S HARMONIOUS HOME, 7:00 AM.
ALAAAN! GET UP NOW!
SHUT UP, COW!!!
ALAN, LEAVE YOUR SISTER ALONE! APOLOGIZE TO HER FOR CALLING HER A HEFFER! AND MAKE ME SOME EGGS!
I CALL 'EM LIKE I SEE 'EM! AND MAKE THEM YOURSELF!
WILL ALL OF YOU JUST SHUT UP?!
ALAN'S HARMONIOUS HOME, 7:30 AM.
AND YOU BETTER MAKE THE BUS ON TIME, 'CAUSE I'M NOT GOING TO DRIVE YOU!
YOU CALL THAT DRIVING?! ME STEERING THE WHEEL WHILE YOU SHAVE YOUR SASQUATCH LEGS AND CURL YOUR EYELASHES??
I'D RATHER TAKE THE BUS!
ALAN, APOLOGIZE TO YOUR SISTER FOR CALLING HER A BIGFOOT!!!
SHE HAS TO STOP LOOKING LIKE A HAIRY BEAST FIRST!
I'M OUTTA HERE!
DON'T SLAM THE DOOR!
SLAM!
GOD-- THESE PEOPLE!
AAH...
ANYWAY, IT'S A BEAUTIFUL DAY! JUST PERFECT FOR SWOONING!
I CAN'T BELIEVE YOU!!! YOU HAVE THE NERVE TO MAKE FUN OF ME LIKE THIS?!
HOW CUTE. SHE THINKS I'M SO GREAT THAT I'D ONLY BE JOKING IF I BOTHERED TO ASK HER OUT!
TRY THE USUAL. FLOWERS, PRESENTS... TELL HER HOW YOU FEEL!
THAT'S RIGHT! GOTTA GET BLEU SOME FLOWERS AND TELL HER SHE'S GOING OUT WITH ME THIS FRIDAY!
SNAP
BLEU FINNEGAN, PREPARE TO BE SWEPT OFF YOUR FEET!

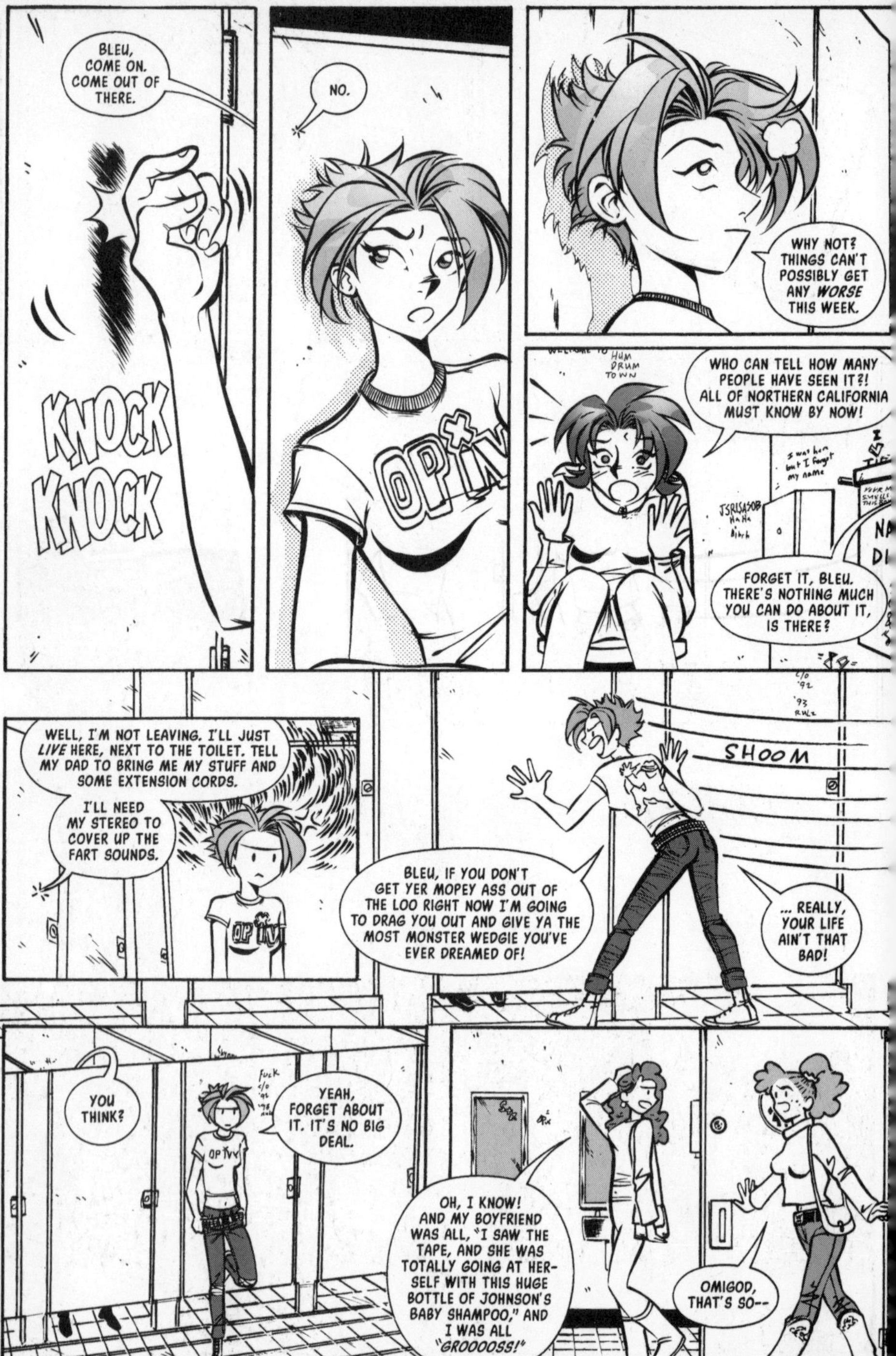
BLEU, COME ON. COME OUT OF THERE.
KNOCK KNOCK
NO.
WHY NOT? THINGS CAN'T POSSIBLY GET ANY *WORSE* THIS WEEK.
HUM DRUM TOWN
WHO CAN TELL HOW MANY PEOPLE HAVE SEEN IT?! ALL OF NORTHERN CALIFORNIA MUST KNOW BY NOW!
FORGET IT, BLEU. THERE'S NOTHING MUCH YOU CAN DO ABOUT IT, IS THERE?
WELL, I'M NOT LEAVING. I'LL JUST *LIVE* HERE, NEXT TO THE TOILET. TELL MY DAD TO BRING ME MY STUFF AND SOME EXTENSION CORDS.
I'LL NEED MY STEREO TO COVER UP THE FART SOUNDS.
SHOOM
BLEU, IF YOU DON'T GET YER MOPEY ASS OUT OF THE LOO RIGHT NOW I'M GOING TO DRAG YOU OUT AND GIVE YA THE MOST MONSTER WEDGIE YOU'VE EVER DREAMED OF!
... REALLY, YOUR LIFE AIN'T THAT BAD!
YOU THINK?
YEAH, FORGET ABOUT IT. IT'S NO BIG DEAL.
OH, I KNOW! AND MY BOYFRIEND WAS ALL, "I SAW THE TAPE, AND SHE WAS TOTALLY GOING AT HERSELF WITH THIS HUGE BOTTLE OF JOHNSON'S BABY SHAMPOO," AND I WAS ALL "*GROOOOSS!*"
OMIGOD, THAT'S SO--

IF THIS WAS IN COLOR, YOU'D SEE THOSE WE
PINK STONEWASHED JEANS. THIS HAPP

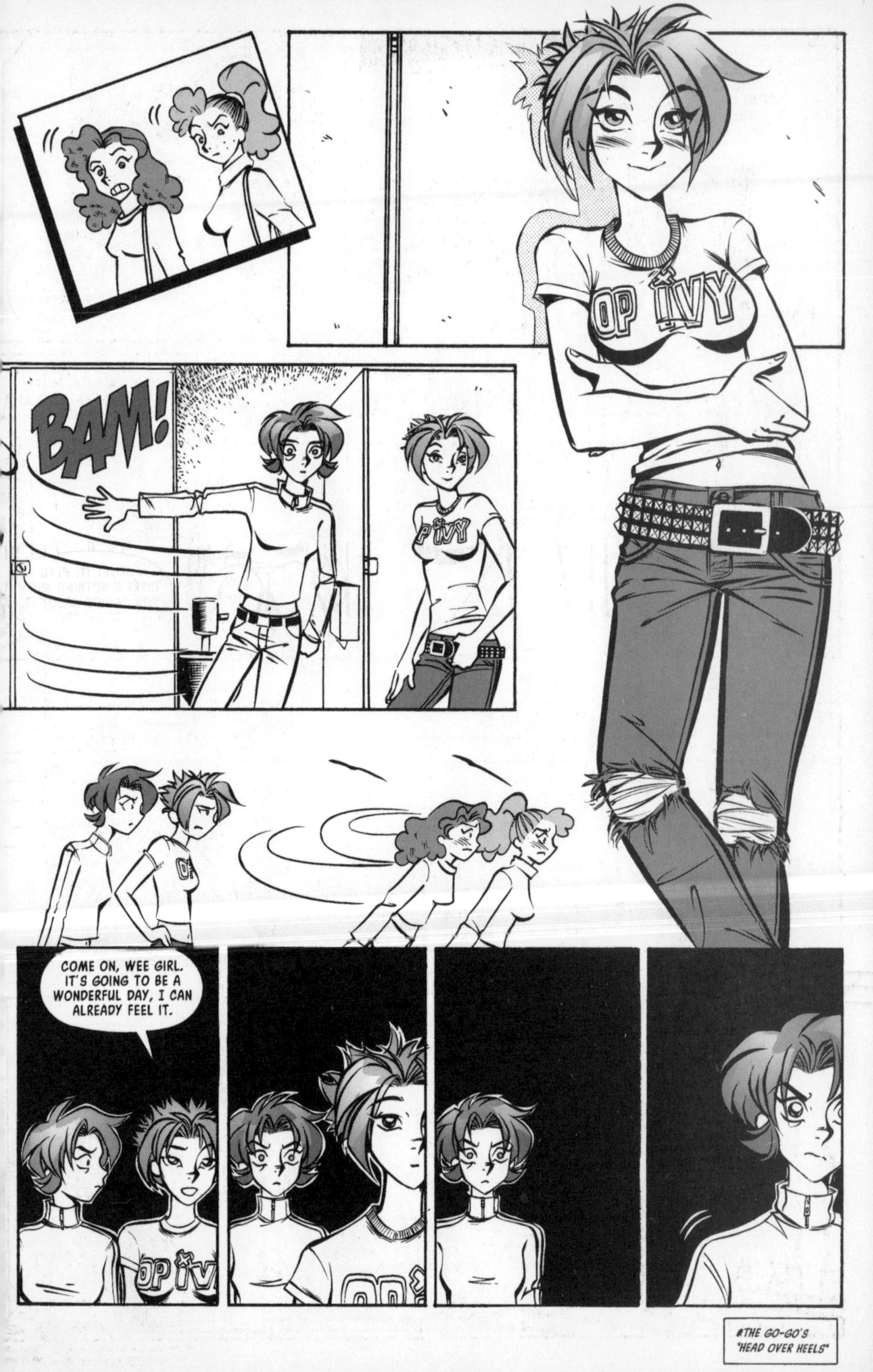
BAM!
COME ON, WEE GIRL. IT'S GOING TO BE A WONDERFUL DAY, I CAN ALREADY FEEL IT.
#THE GO-GO'S "HEAD OVER HEELS"

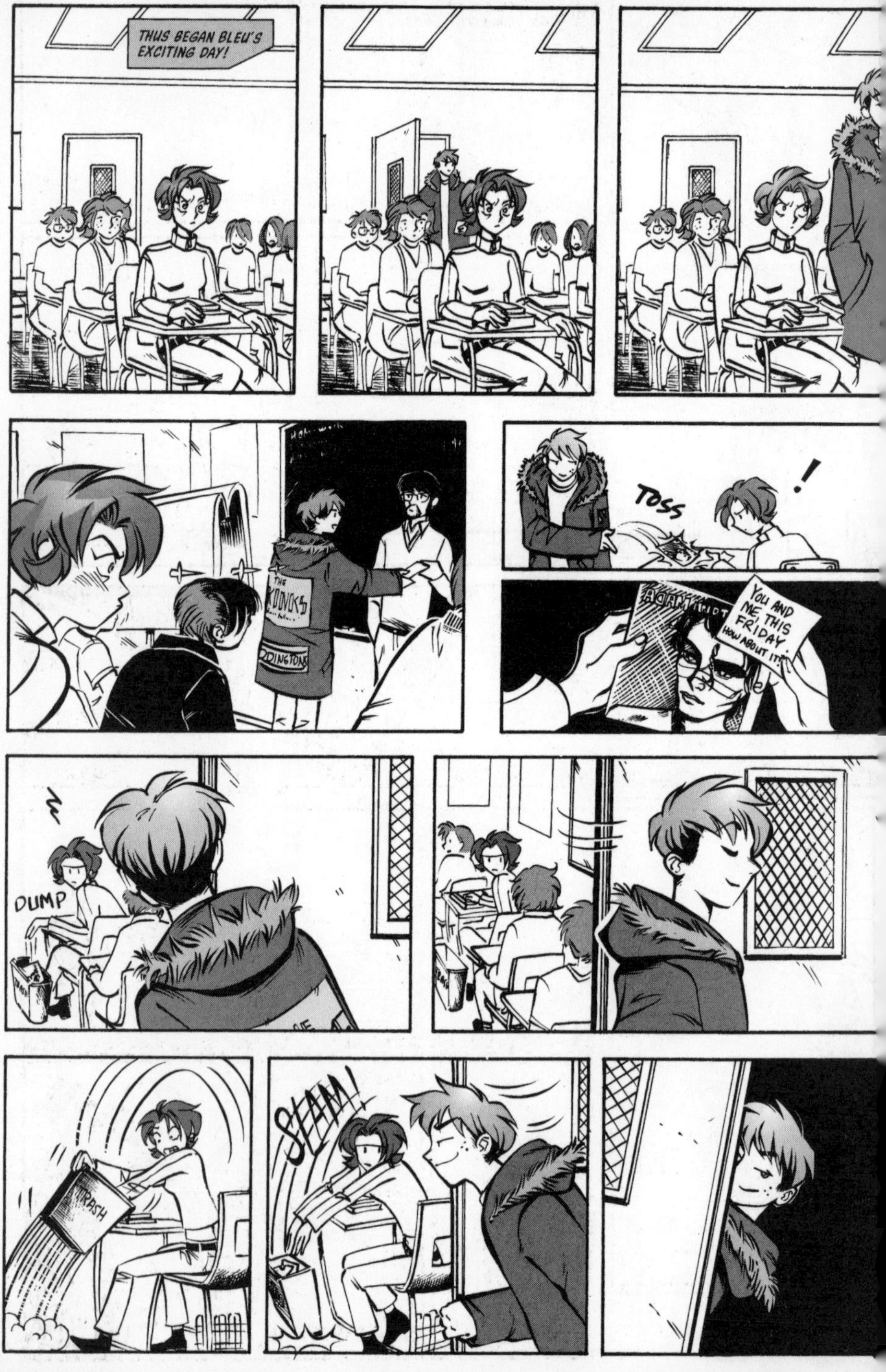
THUS BEGAN BLEU'S EXCITING DAY!
TOSS
!
YOU AND ME, THIS FRIDAY. HOW ABOUT IT?
DUMP
SLAM!

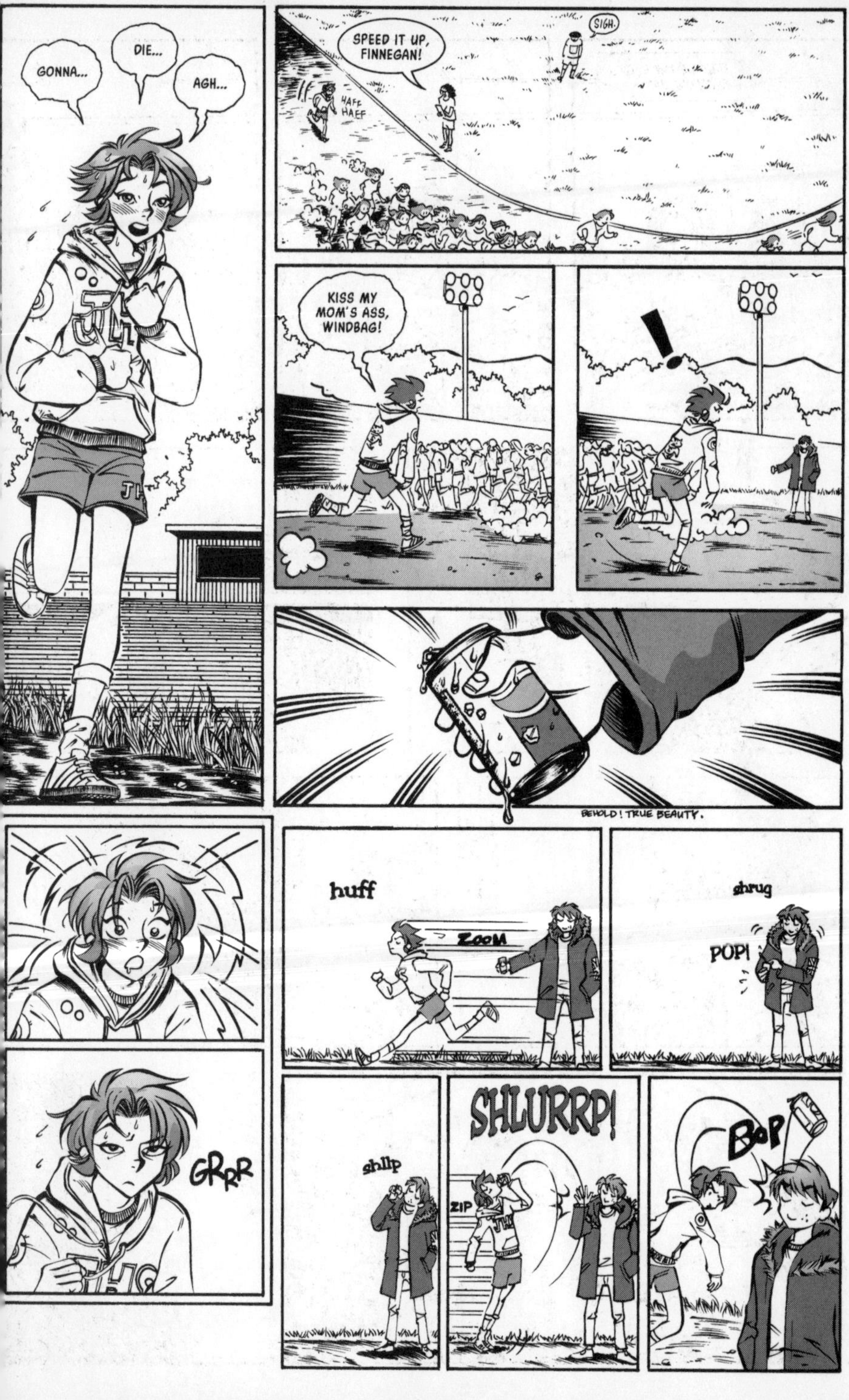

GONNA...
DIE...
AGH...
SPEED IT UP, FINNEGAN!
SIGH.
HAFF HAFF
KISS MY MOM'S ASS, WINDBAG!
!
BEHOLD! TRUE BEAUTY.
huff
ZOOM
shrug
POP!
GRRR
shllp
SHLURRP!
ZIP
BOP

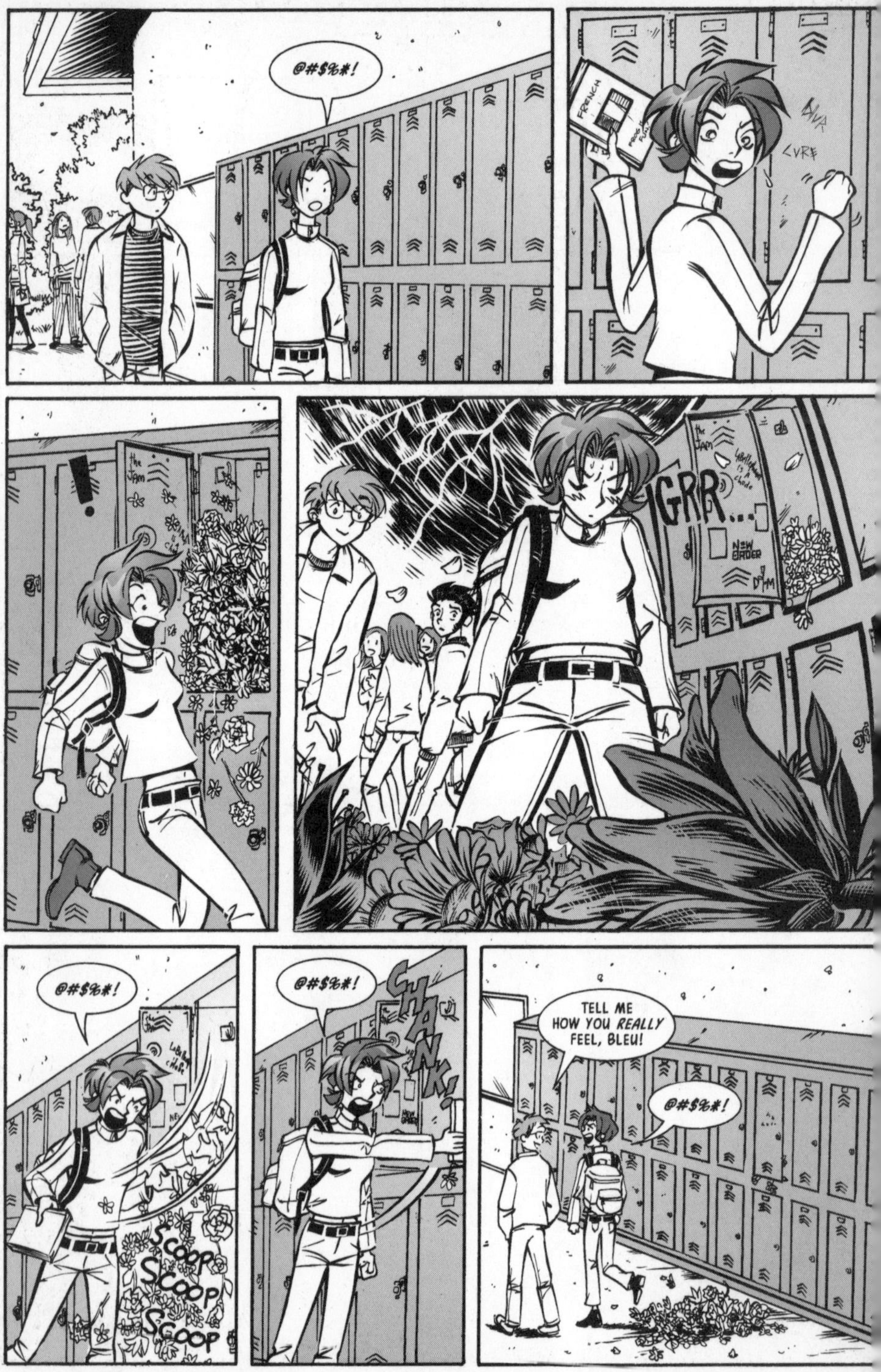
@#$%*!
FRENCH
GRR...
@#$%*!
SCOOP
SCOOP
SCOOP
@#$%*!
SHANK!
TELL ME HOW YOU REALLY FEEL, BLEU!
@#$%*!

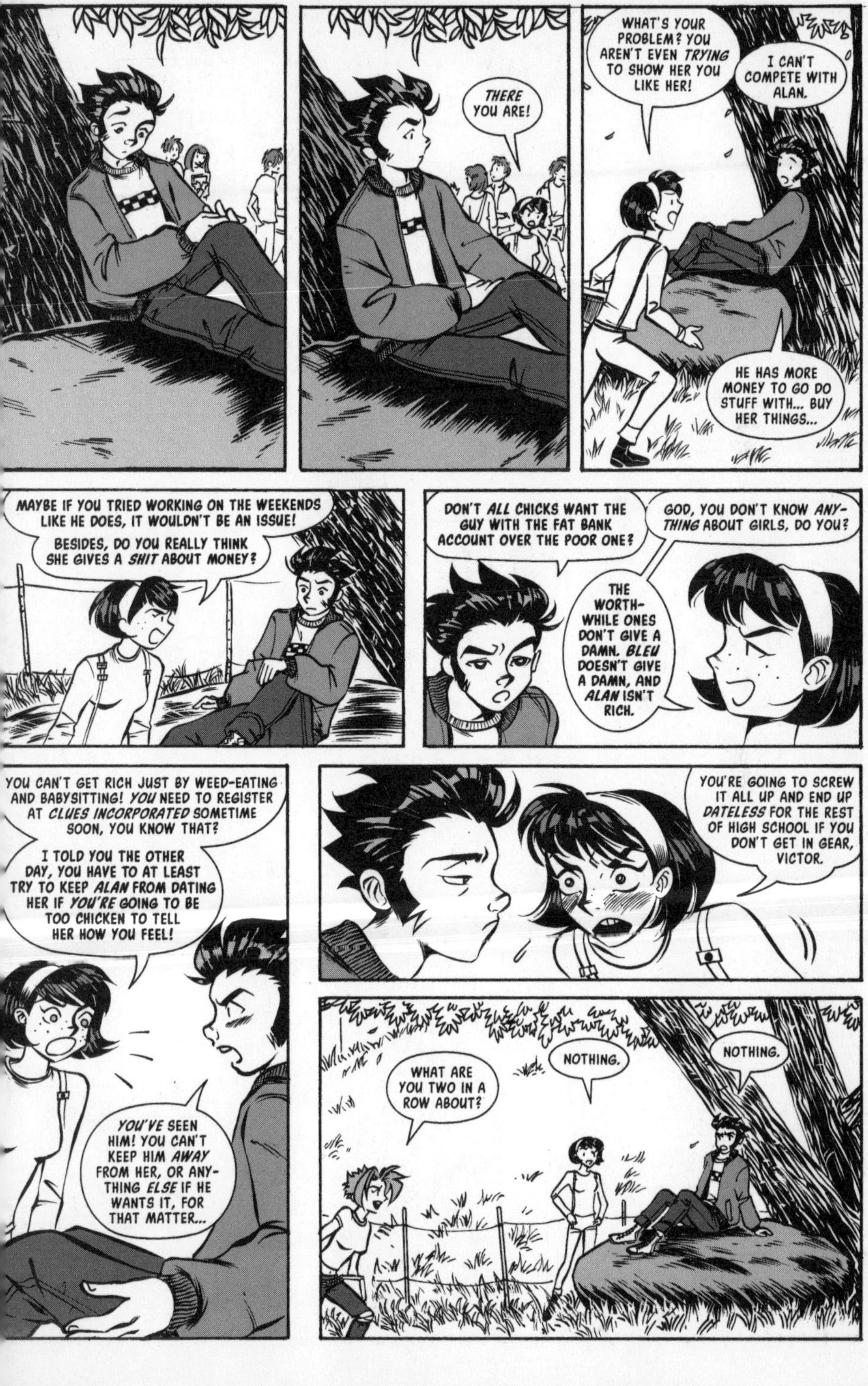
THERE YOU ARE!
WHAT'S YOUR PROBLEM? YOU AREN'T EVEN TRYING TO SHOW HER YOU LIKE HER!
I CAN'T COMPETE WITH ALAN.
HE HAS MORE MONEY TO GO DO STUFF WITH... BUY HER THINGS...
MAYBE IF YOU TRIED WORKING ON THE WEEKENDS LIKE HE DOES, IT WOULDN'T BE AN ISSUE!
BESIDES, DO YOU REALLY THINK SHE GIVES A SHIT ABOUT MONEY?
DON'T ALL CHICKS WANT THE GUY WITH THE FAT BANK ACCOUNT OVER THE POOR ONE?
GOD, YOU DON'T KNOW ANYTHING ABOUT GIRLS, DO YOU?
THE WORTHWHILE ONES DON'T GIVE A DAMN. BLEU DOESN'T GIVE A DAMN, AND ALAN ISN'T RICH.
YOU CAN'T GET RICH JUST BY WEED-EATING AND BABYSITTING! YOU NEED TO REGISTER AT CLUES INCORPORATED SOMETIME SOON, YOU KNOW THAT?
I TOLD YOU THE OTHER DAY, YOU HAVE TO AT LEAST TRY TO KEEP ALAN FROM DATING HER IF YOU'RE GOING TO BE TOO CHICKEN TO TELL HER HOW YOU FEEL!
YOU'VE SEEN HIM! YOU CAN'T KEEP HIM AWAY FROM HER, OR ANYTHING ELSE IF HE WANTS IT, FOR THAT MATTER...
YOU'RE GOING TO SCREW IT ALL UP AND END UP DATELESS FOR THE REST OF HIGH SCHOOL IF YOU DON'T GET IN GEAR, VICTOR.
WHAT ARE YOU TWO IN A ROW ABOUT?
NOTHING.
NOTHING.

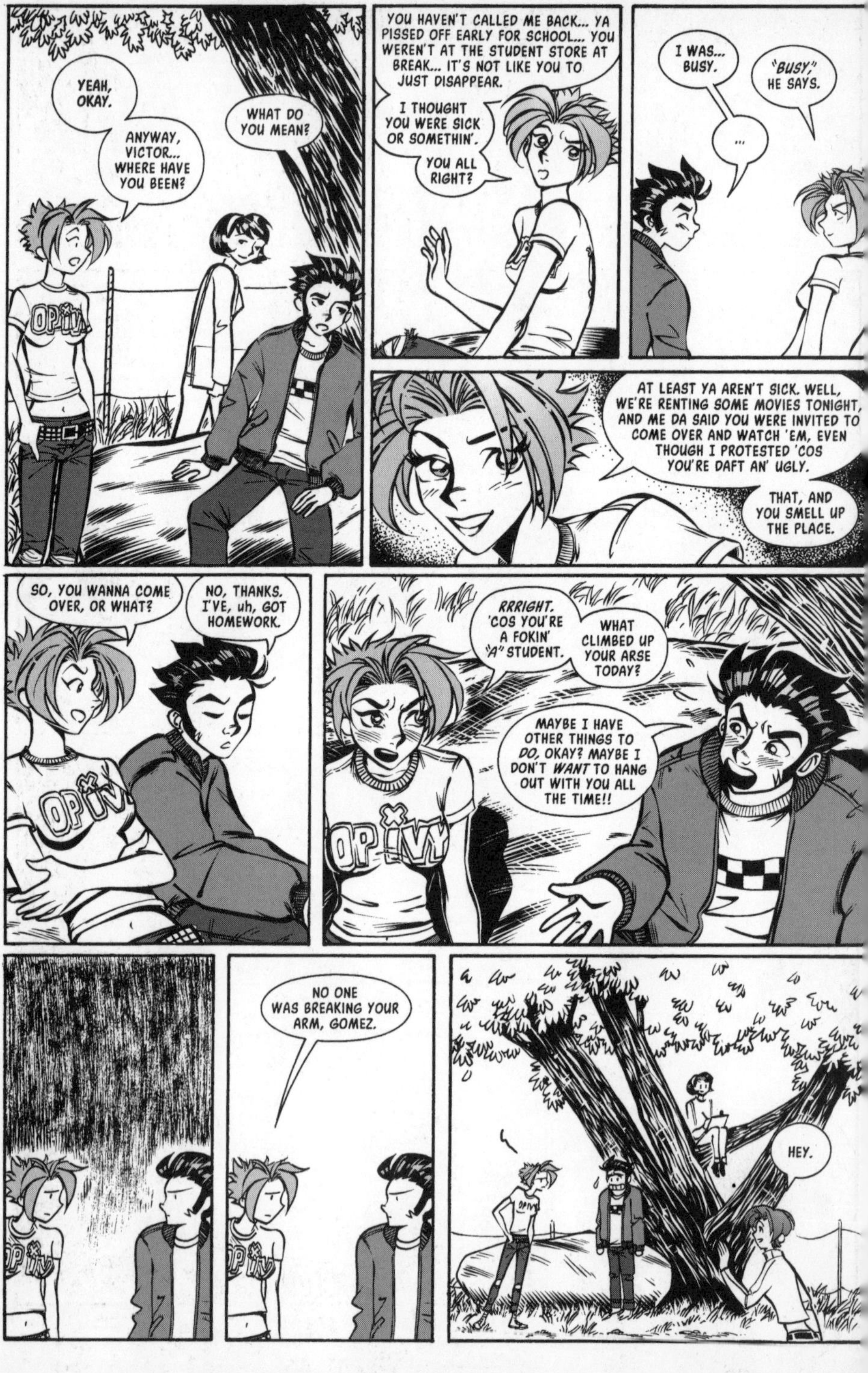

YEAH, OKAY.
ANYWAY, VICTOR... WHERE HAVE YOU BEEN?
WHAT DO YOU MEAN?
YOU HAVEN'T CALLED ME BACK... YA PISSED OFF EARLY FOR SCHOOL... YOU WEREN'T AT THE STUDENT STORE AT BREAK... IT'S NOT LIKE YOU TO JUST DISAPPEAR.
I THOUGHT YOU WERE SICK OR SOMETHIN'.
YOU ALL RIGHT?
I WAS... BUSY.
"BUSY," HE SAYS.
...
AT LEAST YA AREN'T SICK. WELL, WE'RE RENTING SOME MOVIES TONIGHT, AND ME DA SAID YOU WERE INVITED TO COME OVER AND WATCH 'EM, EVEN THOUGH I PROTESTED 'COS YOU'RE DAFT AN' UGLY.
THAT, AND YOU SMELL UP THE PLACE.
SO, YOU WANNA COME OVER, OR WHAT?
NO, THANKS. I'VE, uh, GOT HOMEWORK.
RRRIGHT. 'COS YOU'RE A FOKIN' "A" STUDENT.
WHAT CLIMBED UP YOUR ARSE TODAY?
MAYBE I HAVE OTHER THINGS TO DO, OKAY? MAYBE I DON'T WANT TO HANG OUT WITH YOU ALL THE TIME!!
NO ONE WAS BREAKING YOUR ARM, GOMEZ.
HEY.

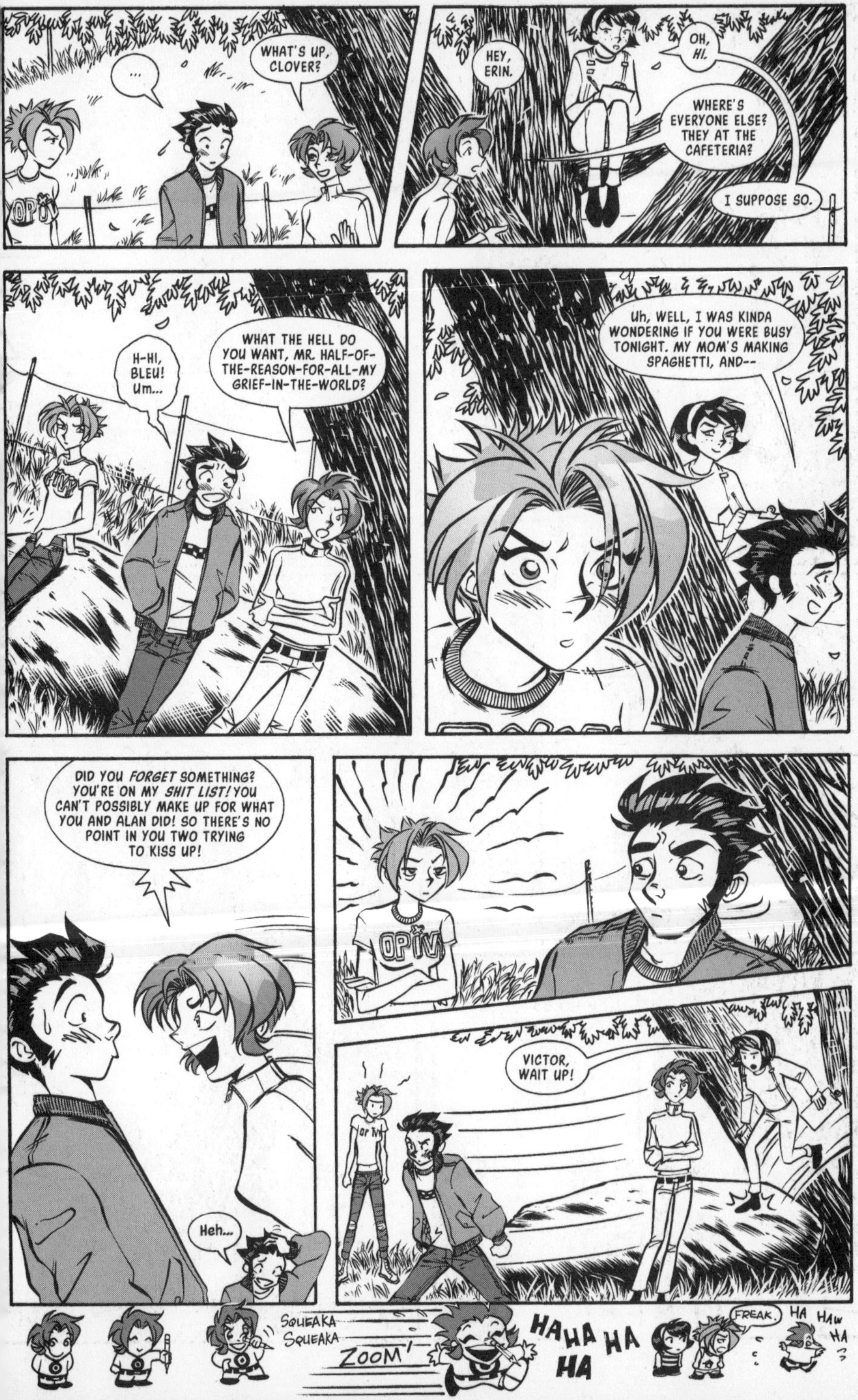
...
WHAT'S UP, CLOVER?
HEY, ERIN.
OH, HI.
WHERE'S EVERYONE ELSE? THEY AT THE CAFETERIA?
I SUPPOSE SO.
H-HI, BLEU! Um...
WHAT THE HELL DO YOU WANT, MR. HALF-OF-THE-REASON-FOR-ALL-MY GRIEF-IN-THE-WORLD?
Uh, WELL, I WAS KINDA WONDERING IF YOU WERE BUSY TONIGHT. MY MOM'S MAKING SPAGHETTI, AND--
DID YOU *FORGET* SOMETHING? YOU'RE ON MY *SHIT LIST!* YOU CAN'T POSSIBLY MAKE UP FOR WHAT YOU AND ALAN DID! SO THERE'S NO POINT IN YOU TWO TRYING TO KISS UP!
Heh...
VICTOR, WAIT UP!
SQUEAKA SQUEAKA
ZOOM!
HA HA HA HA HA
FREAK.
HA HAW HA

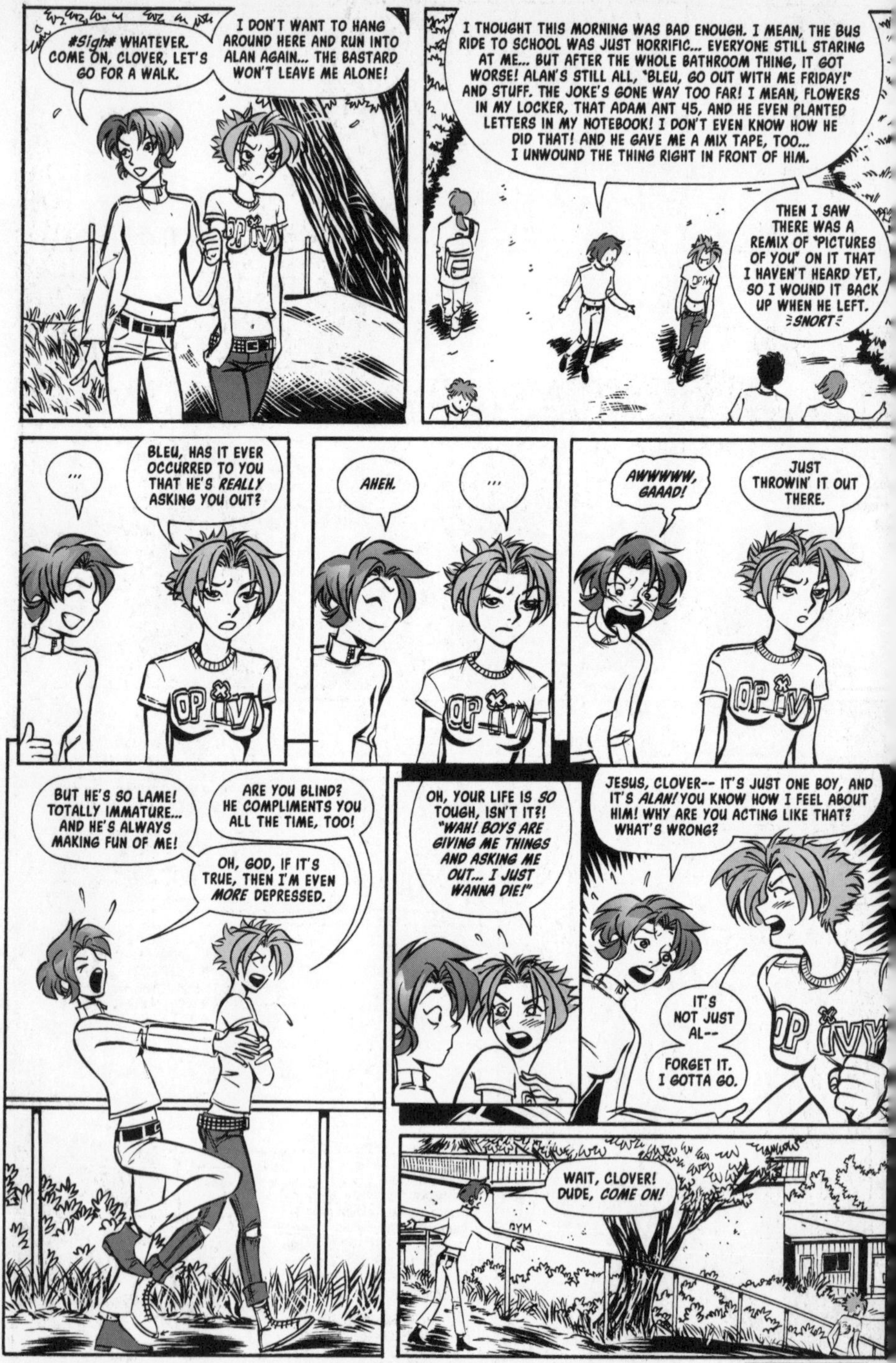

#Sigh# WHATEVER. COME ON, CLOVER, LET'S GO FOR A WALK.
I DON'T WANT TO HANG AROUND HERE AND RUN INTO ALAN AGAIN... THE BASTARD WON'T LEAVE ME ALONE!
I THOUGHT THIS MORNING WAS BAD ENOUGH. I MEAN, THE BUS RIDE TO SCHOOL WAS JUST HORRIFIC... EVERYONE STILL STARING AT ME... BUT AFTER THE WHOLE BATHROOM THING, IT GOT WORSE! ALAN'S STILL ALL, "BLEU, GO OUT WITH ME FRIDAY!" AND STUFF. THE JOKE'S GONE WAY TOO FAR! I MEAN, FLOWERS IN MY LOCKER, THAT ADAM ANT 45, AND HE EVEN PLANTED LETTERS IN MY NOTEBOOK! I DON'T EVEN KNOW HOW HE DID THAT! AND HE GAVE ME A MIX TAPE, TOO... I UNWOUND THE THING RIGHT IN FRONT OF HIM.
THEN I SAW THERE WAS A REMIX OF "PICTURES OF YOU" ON IT THAT I HAVEN'T HEARD YET, SO I WOUND IT BACK UP WHEN HE LEFT.
SNORT
...
BLEU, HAS IT EVER OCCURRED TO YOU THAT HE'S REALLY ASKING YOU OUT?
AHEH.
...
AWWWWW, GAAAD!
JUST THROWIN' IT OUT THERE.
BUT HE'S SO LAME! TOTALLY IMMATURE... AND HE'S ALWAYS MAKING FUN OF ME!
ARE YOU BLIND? HE COMPLIMENTS YOU ALL THE TIME, TOO!
OH, GOD, IF IT'S TRUE, THEN I'M EVEN MORE DEPRESSED.
OH, YOUR LIFE IS SO TOUGH, ISN'T IT?! "WAH! BOYS ARE GIVING ME THINGS AND ASKING ME OUT... I JUST WANNA DIE!"
JESUS, CLOVER-- IT'S JUST ONE BOY, AND IT'S ALAN! YOU KNOW HOW I FEEL ABOUT HIM! WHY ARE YOU ACTING LIKE THAT? WHAT'S WRONG?
IT'S NOT JUST AL--
FORGET IT. I GOTTA GO.
WAIT, CLOVER! DUDE, COME ON!
GYM

#BUZZCOCKS "EVER FALLEN IN LOVE?"

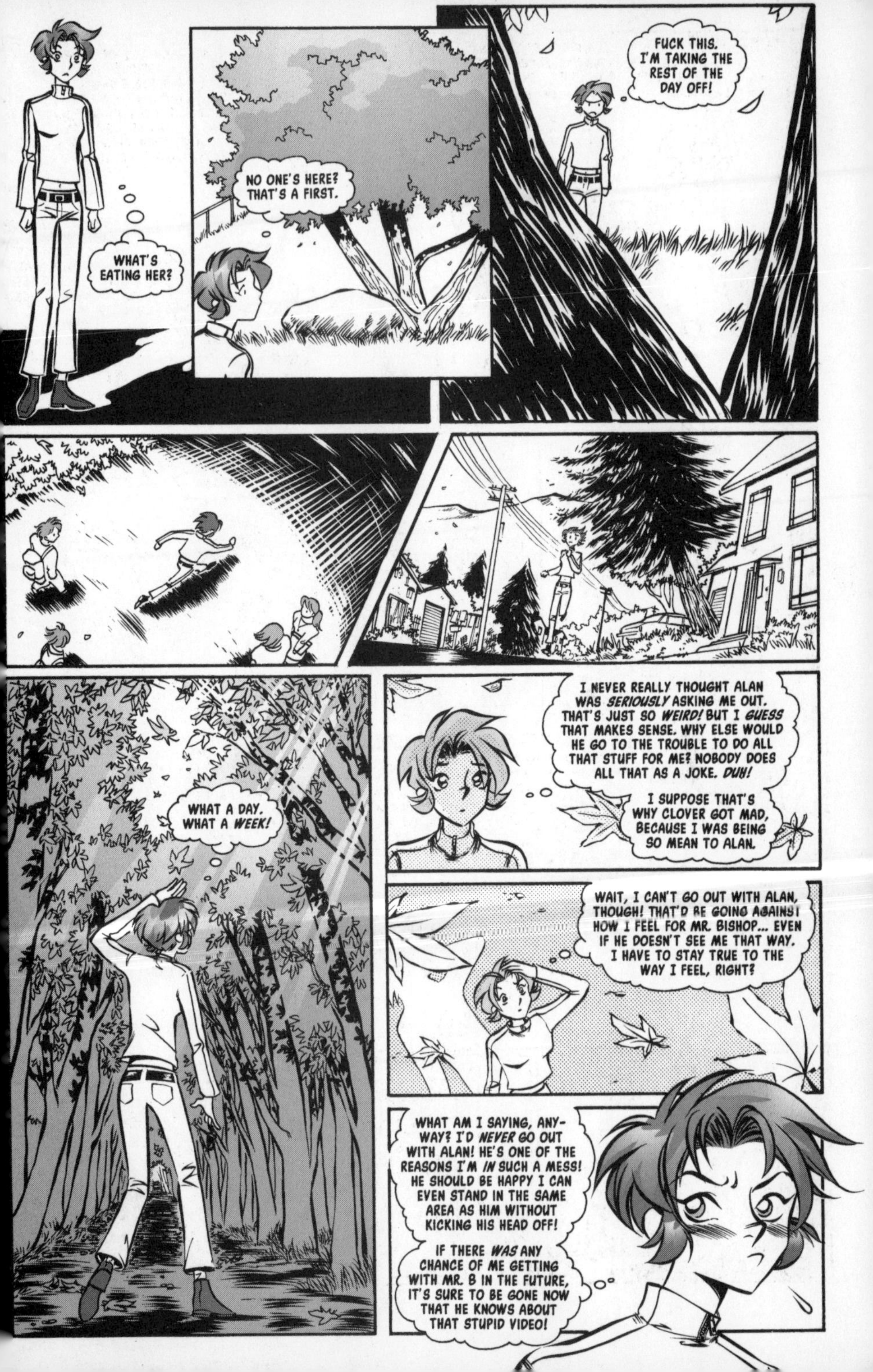
WHAT'S EATING HER?
NO ONE'S HERE? THAT'S A FIRST.
FUCK THIS. I'M TAKING THE REST OF THE DAY OFF!
WHAT A DAY. WHAT A WEEK!
I NEVER REALLY THOUGHT ALAN WAS SERIOUSLY ASKING ME OUT. THAT'S JUST SO WEIRD! BUT I GUESS THAT MAKES SENSE. WHY ELSE WOULD HE GO TO THE TROUBLE TO DO ALL THAT STUFF FOR ME? NOBODY DOES ALL THAT AS A JOKE. DUH!
I SUPPOSE THAT'S WHY CLOVER GOT MAD, BECAUSE I WAS BEING SO MEAN TO ALAN.
WAIT, I CAN'T GO OUT WITH ALAN, THOUGH! THAT'D BE GOING AGAINST HOW I FEEL FOR MR. BISHOP... EVEN IF HE DOESN'T SEE ME THAT WAY. I HAVE TO STAY TRUE TO THE WAY I FEEL, RIGHT?
WHAT AM I SAYING, ANY-WAY? I'D NEVER GO OUT WITH ALAN! HE'S ONE OF THE REASONS I'M IN SUCH A MESS! HE SHOULD BE HAPPY I CAN EVEN STAND IN THE SAME AREA AS HIM WITHOUT KICKING HIS HEAD OFF!
IF THERE WAS ANY CHANCE OF ME GETTING WITH MR. B IN THE FUTURE, IT'S SURE TO BE GONE NOW THAT HE KNOWS ABOUT THAT STUPID VIDEO!

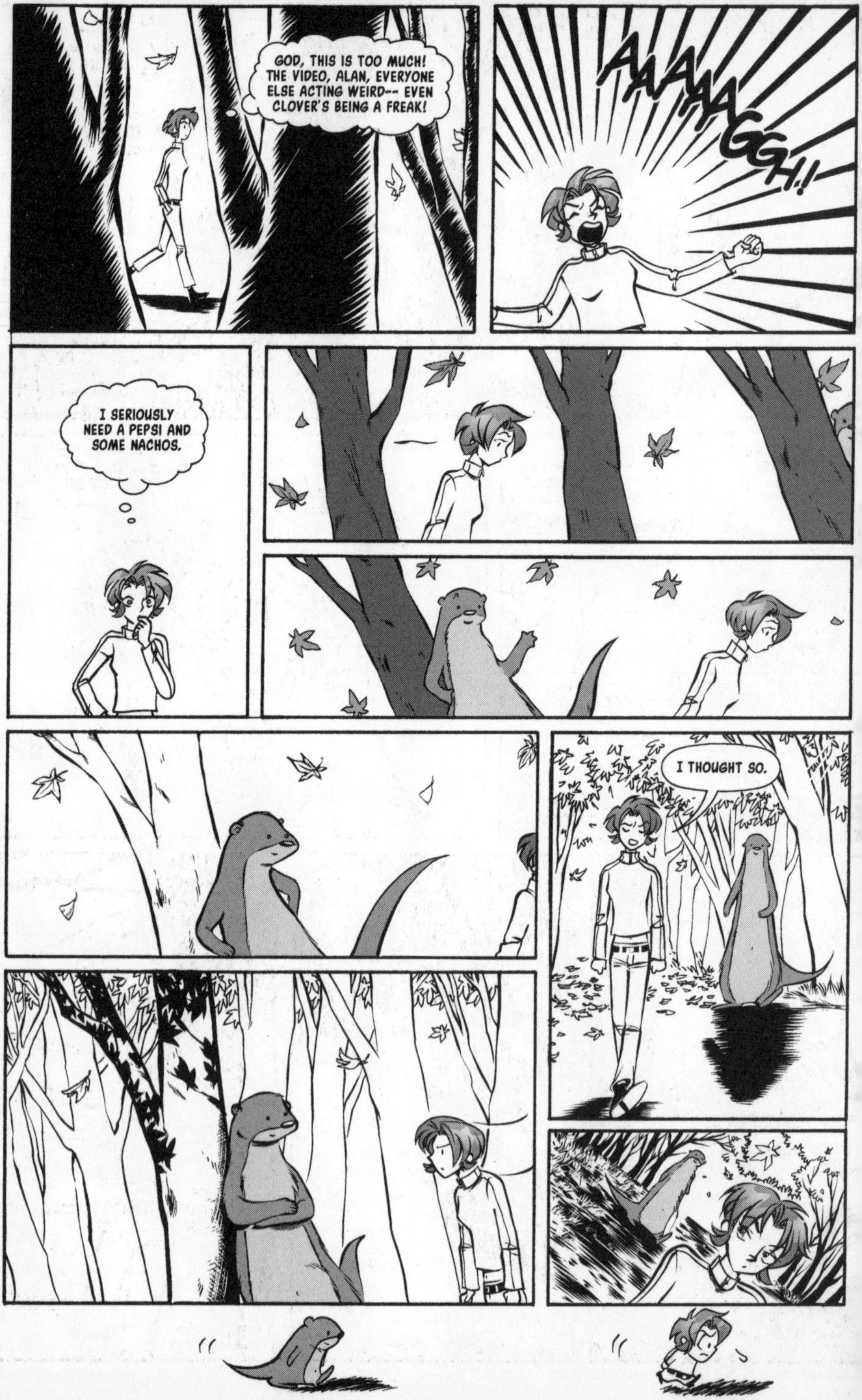
GOD, THIS IS TOO MUCH! THE VIDEO, ALAN, EVERYONE ELSE ACTING WEIRD-- EVEN CLOVER'S BEING A FREAK!
AAAAAAGGGH!!
I SERIOUSLY NEED A PEPSI AND SOME NACHOS.
I THOUGHT SO.

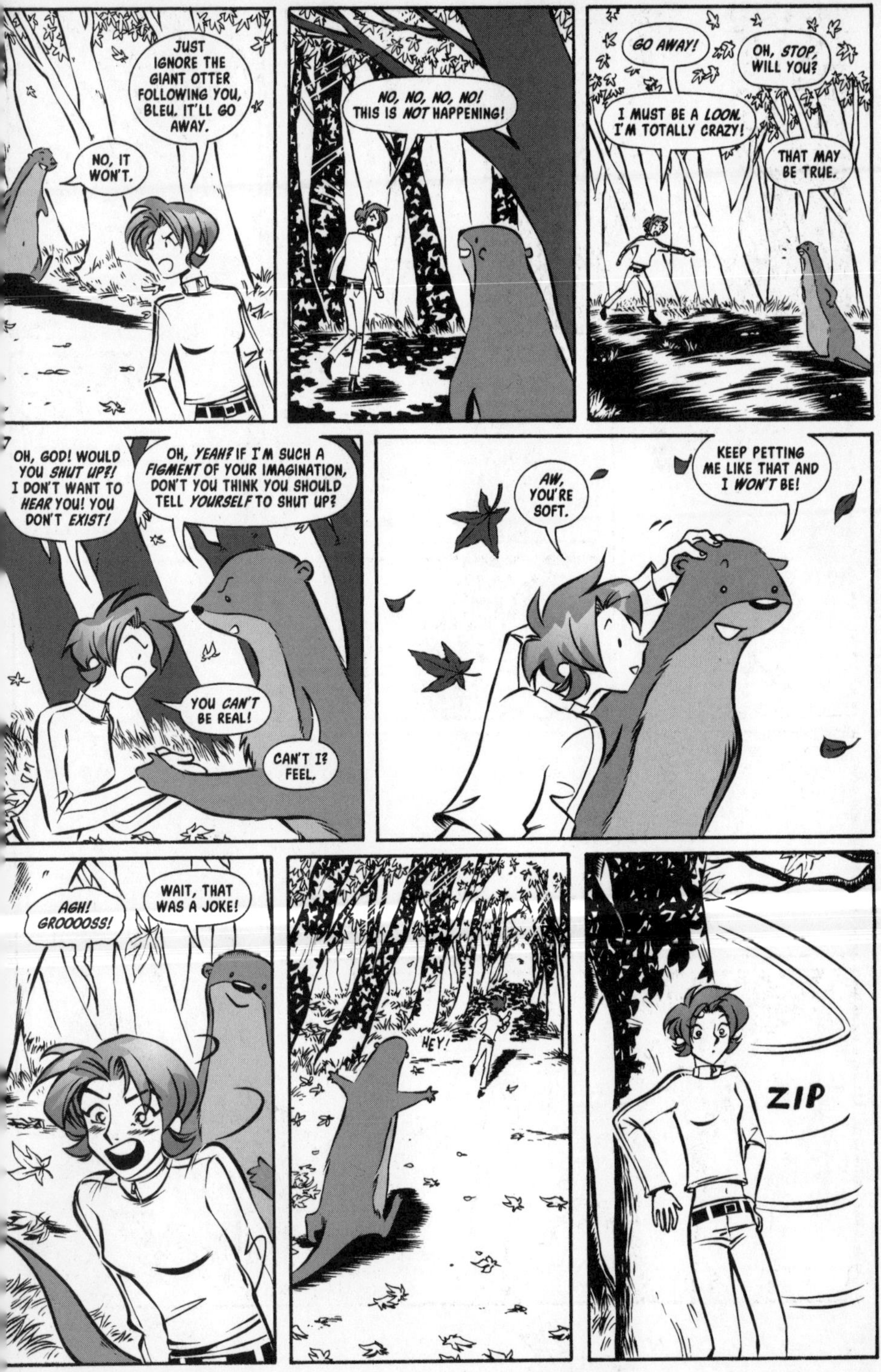
JUST IGNORE THE GIANT OTTER FOLLOWING YOU, BLEU. IT'LL GO AWAY.
NO, IT WON'T.
NO, NO, NO, NO! THIS IS NOT HAPPENING!
GO AWAY!
I MUST BE A LOON. I'M TOTALLY CRAZY!
OH, STOP, WILL YOU?
THAT MAY BE TRUE.
OH, GOD! WOULD YOU SHUT UP?! I DON'T WANT TO HEAR YOU! YOU DON'T EXIST!
OH, YEAH? IF I'M SUCH A FIGMENT OF YOUR IMAGINATION, DON'T YOU THINK YOU SHOULD TELL YOURSELF TO SHUT UP?
YOU CAN'T BE REAL!
CAN'T I? FEEL.
AW, YOU'RE SOFT.
KEEP PETTING ME LIKE THAT AND I WON'T BE!
AGH! GROOOOSS!
WAIT, THAT WAS A JOKE!
HEY!
ZIP

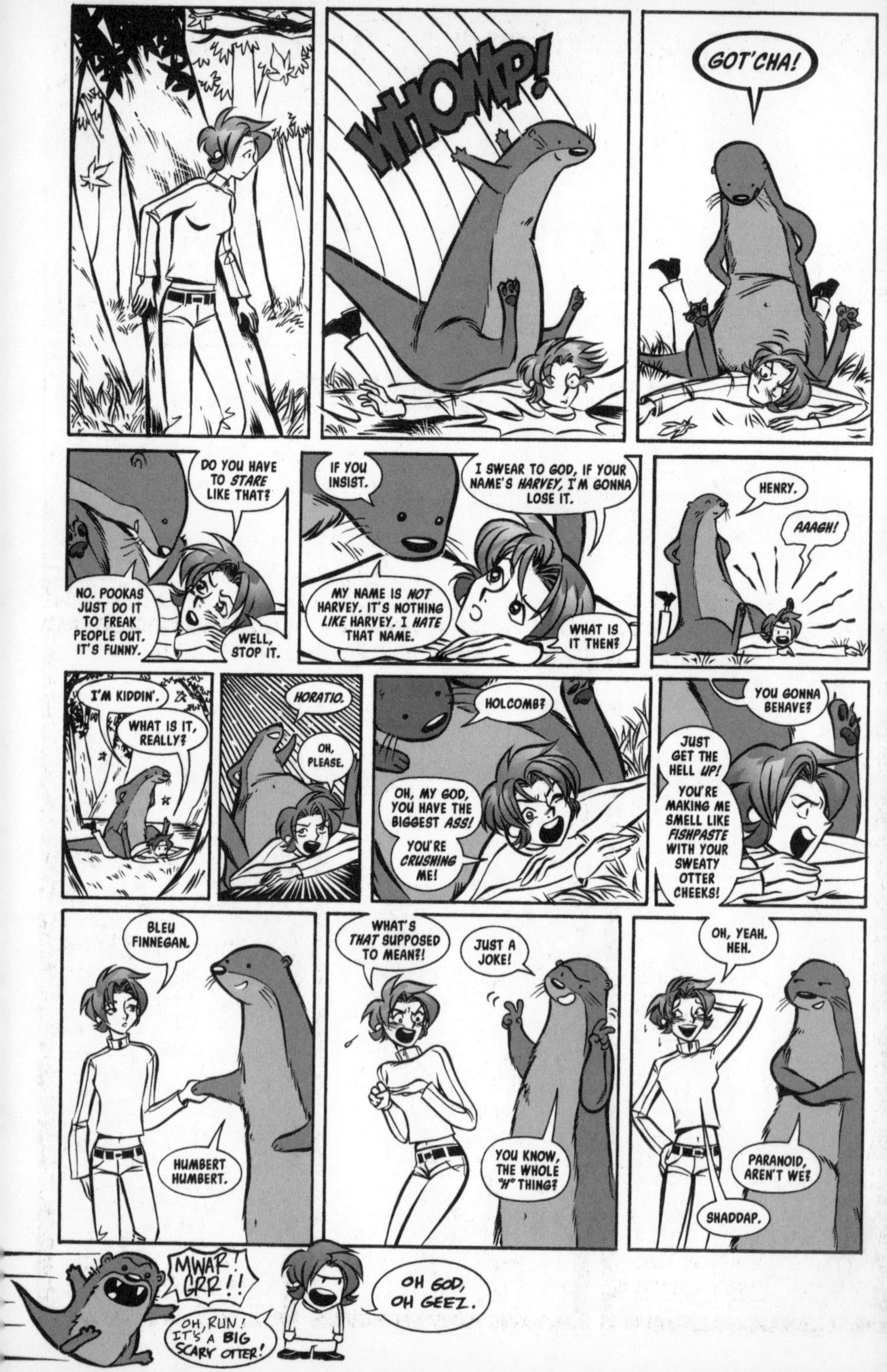
WHOMP!
GOT'CHA!
DO YOU HAVE TO STARE LIKE THAT?
NO. POOKAS JUST DO IT TO FREAK PEOPLE OUT. IT'S FUNNY.
WELL, STOP IT.
IF YOU INSIST.
I SWEAR TO GOD, IF YOUR NAME'S HARVEY, I'M GONNA LOSE IT.
MY NAME IS NOT HARVEY. IT'S NOTHING LIKE HARVEY. I HATE THAT NAME.
WHAT IS IT THEN?
HENRY.
AAAGH!
I'M KIDDIN'.
WHAT IS IT, REALLY?
HORATIO.
OH, PLEASE.
HOLCOMB?
OH, MY GOD, YOU HAVE THE BIGGEST ASS!
YOU'RE CRUSHING ME!
YOU GONNA BEHAVE?
JUST GET THE HELL UP!
YOU'RE MAKING ME SMELL LIKE FISHPASTE WITH YOUR SWEATY OTTER CHEEKS!
BLEU FINNEGAN.
HUMBERT HUMBERT.
WHAT'S THAT SUPPOSED TO MEAN?!
JUST A JOKE!
YOU KNOW, THE WHOLE "H" THING?
OH, YEAH. HEH.
PARANOID, AREN'T WE?
SHADDAP.
MWAR! GRR!!
OH, RUN! IT'S A BIG SCARY OTTER!
OH GOD, OH GEEZ.

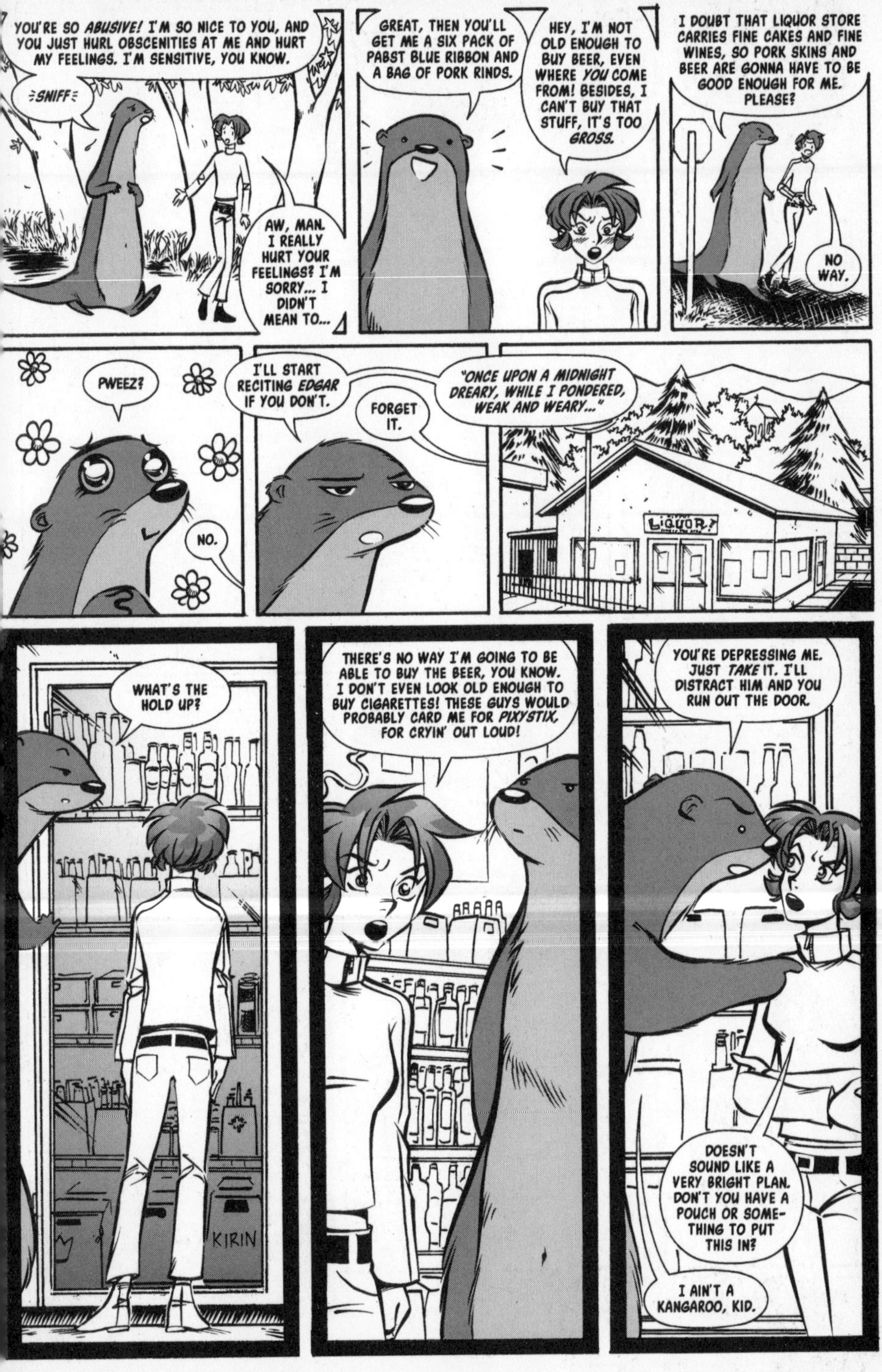
YOU'RE SO ABUSIVE! I'M SO NICE TO YOU, AND YOU JUST HURL OBSCENITIES AT ME AND HURT MY FEELINGS. I'M SENSITIVE, YOU KNOW.
SNIFF
AW, MAN. I REALLY HURT YOUR FEELINGS? I'M SORRY... I DIDN'T MEAN TO...
GREAT, THEN YOU'LL GET ME A SIX PACK OF PABST BLUE RIBBON AND A BAG OF PORK RINDS.
HEY, I'M NOT OLD ENOUGH TO BUY BEER, EVEN WHERE YOU COME FROM! BESIDES, I CAN'T BUY THAT STUFF, IT'S TOO GROSS.
I DOUBT THAT LIQUOR STORE CARRIES FINE CAKES AND FINE WINES, SO PORK SKINS AND BEER ARE GONNA HAVE TO BE GOOD ENOUGH FOR ME. PLEASE?
NO WAY.
PWEEZ?
NO.
I'LL START RECITING EDGAR IF YOU DON'T.
FORGET IT.
"ONCE UPON A MIDNIGHT DREARY, WHILE I PONDERED, WEAK AND WEARY..."
LIQUOR
WHAT'S THE HOLD UP?
KIRIN
THERE'S NO WAY I'M GOING TO BE ABLE TO BUY THE BEER, YOU KNOW. I DON'T EVEN LOOK OLD ENOUGH TO BUY CIGARETTES! THESE GUYS WOULD PROBABLY CARD ME FOR PIXYSTIX, FOR CRYIN' OUT LOUD!
YOU'RE DEPRESSING ME. JUST TAKE IT. I'LL DISTRACT HIM AND YOU RUN OUT THE DOOR.
DOESN'T SOUND LIKE A VERY BRIGHT PLAN. DON'T YOU HAVE A POUCH OR SOMETHING TO PUT THIS IN?
I AIN'T A KANGAROO, KID.

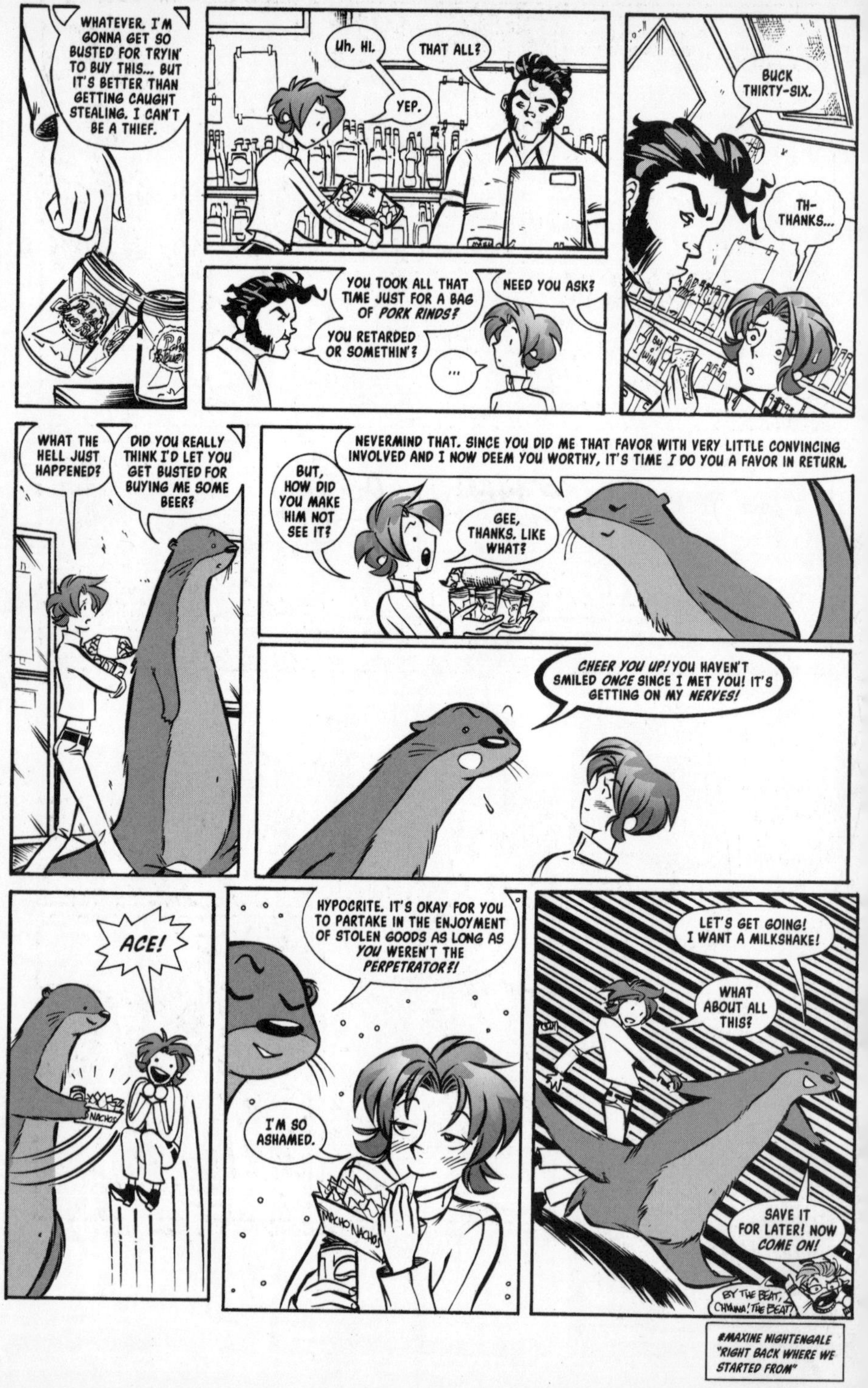
WHATEVER. I'M GONNA GET SO BUSTED FOR TRYIN' TO BUY THIS... BUT IT'S BETTER THAN GETTING CAUGHT STEALING. I CAN'T BE A THIEF.
UH, HI.
THAT ALL?
YEP.
BUCK THIRTY-SIX.
TH- THANKS...
YOU TOOK ALL THAT TIME JUST FOR A BAG OF PORK RINDS?
NEED YOU ASK?
YOU RETARDED OR SOMETHIN'?
...
WHAT THE HELL JUST HAPPENED?
DID YOU REALLY THINK I'D LET YOU GET BUSTED FOR BUYING ME SOME BEER?
NEVERMIND THAT. SINCE YOU DID ME THAT FAVOR WITH VERY LITTLE CONVINCING INVOLVED AND I NOW DEEM YOU WORTHY, IT'S TIME I DO YOU A FAVOR IN RETURN.
BUT, HOW DID YOU MAKE HIM NOT SEE IT?
GEE, THANKS. LIKE WHAT?
CHEER YOU UP! YOU HAVEN'T SMILED ONCE SINCE I MET YOU! IT'S GETTING ON MY NERVES!
ACE!
NACHOS
HYPOCRITE. IT'S OKAY FOR YOU TO PARTAKE IN THE ENJOYMENT OF STOLEN GOODS AS LONG AS YOU WEREN'T THE PERPETRATOR?!
I'M SO ASHAMED.
MACHO NACHOS
LET'S GET GOING! I WANT A MILKSHAKE!
WHAT ABOUT ALL THIS?
SAVE IT FOR LATER! NOW COME ON!
BY THE BEAT, CHYANA! THE BEAT!

#MAXINE NIGHTENGALE "RIGHT BACK WHERE WE STARTED FROM"

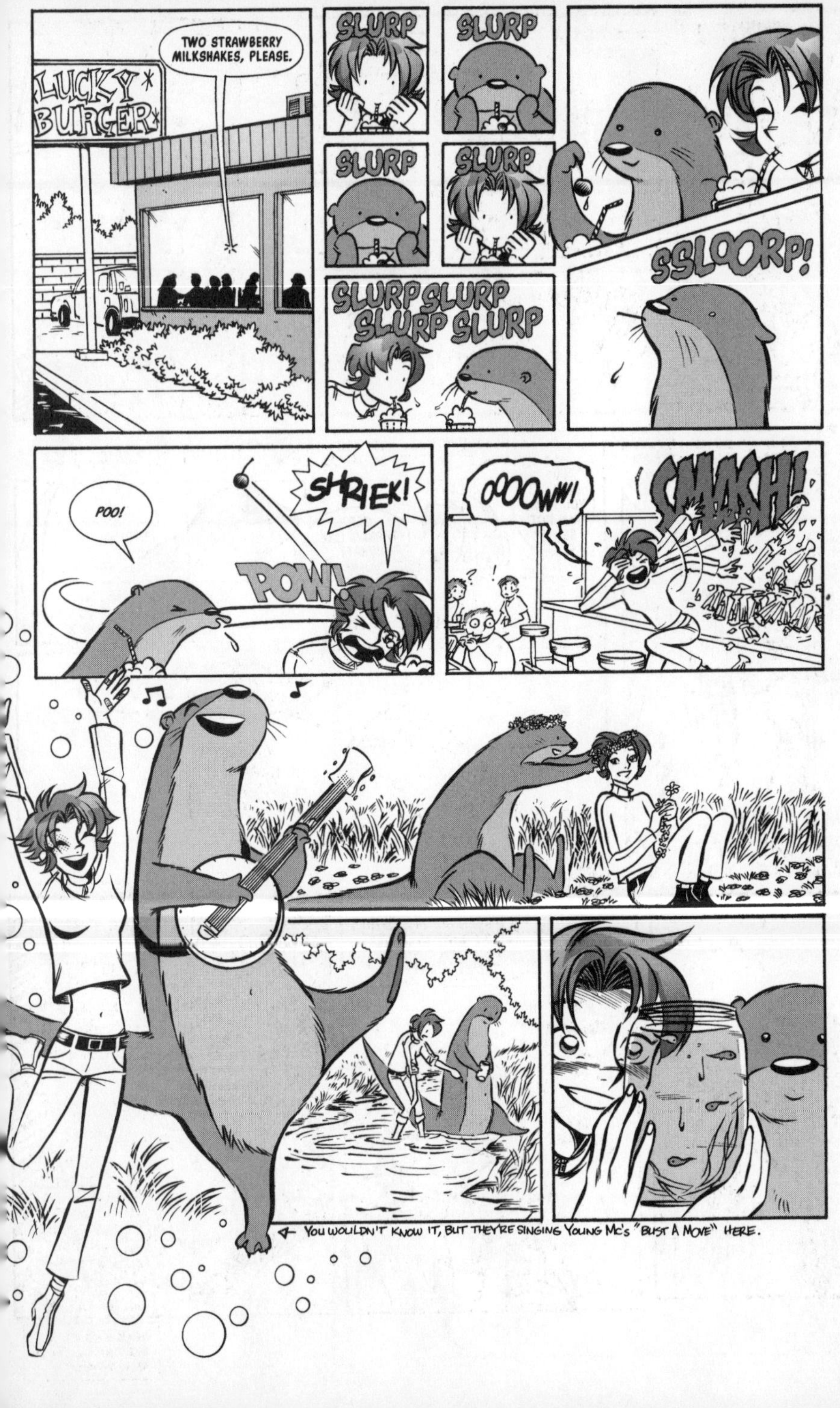
LUCKY BURGER
TWO STRAWBERRY MILKSHAKES, PLEASE.
SLURP
SLURP
SLURP
SLURP
SLURP SLURP SLURP SLURP
SSLOORP!
POO!
SHRIEK!
POW!
OOOOW!!
SMASH!
You wouldn't know it, but they're singing Young Mc's "Bust A Move" here.

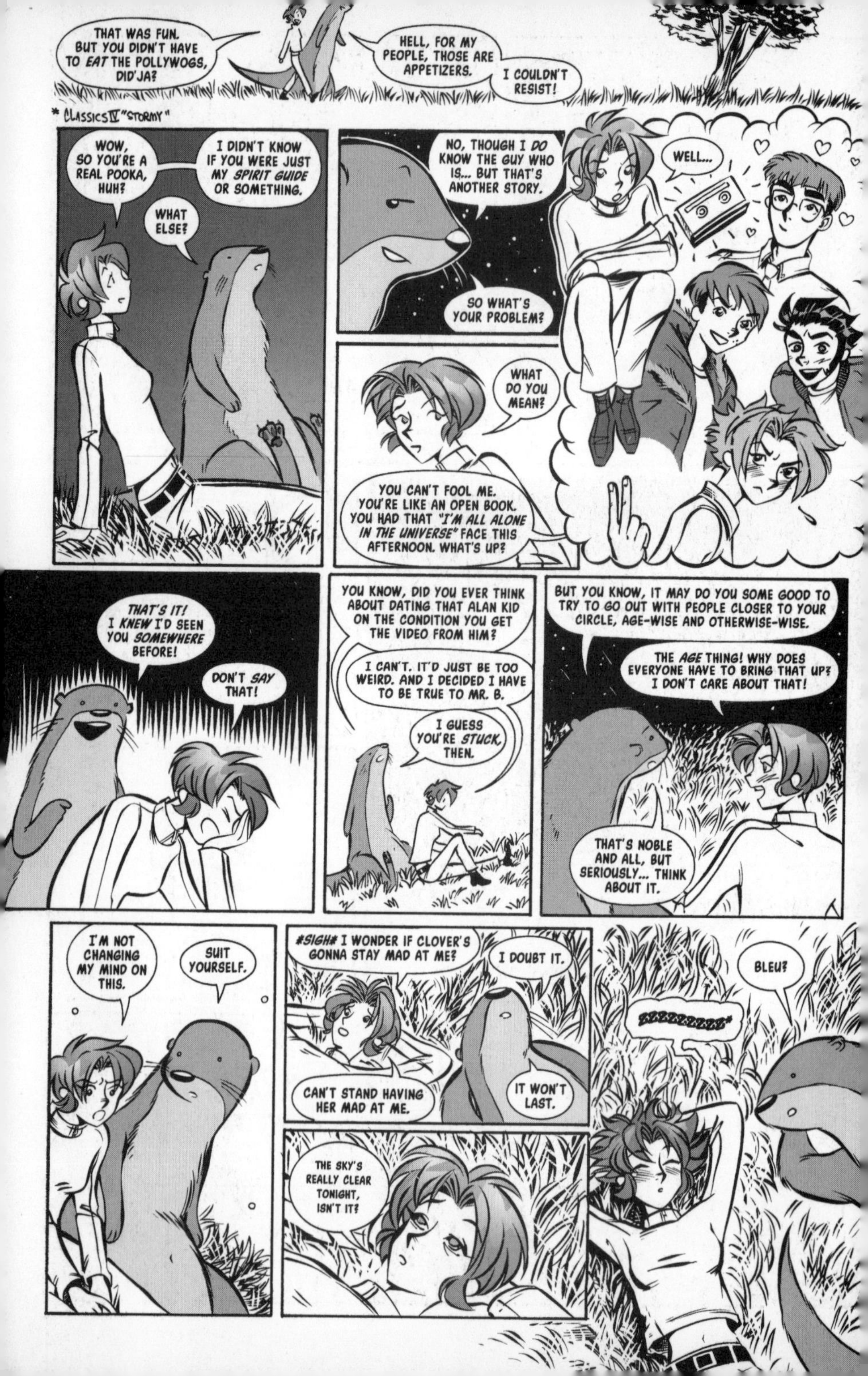
THAT WAS FUN. BUT YOU DIDN'T HAVE TO EAT THE POLLYWOGS, DID'JA?
HELL, FOR MY PEOPLE, THOSE ARE APPETIZERS.
I COULDN'T RESIST!
* CLASSICS IV "STORMY"
WOW, SO YOU'RE A REAL POOKA, HUH?
I DIDN'T KNOW IF YOU WERE JUST MY SPIRIT GUIDE OR SOMETHING.
WHAT ELSE?
NO, THOUGH I DO KNOW THE GUY WHO IS... BUT THAT'S ANOTHER STORY.
SO WHAT'S YOUR PROBLEM?
WHAT DO YOU MEAN?
YOU CAN'T FOOL ME. YOU'RE LIKE AN OPEN BOOK. YOU HAD THAT "I'M ALL ALONE IN THE UNIVERSE" FACE THIS AFTERNOON. WHAT'S UP?
WELL...
THAT'S IT! I KNEW I'D SEEN YOU SOMEWHERE BEFORE!
DON'T SAY THAT!
YOU KNOW, DID YOU EVER THINK ABOUT DATING THAT ALAN KID ON THE CONDITION YOU GET THE VIDEO FROM HIM?
I CAN'T. IT'D JUST BE TOO WEIRD. AND I DECIDED I HAVE TO BE TRUE TO MR. B.
I GUESS YOU'RE STUCK, THEN.
BUT YOU KNOW, IT MAY DO YOU SOME GOOD TO TRY TO GO OUT WITH PEOPLE CLOSER TO YOUR CIRCLE, AGE-WISE AND OTHERWISE-WISE.
THE AGE THING! WHY DOES EVERYONE HAVE TO BRING THAT UP? I DON'T CARE ABOUT THAT!
THAT'S NOBLE AND ALL, BUT SERIOUSLY... THINK ABOUT IT.
I'M NOT CHANGING MY MIND ON THIS.
SUIT YOURSELF.
#SIGH# I WONDER IF CLOVER'S GONNA STAY MAD AT ME?
I DOUBT IT.
CAN'T STAND HAVING HER MAD AT ME.
IT WON'T LAST.
THE SKY'S REALLY CLEAR TONIGHT, ISN'T IT?
BLEU?
ZZZZZZZZZZ*

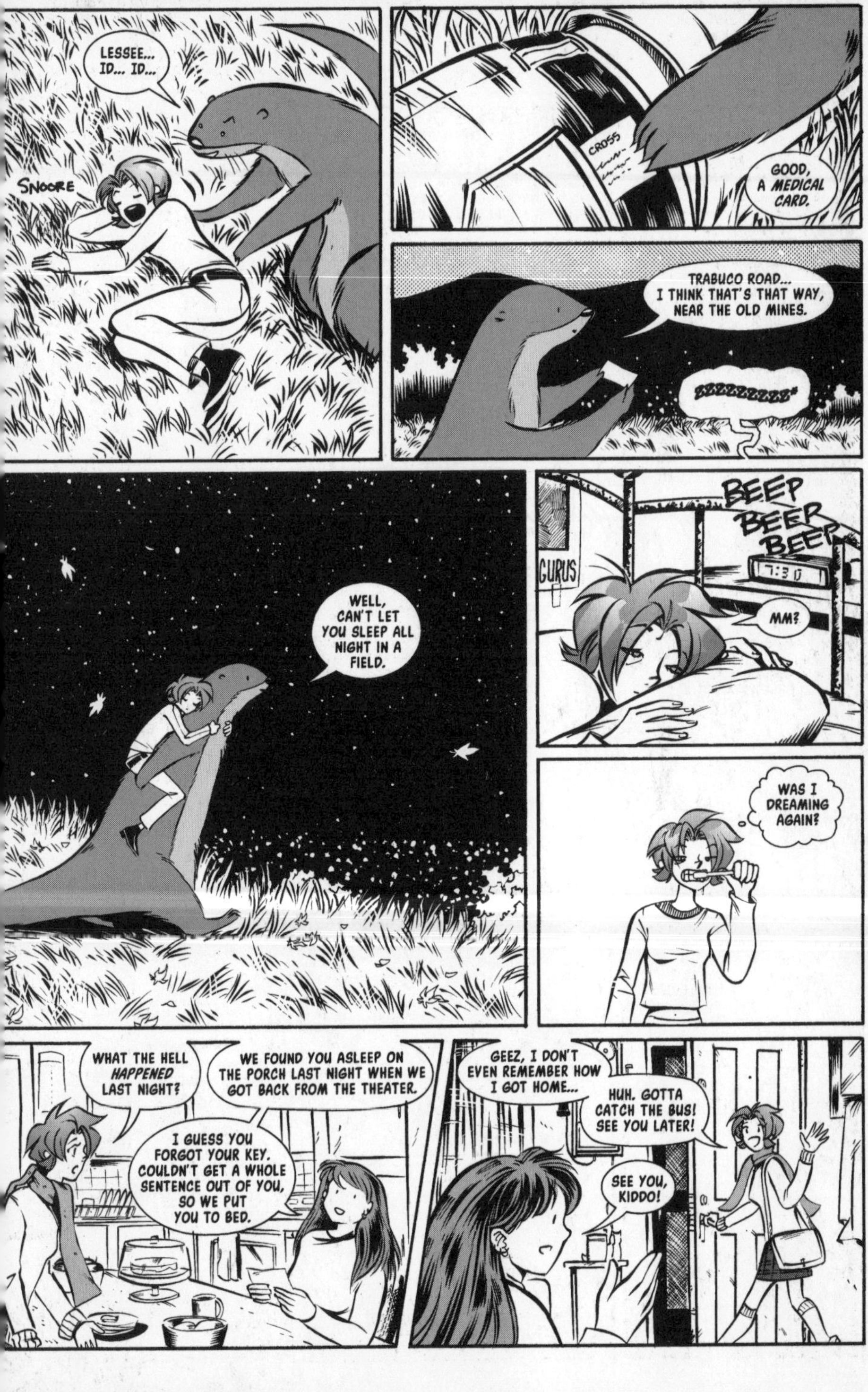
LESSEE... ID... ID...
SNOORE
CROSS
GOOD, A MEDICAL CARD.
TRABUCO ROAD... I THINK THAT'S THAT WAY, NEAR THE OLD MINES.
ZZZZZZZZZ*
WELL, CAN'T LET YOU SLEEP ALL NIGHT IN A FIELD.
BEEP BEEP BEEP
GURUS
7:30
MM?
WAS I DREAMING AGAIN?
WHAT THE HELL HAPPENED LAST NIGHT?
WE FOUND YOU ASLEEP ON THE PORCH LAST NIGHT WHEN WE GOT BACK FROM THE THEATER.
I GUESS YOU FORGOT YOUR KEY. COULDN'T GET A WHOLE SENTENCE OUT OF YOU, SO WE PUT YOU TO BED.
GEEZ, I DON'T EVEN REMEMBER HOW I GOT HOME...
HUH. GOTTA CATCH THE BUS! SEE YOU LATER!
SEE YOU, KIDDO!

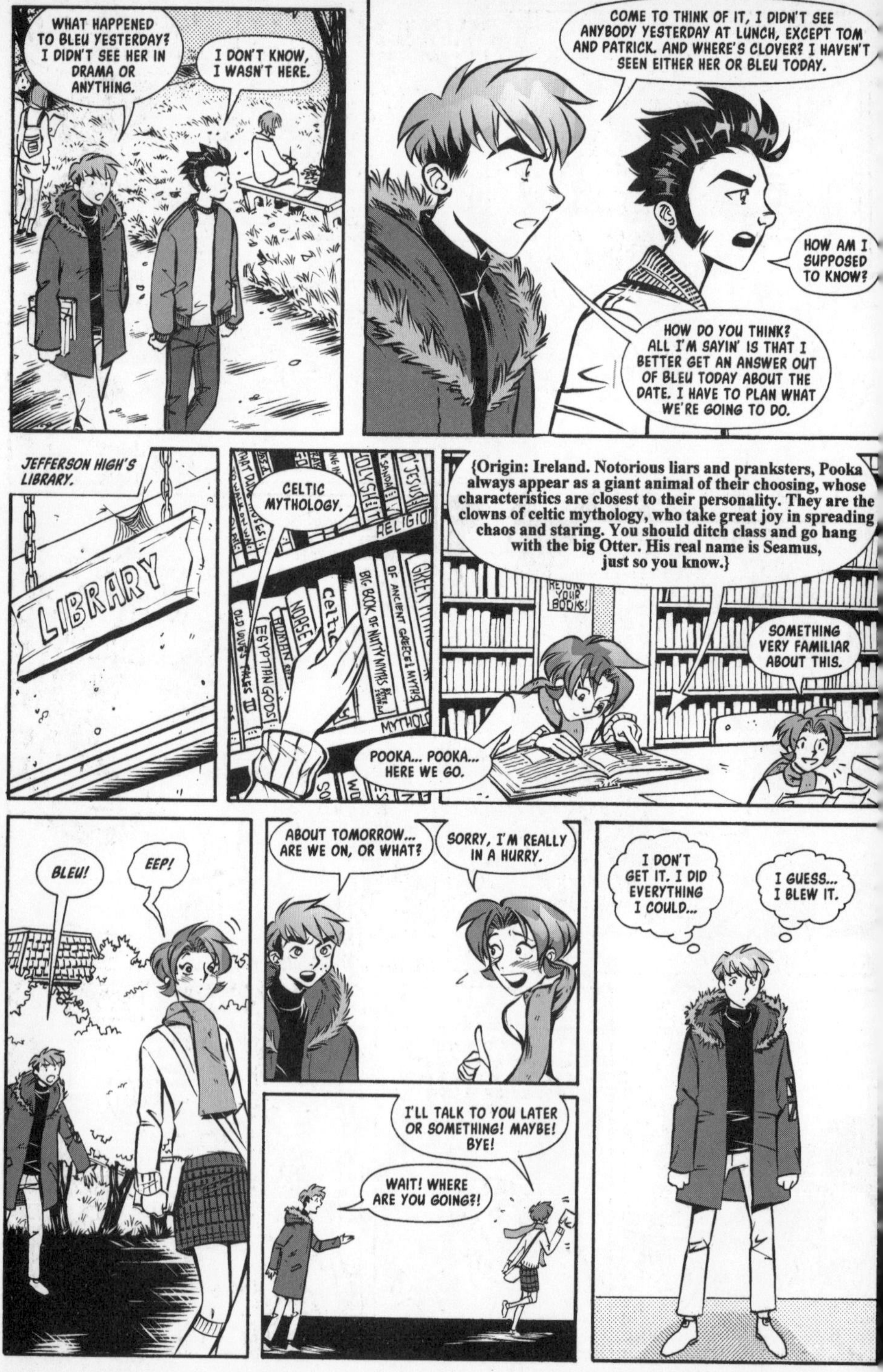
WHAT HAPPENED TO BLEU YESTERDAY? I DIDN'T SEE HER IN DRAMA OR ANYTHING.
I DON'T KNOW, I WASN'T HERE.
COME TO THINK OF IT, I DIDN'T SEE ANYBODY YESTERDAY AT LUNCH, EXCEPT TOM AND PATRICK. AND WHERE'S CLOVER? I HAVEN'T SEEN EITHER HER OR BLEU TODAY.
HOW AM I SUPPOSED TO KNOW?
HOW DO YOU THINK? ALL I'M SAYIN' IS THAT I BETTER GET AN ANSWER OUT OF BLEU TODAY ABOUT THE DATE. I HAVE TO PLAN WHAT WE'RE GOING TO DO.
JEFFERSON HIGH'S LIBRARY.
LIBRARY
CELTIC MYTHOLOGY.
RELIGION
HOLY SHEIT
BIG BOOK OF NUTTY NYMPHS
OF ANCIENT GREECE & MYTHS
EGYPTIAN GODS
OLD LOUIE'S TALES III
NORSE
Celtic
MYTHOLO
{Origin: Ireland. Notorious liars and pranksters, Pooka always appear as a giant animal of their choosing, whose characteristics are closest to their personality. They are the clowns of celtic mythology, who take great joy in spreading chaos and staring. You should ditch class and go hang with the big Otter. His real name is Seamus, just so you know.}
RETURN YOUR BOOKS!
SOMETHING VERY FAMILIAR ABOUT THIS.
POOKA... POOKA... HERE WE GO.
BLEU!
EEP!
ABOUT TOMORROW... ARE WE ON, OR WHAT?
SORRY, I'M REALLY IN A HURRY.
I'LL TALK TO YOU LATER OR SOMETHING! MAYBE! BYE!
WAIT! WHERE ARE YOU GOING?!
I DON'T GET IT. I DID EVERYTHING I COULD...
I GUESS... I BLEW IT.

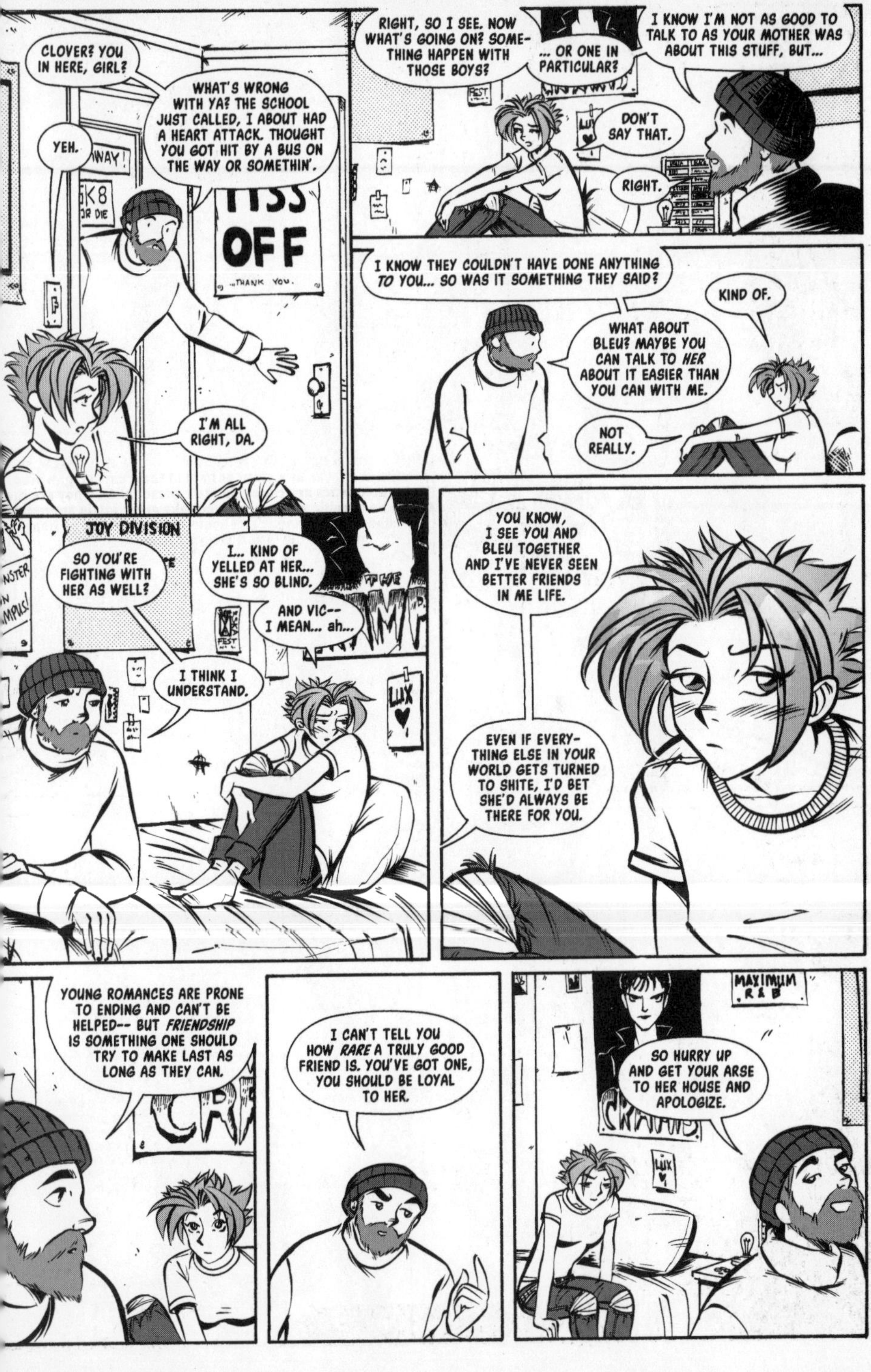
CLOVER? YOU IN HERE, GIRL?
YEH.
WHAT'S WRONG WITH YA? THE SCHOOL JUST CALLED, I ABOUT HAD A HEART ATTACK. THOUGHT YOU GOT HIT BY A BUS ON THE WAY OR SOMETHIN'.
OFF
THANK YOU.
I'M ALL RIGHT, DA.
RIGHT, SO I SEE. NOW WHAT'S GOING ON? SOMETHING HAPPEN WITH THOSE BOYS?
... OR ONE IN PARTICULAR?
I KNOW I'M NOT AS GOOD TO TALK TO AS YOUR MOTHER WAS ABOUT THIS STUFF, BUT...
DON'T SAY THAT.
RIGHT.
I KNOW THEY COULDN'T HAVE DONE ANYTHING TO YOU... SO WAS IT SOMETHING THEY SAID?
KIND OF.
WHAT ABOUT BLEU? MAYBE YOU CAN TALK TO HER ABOUT IT EASIER THAN YOU CAN WITH ME.
NOT REALLY.
JOY DIVISION
SO YOU'RE FIGHTING WITH HER AS WELL?
I... KIND OF YELLED AT HER... SHE'S SO BLIND.
AND VIC-- I MEAN... ah...
I THINK I UNDERSTAND.
LUX
YOU KNOW, I SEE YOU AND BLEU TOGETHER AND I'VE NEVER SEEN BETTER FRIENDS IN ME LIFE.
EVEN IF EVERYTHING ELSE IN YOUR WORLD GETS TURNED TO SHITE, I'D BET SHE'D ALWAYS BE THERE FOR YOU.
YOUNG ROMANCES ARE PRONE TO ENDING AND CAN'T BE HELPED-- BUT FRIENDSHIP IS SOMETHING ONE SHOULD TRY TO MAKE LAST AS LONG AS THEY CAN.
I CAN'T TELL YOU HOW RARE A TRULY GOOD FRIEND IS. YOU'VE GOT ONE, YOU SHOULD BE LOYAL TO HER.
MAXIMUM R&B
SO HURRY UP AND GET YOUR ARSE TO HER HOUSE AND APOLOGIZE.

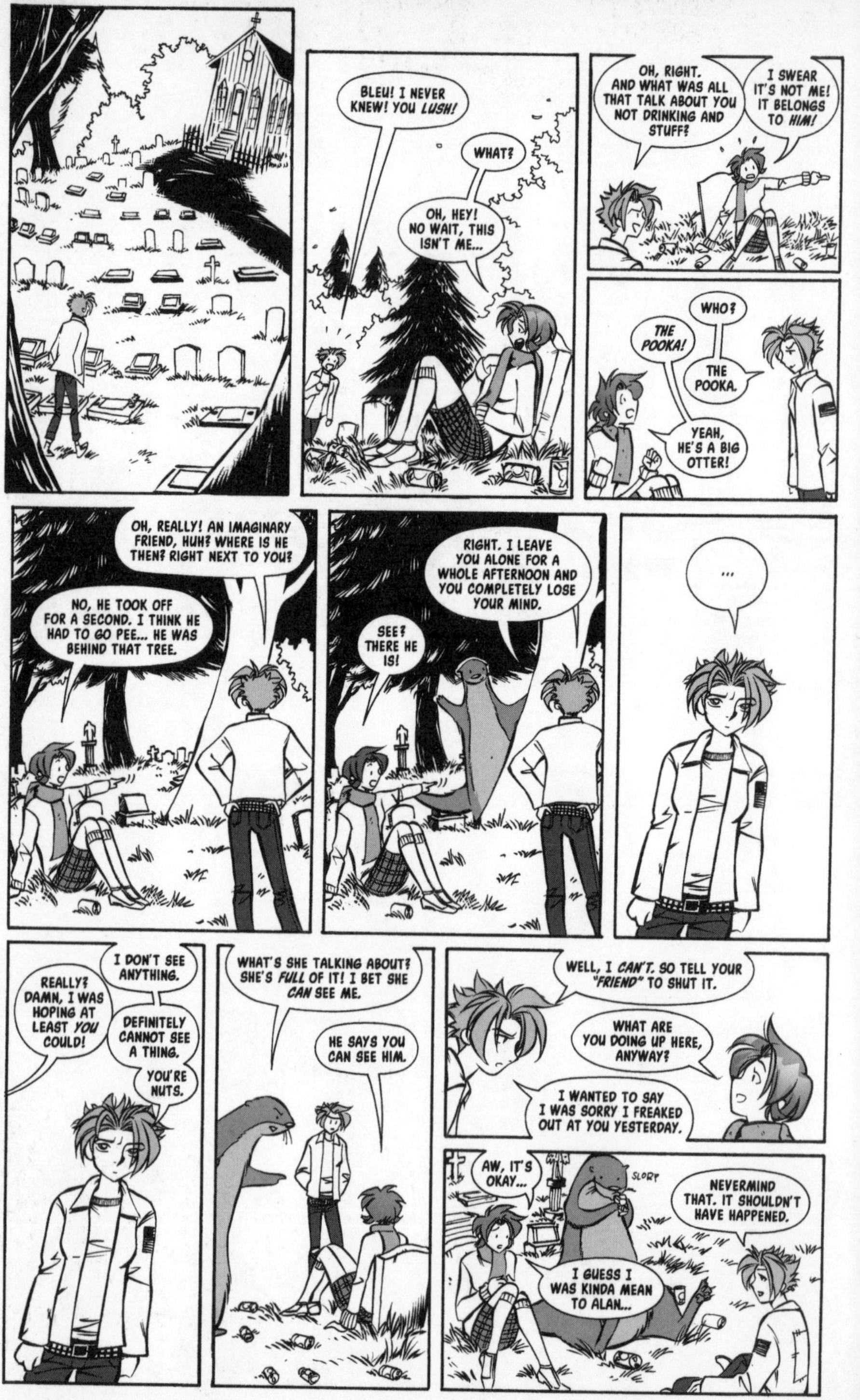

BLEU! I NEVER KNEW! YOU LUSH!
WHAT?
OH, HEY! NO WAIT, THIS ISN'T ME...
OH, RIGHT. AND WHAT WAS ALL THAT TALK ABOUT YOU NOT DRINKING AND STUFF?
I SWEAR IT'S NOT ME! IT BELONGS TO HIM!
WHO?
THE POOKA!
THE POOKA.
YEAH, HE'S A BIG OTTER!
OH, REALLY! AN IMAGINARY FRIEND, HUH? WHERE IS HE THEN? RIGHT NEXT TO YOU?
NO, HE TOOK OFF FOR A SECOND. I THINK HE HAD TO GO PEE... HE WAS BEHIND THAT TREE.
RIGHT. I LEAVE YOU ALONE FOR A WHOLE AFTERNOON AND YOU COMPLETELY LOSE YOUR MIND.
SEE? THERE HE IS!
...
I DON'T SEE ANYTHING.
REALLY? DAMN, I WAS HOPING AT LEAST YOU COULD!
DEFINITELY CANNOT SEE A THING.
YOU'RE NUTS.
WHAT'S SHE TALKING ABOUT? SHE'S FULL OF IT! I BET SHE CAN SEE ME.
HE SAYS YOU CAN SEE HIM.
WELL, I CAN'T. SO TELL YOUR "FRIEND" TO SHUT IT.
WHAT ARE YOU DOING UP HERE, ANYWAY?
I WANTED TO SAY I WAS SORRY I FREAKED OUT AT YOU YESTERDAY.
AW, IT'S OKAY...
SLORP
NEVERMIND THAT. IT SHOULDN'T HAVE HAPPENED.
I GUESS I WAS KINDA MEAN TO ALAN...

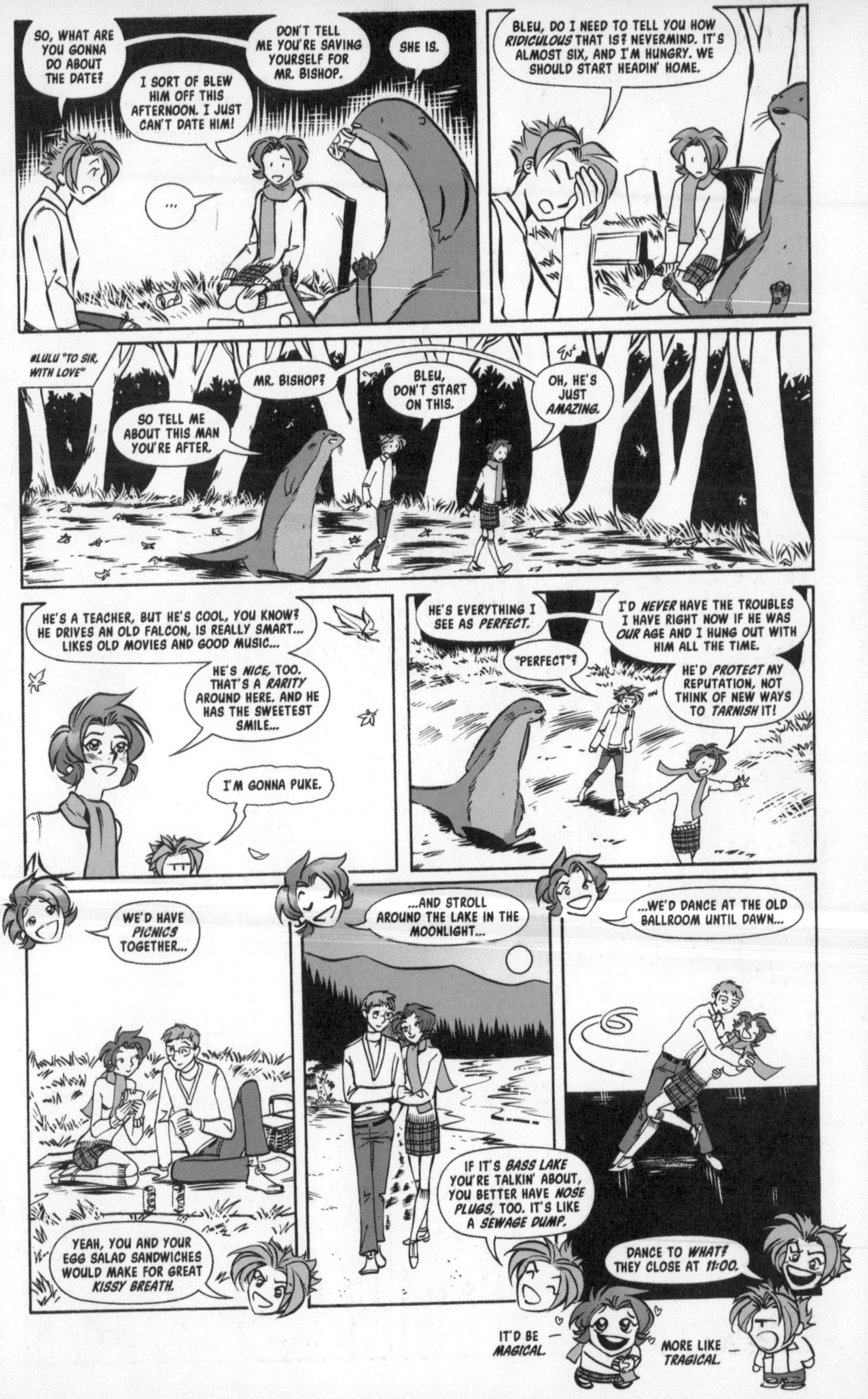
SO, WHAT ARE YOU GONNA DO ABOUT THE DATE?
DON'T TELL ME YOU'RE SAVING YOURSELF FOR MR. BISHOP.
SHE IS.
I SORT OF BLEW HIM OFF THIS AFTERNOON. I JUST CAN'T DATE HIM!
...
BLEU, DO I NEED TO TELL YOU HOW RIDICULOUS THAT IS? NEVERMIND. IT'S ALMOST SIX, AND I'M HUNGRY. WE SHOULD START HEADIN' HOME.
#LULU "TO SIR, WITH LOVE"
SO TELL ME ABOUT THIS MAN YOU'RE AFTER.
MR. BISHOP?
BLEU, DON'T START ON THIS.
OH, HE'S JUST AMAZING.
HE'S A TEACHER, BUT HE'S COOL, YOU KNOW? HE DRIVES AN OLD FALCON, IS REALLY SMART... LIKES OLD MOVIES AND GOOD MUSIC...
HE'S NICE, TOO. THAT'S A RARITY AROUND HERE. AND HE HAS THE SWEETEST SMILE...
I'M GONNA PUKE.
HE'S EVERYTHING I SEE AS PERFECT.
"PERFECT"?
I'D NEVER HAVE THE TROUBLES I HAVE RIGHT NOW IF HE WAS OUR AGE AND I HUNG OUT WITH HIM ALL THE TIME.
HE'D PROTECT MY REPUTATION, NOT THINK OF NEW WAYS TO TARNISH IT!
WE'D HAVE PICNICS TOGETHER...
YEAH, YOU AND YOUR EGG SALAD SANDWICHES WOULD MAKE FOR GREAT KISSY BREATH.
...AND STROLL AROUND THE LAKE IN THE MOONLIGHT...
IF IT'S BASS LAKE YOU'RE TALKIN' ABOUT, YOU BETTER HAVE NOSE PLUGS, TOO. IT'S LIKE A SEWAGE DUMP.
...WE'D DANCE AT THE OLD BALLROOM UNTIL DAWN...
DANCE TO WHAT? THEY CLOSE AT 11:00.
IT'D BE — MAGICAL.
MORE LIKE — TRAGICAL.

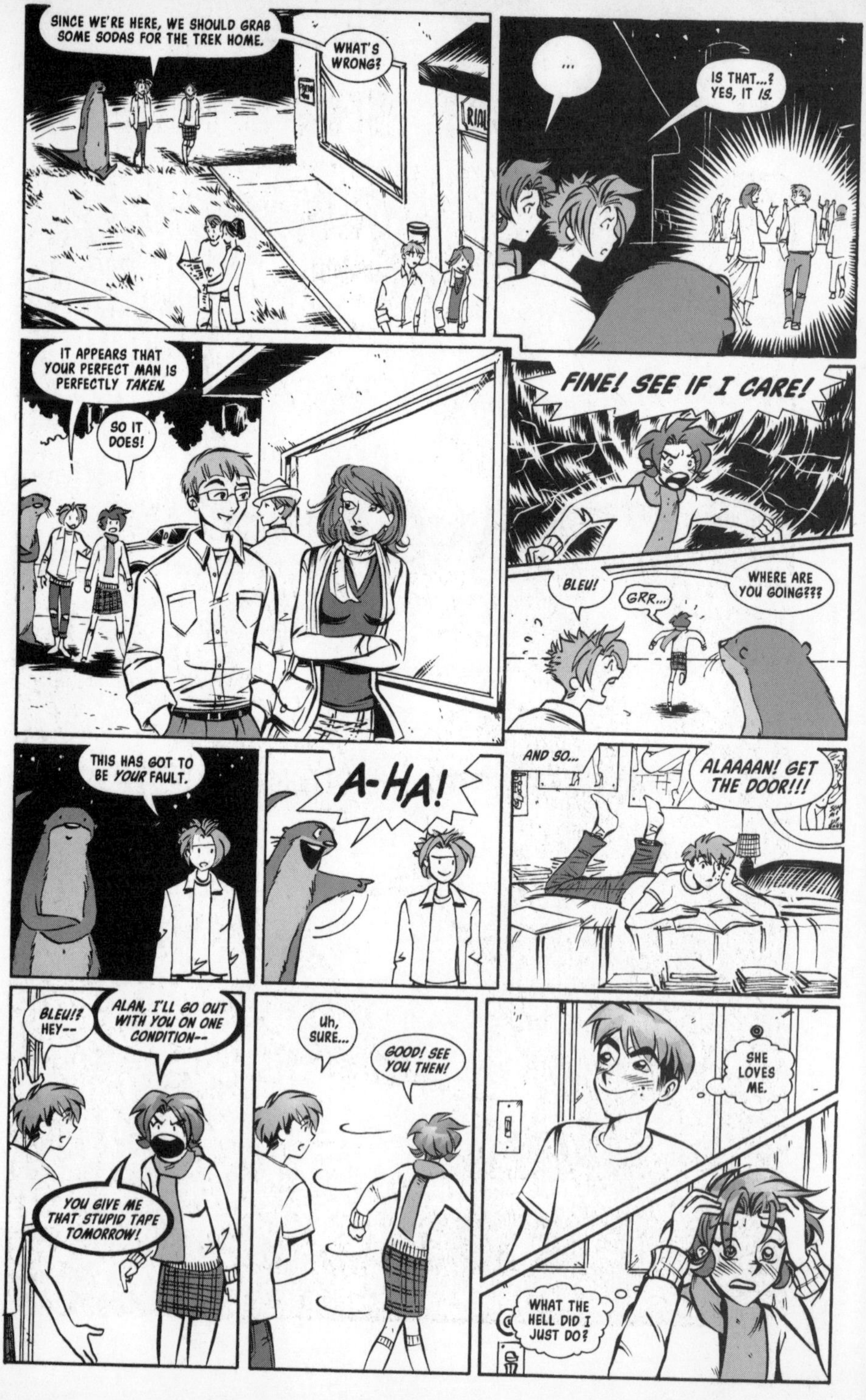
SINCE WE'RE HERE, WE SHOULD GRAB SOME SODAS FOR THE TREK HOME.
WHAT'S WRONG?
...
IS THAT...? YES, IT *IS*.
IT APPEARS THAT YOUR PERFECT MAN IS PERFECTLY *TAKEN*.
SO IT DOES!
FINE! SEE IF I CARE!
BLEU!
GRR...
WHERE ARE YOU GOING???
THIS HAS GOT TO BE *YOUR* FAULT.
A-HA!
AND SO...
ALAAAAN! GET THE DOOR!!!
BLEU!? HEY--
ALAN, I'LL GO OUT WITH YOU ON ONE CONDITION--
YOU GIVE ME THAT STUPID TAPE TOMORROW!
Uh, SURE...
GOOD! SEE YOU THEN!
SHE LOVES ME.
WHAT THE HELL DID I JUST DO?

chapter four:
"HANDS OFF, SHE'S MINE"

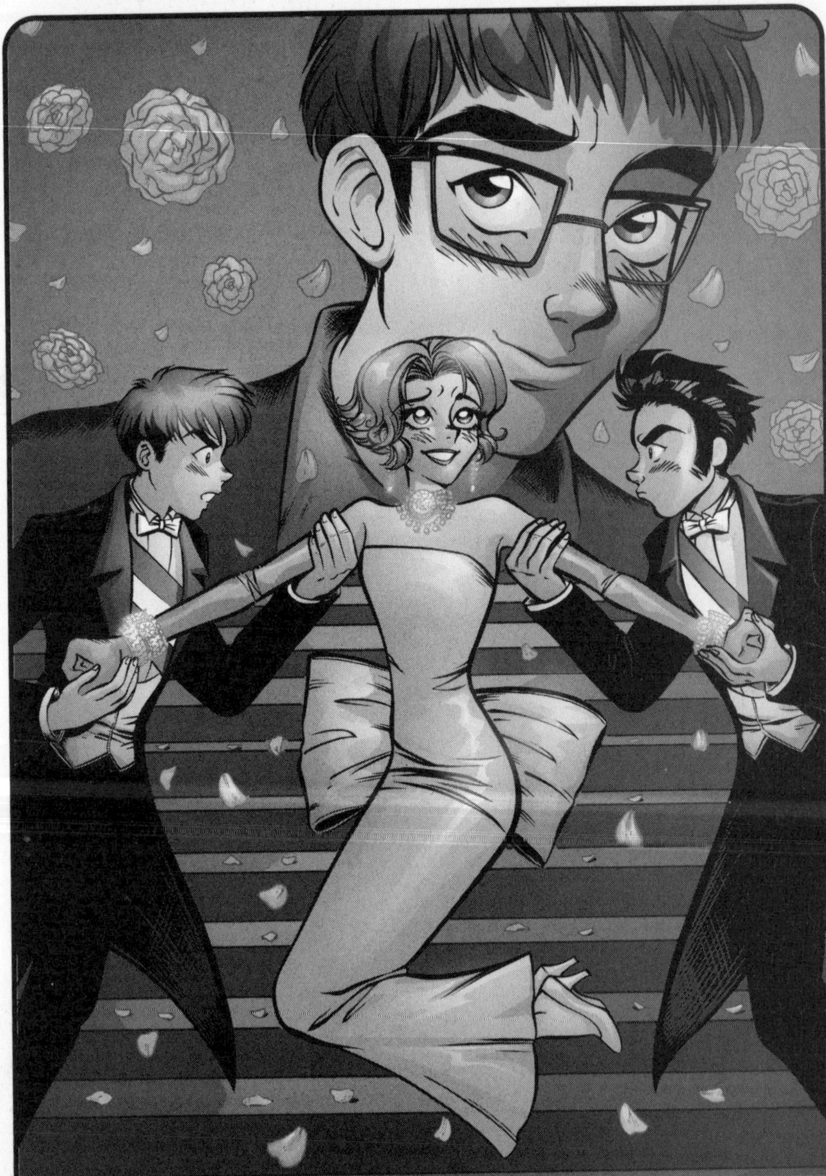

YOU AND YOUR FUCKIN' BOOK! GIVIN' ME A FUCKIN' ULCER! FUCKIN' FUCKIN' FUCK BLUE FUCKIN' MONDAY!!!!

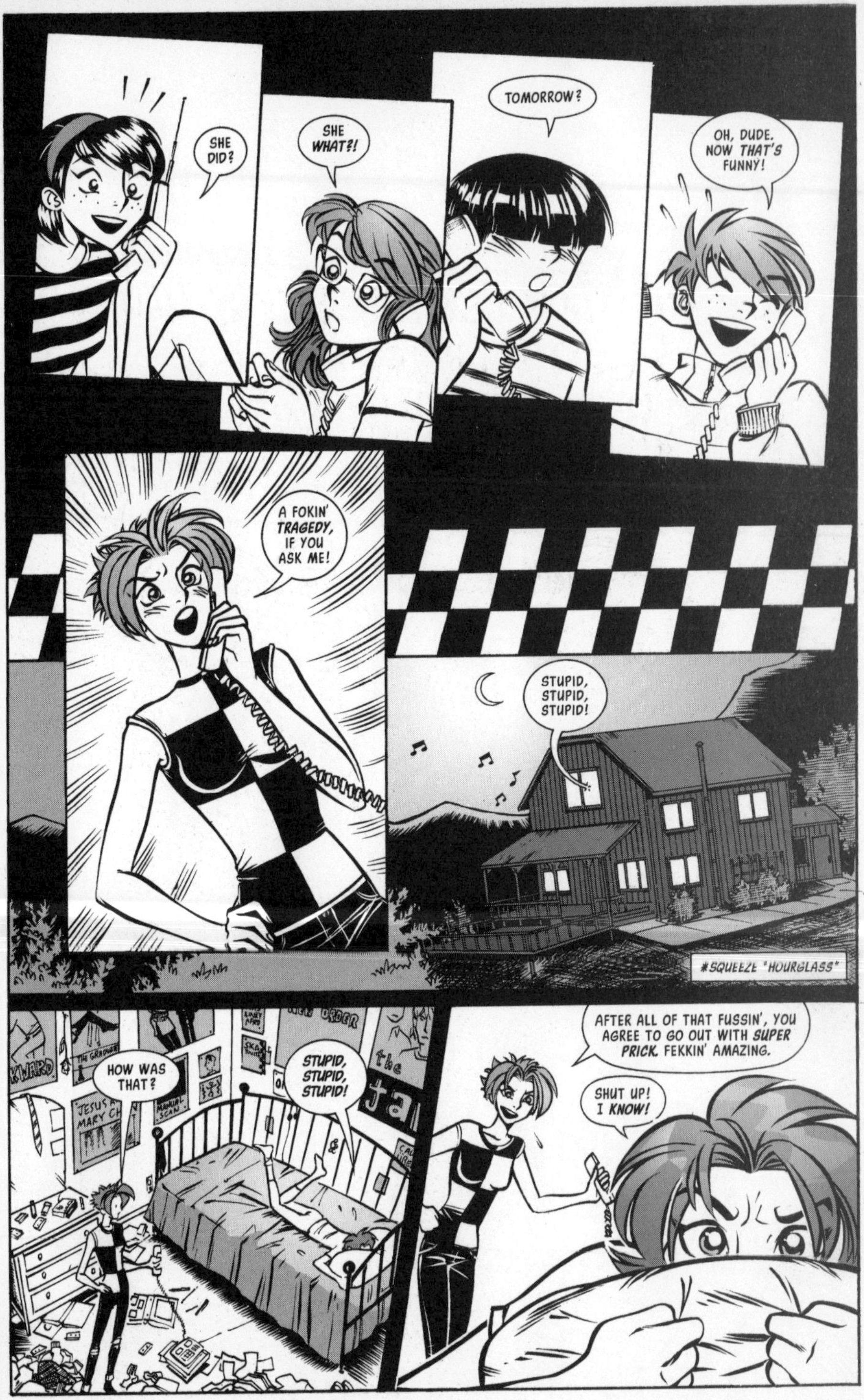
SHE DID?
SHE WHAT?!
TOMORROW?
OH, DUDE. NOW THAT'S FUNNY!
A FOKIN' TRAGEDY, IF YOU ASK ME!
STUPID, STUPID, STUPID!
*SQUEEZE "HOURGLASS"
HOW WAS THAT?
STUPID, STUPID, STUPID!
AFTER ALL OF THAT FUSSIN', YOU AGREE TO GO OUT WITH SUPER PRICK. FEKKIN' AMAZING.
SHUT UP! I KNOW!

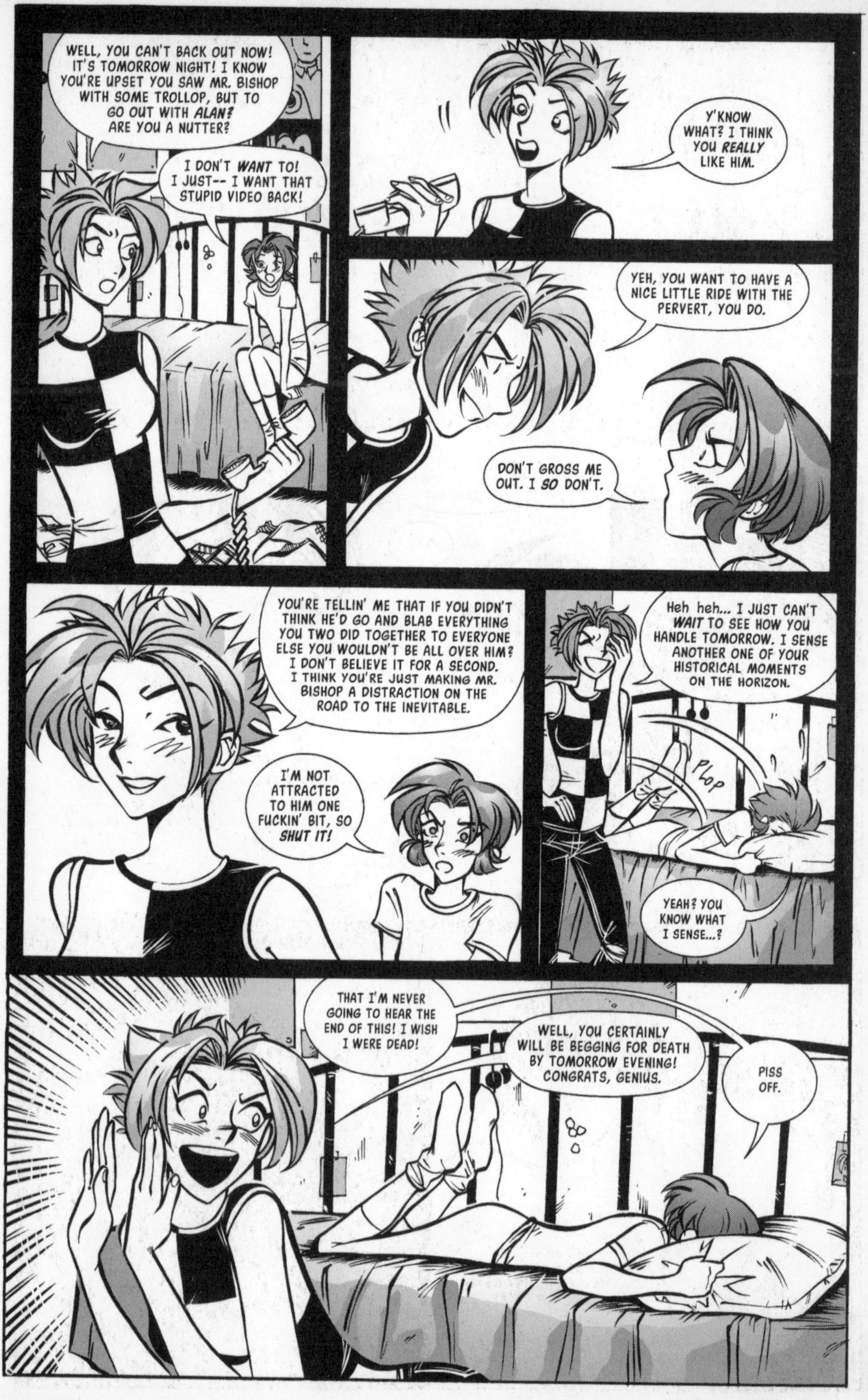
WELL, YOU CAN'T BACK OUT NOW! IT'S TOMORROW NIGHT! I KNOW YOU'RE UPSET YOU SAW MR. BISHOP WITH SOME TROLLOP, BUT TO GO OUT WITH ALAN? ARE YOU A NUTTER?
I DON'T WANT TO! I JUST-- I WANT THAT STUPID VIDEO BACK!
Y'KNOW WHAT? I THINK YOU REALLY LIKE HIM.
YEH, YOU WANT TO HAVE A NICE LITTLE RIDE WITH THE PERVERT, YOU DO.
DON'T GROSS ME OUT. I SO DON'T.
YOU'RE TELLIN' ME THAT IF YOU DIDN'T THINK HE'D GO AND BLAB EVERYTHING YOU TWO DID TOGETHER TO EVERYONE ELSE YOU WOULDN'T BE ALL OVER HIM? I DON'T BELIEVE IT FOR A SECOND. I THINK YOU'RE JUST MAKING MR. BISHOP A DISTRACTION ON THE ROAD TO THE INEVITABLE.
I'M NOT ATTRACTED TO HIM ONE FUCKIN' BIT, SO SHUT IT!
Heh heh... I JUST CAN'T WAIT TO SEE HOW YOU HANDLE TOMORROW. I SENSE ANOTHER ONE OF YOUR HISTORICAL MOMENTS ON THE HORIZON.
PLOP
YEAH? YOU KNOW WHAT I SENSE...?
THAT I'M NEVER GOING TO HEAR THE END OF THIS! I WISH I WERE DEAD!
WELL, YOU CERTAINLY WILL BE BEGGING FOR DEATH BY TOMORROW EVENING! CONGRATS, GENIUS.
PISS OFF.

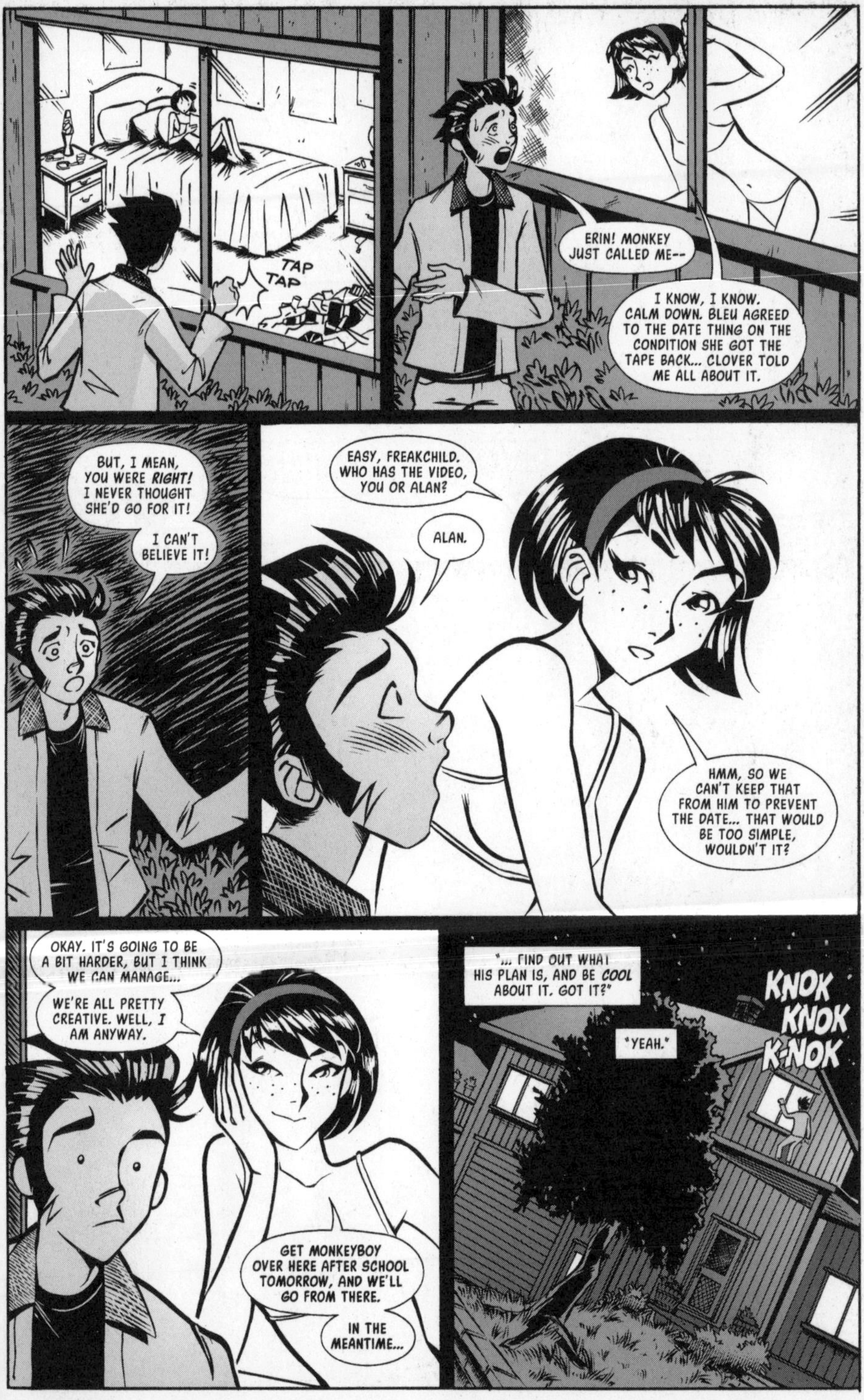
TAP
TAP
ERIN! MONKEY JUST CALLED ME--
I KNOW, I KNOW. CALM DOWN. BLEU AGREED TO THE DATE THING ON THE CONDITION SHE GOT THE TAPE BACK... CLOVER TOLD ME ALL ABOUT IT.
BUT, I MEAN, YOU WERE RIGHT! I NEVER THOUGHT SHE'D GO FOR IT!
I CAN'T BELIEVE IT!
EASY, FREAKCHILD. WHO HAS THE VIDEO, YOU OR ALAN?
ALAN.
HMM, SO WE CAN'T KEEP THAT FROM HIM TO PREVENT THE DATE... THAT WOULD BE TOO SIMPLE, WOULDN'T IT?
OKAY. IT'S GOING TO BE A BIT HARDER, BUT I THINK WE CAN MANAGE...
WE'RE ALL PRETTY CREATIVE. WELL, I AM ANYWAY.
GET MONKEYBOY OVER HERE AFTER SCHOOL TOMORROW, AND WE'LL GO FROM THERE.
IN THE MEANTIME...
"... FIND OUT WHAT HIS PLAN IS, AND BE COOL ABOUT IT. GOT IT?"
"YEAH."
KNOK
KNOK
K-NOK

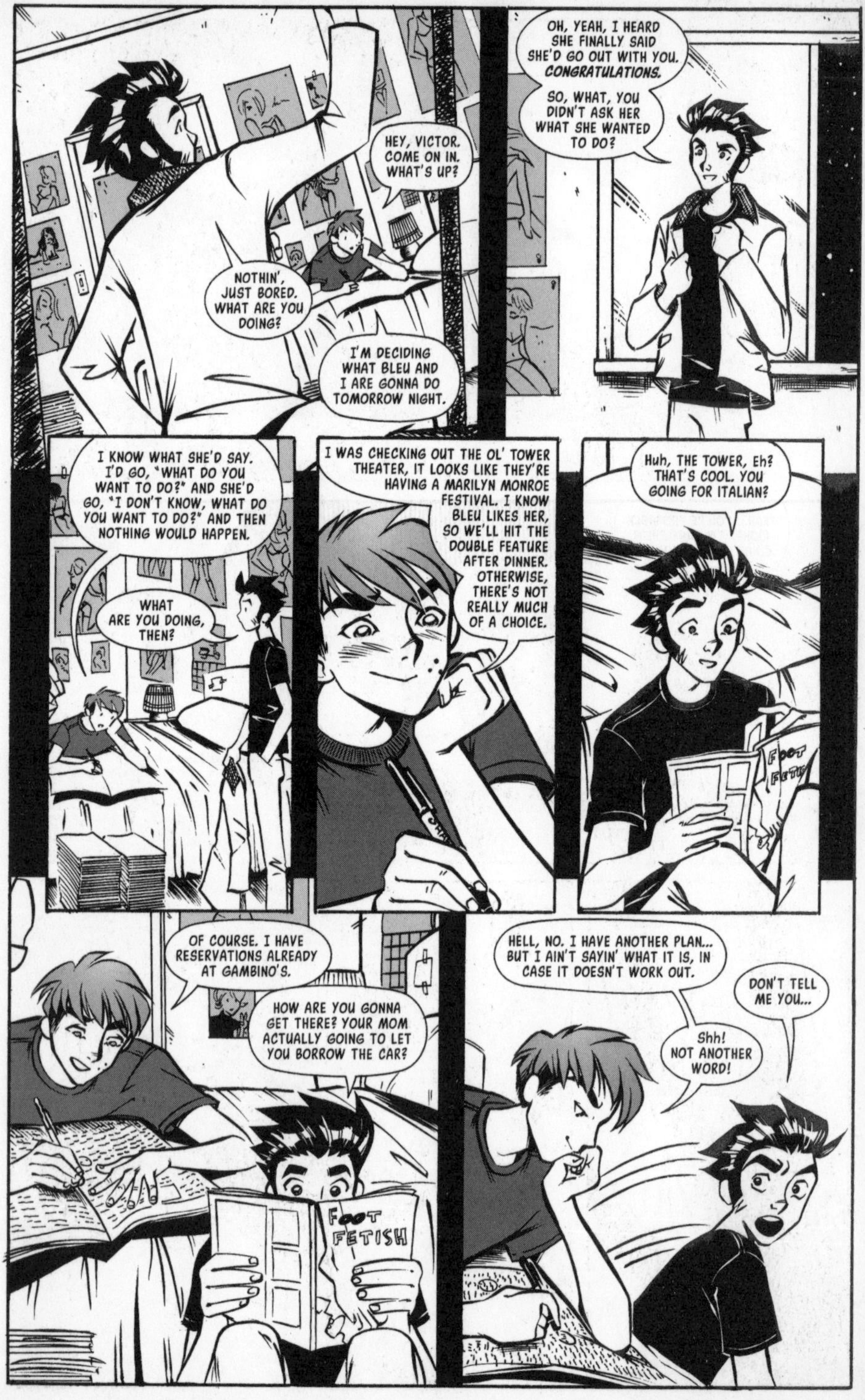
HEY, VICTOR. COME ON IN. WHAT'S UP?
NOTHIN', JUST BORED. WHAT ARE YOU DOING?
I'M DECIDING WHAT BLEU AND I ARE GONNA DO TOMORROW NIGHT.
OH, YEAH, I HEARD SHE FINALLY SAID SHE'D GO OUT WITH YOU. CONGRATULATIONS.
SO, WHAT, YOU DIDN'T ASK HER WHAT SHE WANTED TO DO?
I KNOW WHAT SHE'D SAY. I'D GO, "WHAT DO YOU WANT TO DO?" AND SHE'D GO, "I DON'T KNOW, WHAT DO YOU WANT TO DO?" AND THEN NOTHING WOULD HAPPEN.
WHAT ARE YOU DOING, THEN?
I WAS CHECKING OUT THE OL' TOWER THEATER, IT LOOKS LIKE THEY'RE HAVING A MARILYN MONROE FESTIVAL. I KNOW BLEU LIKES HER, SO WE'LL HIT THE DOUBLE FEATURE AFTER DINNER. OTHERWISE, THERE'S NOT REALLY MUCH OF A CHOICE.
Huh, THE TOWER, Eh? THAT'S COOL. YOU GOING FOR ITALIAN?
OF COURSE. I HAVE RESERVATIONS ALREADY AT GAMBINO'S.
HOW ARE YOU GONNA GET THERE? YOUR MOM ACTUALLY GOING TO LET YOU BORROW THE CAR?
FOOT FETISH
HELL, NO. I HAVE ANOTHER PLAN... BUT I AIN'T SAYIN' WHAT IT IS, IN CASE IT DOESN'T WORK OUT.
DON'T TELL ME YOU...
Shh! NOT ANOTHER WORD!

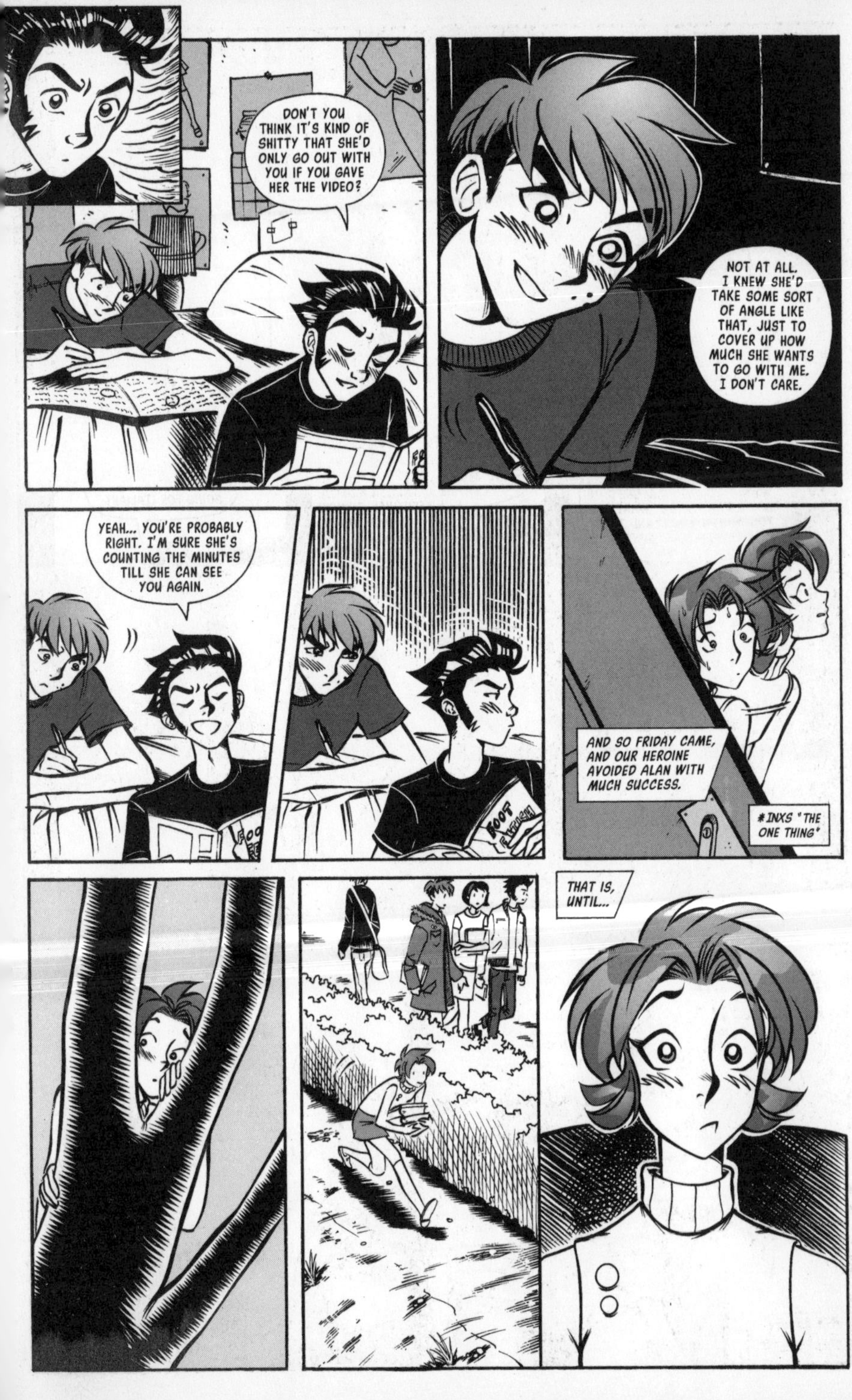
DON'T YOU THINK IT'S KIND OF SHITTY THAT SHE'D ONLY GO OUT WITH YOU IF YOU GAVE HER THE VIDEO?
NOT AT ALL. I KNEW SHE'D TAKE SOME SORT OF ANGLE LIKE THAT, JUST TO COVER UP HOW MUCH SHE WANTS TO GO WITH ME. I DON'T CARE.
YEAH... YOU'RE PROBABLY RIGHT. I'M SURE SHE'S COUNTING THE MINUTES TILL SHE CAN SEE YOU AGAIN.
AND SO FRIDAY CAME, AND OUR HEROINE AVOIDED ALAN WITH MUCH SUCCESS.
#INXS "THE ONE THING"
THAT IS, UNTIL...

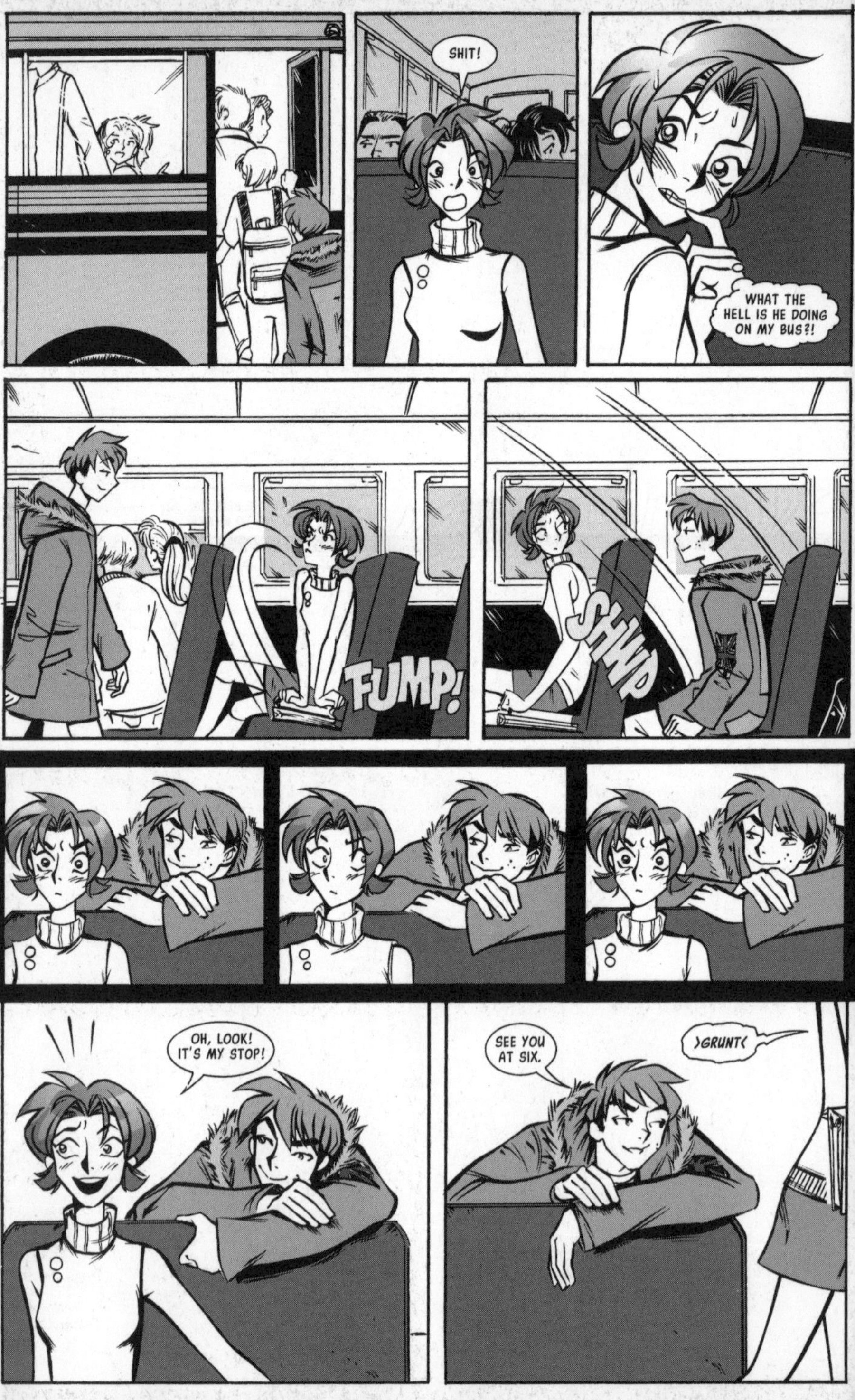
SHIT!
WHAT THE HELL IS HE DOING ON MY BUS?!
FUMP!
SHWP
OH, LOOK! IT'S MY STOP!
SEE YOU AT SIX.
>GRUNT<

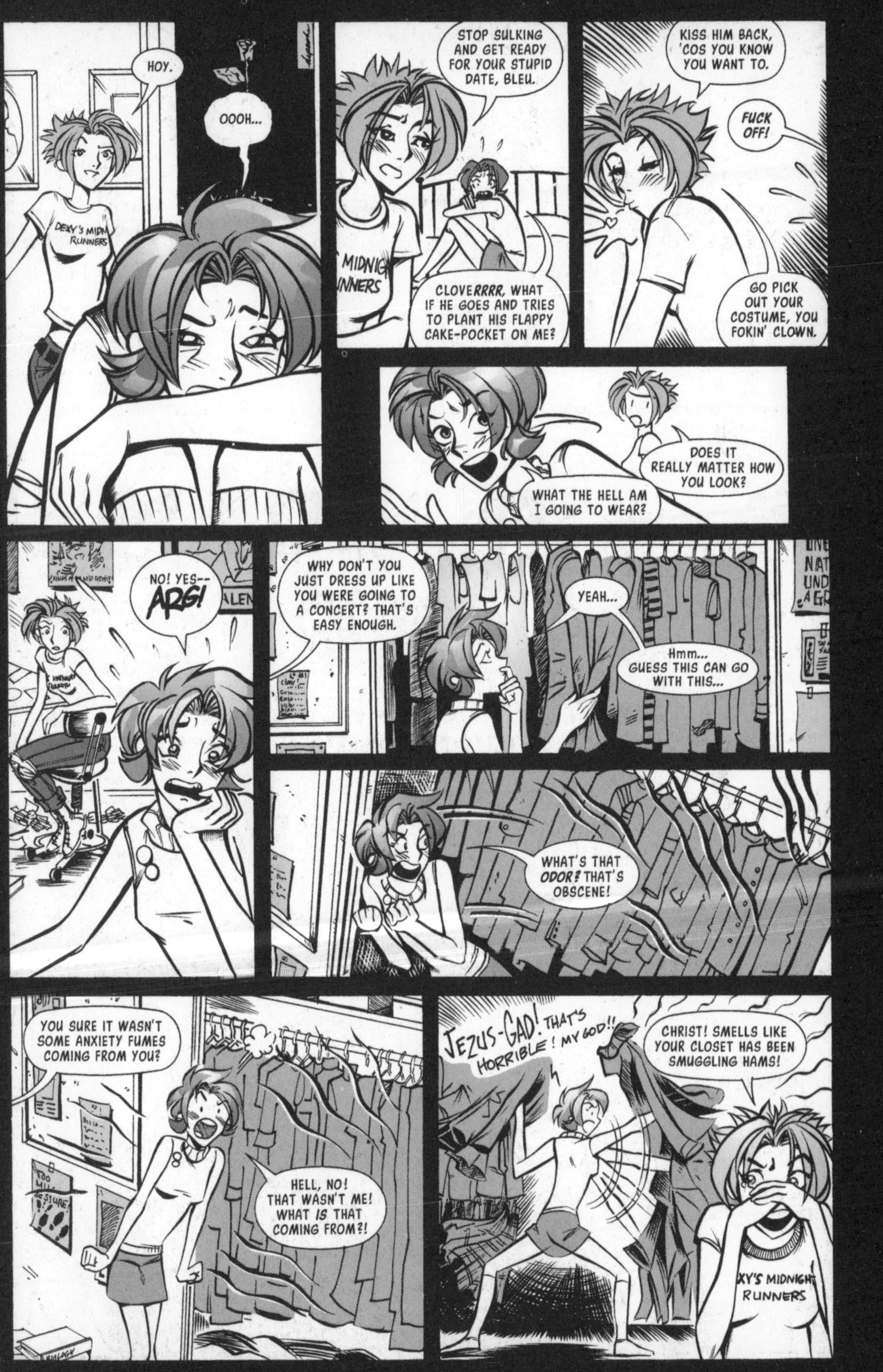
HOY.
OOOH...
STOP SULKING AND GET READY FOR YOUR STUPID DATE, BLEU.
CLOVERRRR, WHAT IF HE GOES AND TRIES TO PLANT HIS FLAPPY CAKE-POCKET ON ME?
KISS HIM BACK, 'COS YOU KNOW YOU WANT TO.
FUCK OFF!
GO PICK OUT YOUR COSTUME, YOU FOKIN' CLOWN.
WHAT THE HELL AM I GOING TO WEAR?
DOES IT REALLY MATTER HOW YOU LOOK?
NO! YES-- ARG!
WHY DON'T YOU JUST DRESS UP LIKE YOU WERE GOING TO A CONCERT? THAT'S EASY ENOUGH.
YEAH...
Hmm... GUESS THIS CAN GO WITH THIS...
WHAT'S THAT ODOR? THAT'S OBSCENE!
YOU SURE IT WASN'T SOME ANXIETY FUMES COMING FROM YOU?
HELL, NO! THAT WASN'T ME! WHAT IS THAT COMING FROM?!
JEZUS-GAD! THAT'S HORRIBLE! MY GOD!!
CHRIST! SMELLS LIKE YOUR CLOSET HAS BEEN SMUGGLING HAMS!

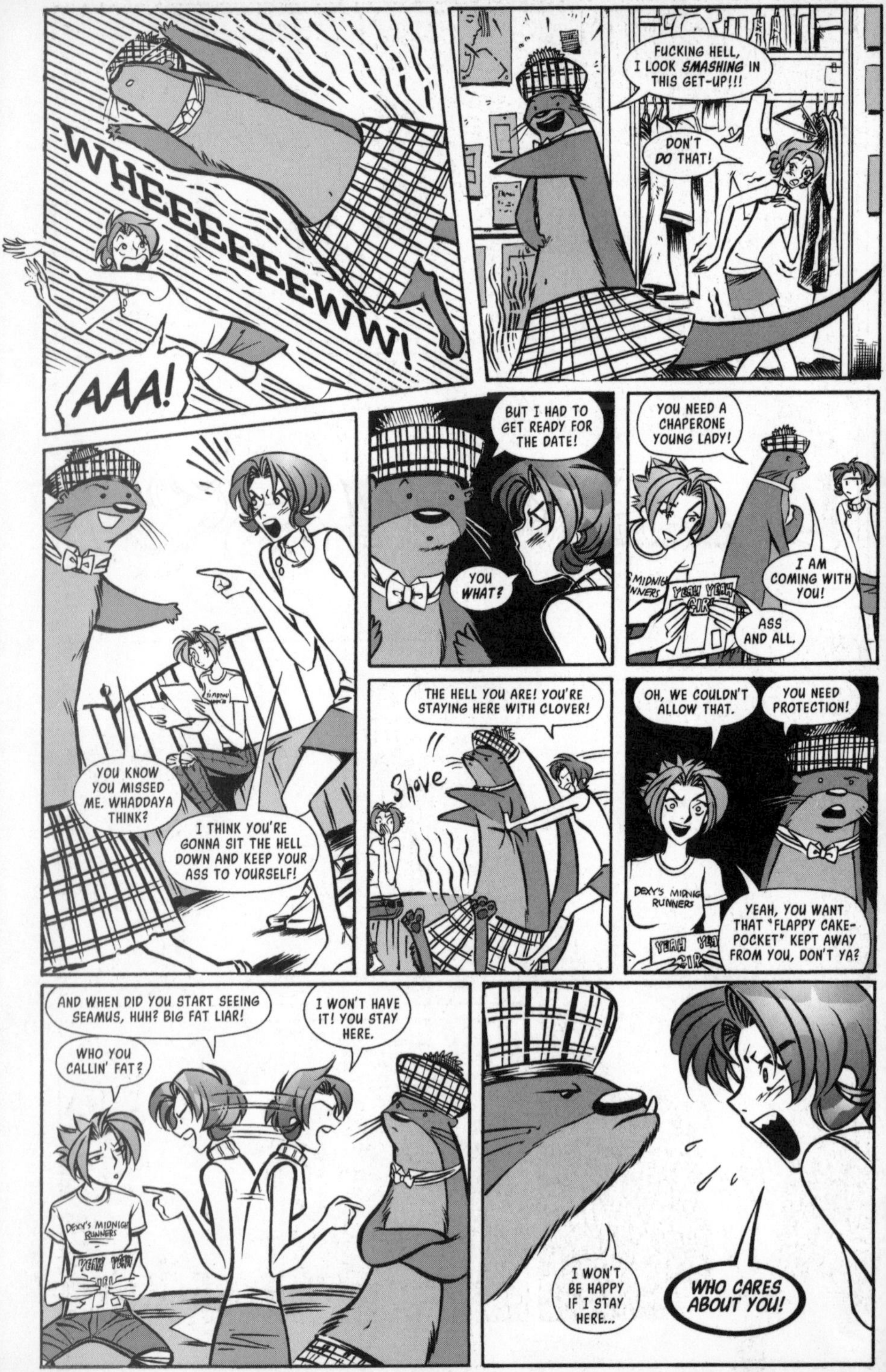
WHEEEEEEEWW!
AAA!
FUCKING HELL, I LOOK SMASHING IN THIS GET-UP!!!
DON'T DO THAT!
YOU KNOW YOU MISSED ME. WHADDAYA THINK?
I THINK YOU'RE GONNA SIT THE HELL DOWN AND KEEP YOUR ASS TO YOURSELF!
BUT I HAD TO GET READY FOR THE DATE!
YOU WHAT?
YOU NEED A CHAPERONE YOUNG LADY!
I AM COMING WITH YOU!
ASS AND ALL.
THE HELL YOU ARE! YOU'RE STAYING HERE WITH CLOVER!
Shove
OH, WE COULDN'T ALLOW THAT.
YOU NEED PROTECTION!
YEAH, YOU WANT THAT "FLAPPY CAKE-POCKET" KEPT AWAY FROM YOU, DON'T YA?
AND WHEN DID YOU START SEEING SEAMUS, HUH? BIG FAT LIAR!
WHO YOU CALLIN' FAT?
I WON'T HAVE IT! YOU STAY HERE.
I WON'T BE HAPPY IF I STAY HERE...
WHO CARES ABOUT YOU!

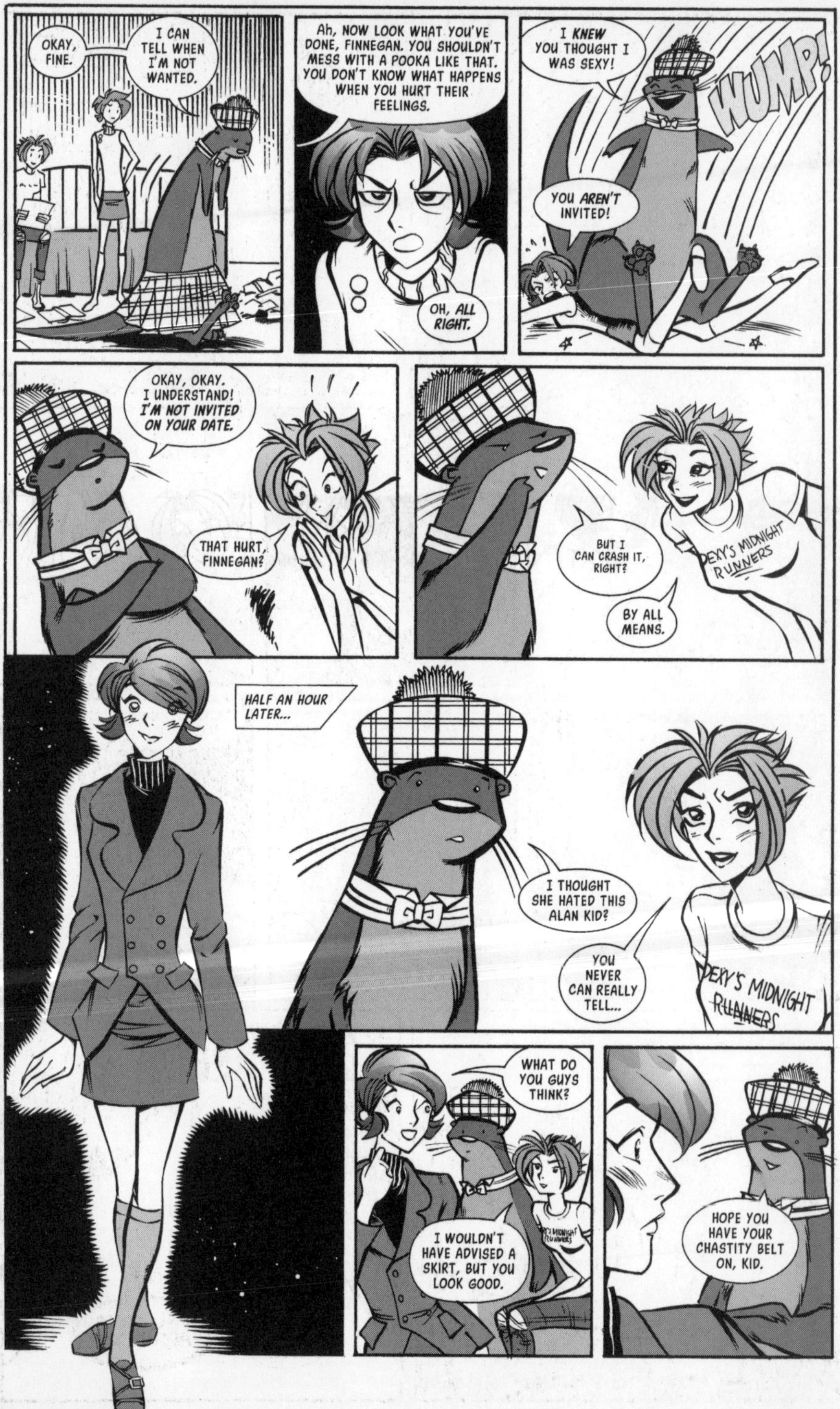
OKAY, FINE.
I CAN TELL WHEN I'M NOT WANTED.
Ah, NOW LOOK WHAT YOU'VE DONE, FINNEGAN. YOU SHOULDN'T MESS WITH A POOKA LIKE THAT. YOU DON'T KNOW WHAT HAPPENS WHEN YOU HURT THEIR FEELINGS.
OH, ALL RIGHT.
I KNEW YOU THOUGHT I WAS SEXY!
WUMP!
YOU AREN'T INVITED!
OKAY, OKAY. I UNDERSTAND! I'M NOT INVITED ON YOUR DATE.
THAT HURT, FINNEGAN?
BUT I CAN CRASH IT, RIGHT?
DEXY'S MIDNIGHT RUNNERS
BY ALL MEANS.
HALF AN HOUR LATER...
I THOUGHT SHE HATED THIS ALAN KID?
YOU NEVER CAN REALLY TELL...
DEXY'S MIDNIGHT RUNNERS
WHAT DO YOU GUYS THINK?
I WOULDN'T HAVE ADVISED A SKIRT, BUT YOU LOOK GOOD.
HOPE YOU HAVE YOUR CHASTITY BELT ON, KID.

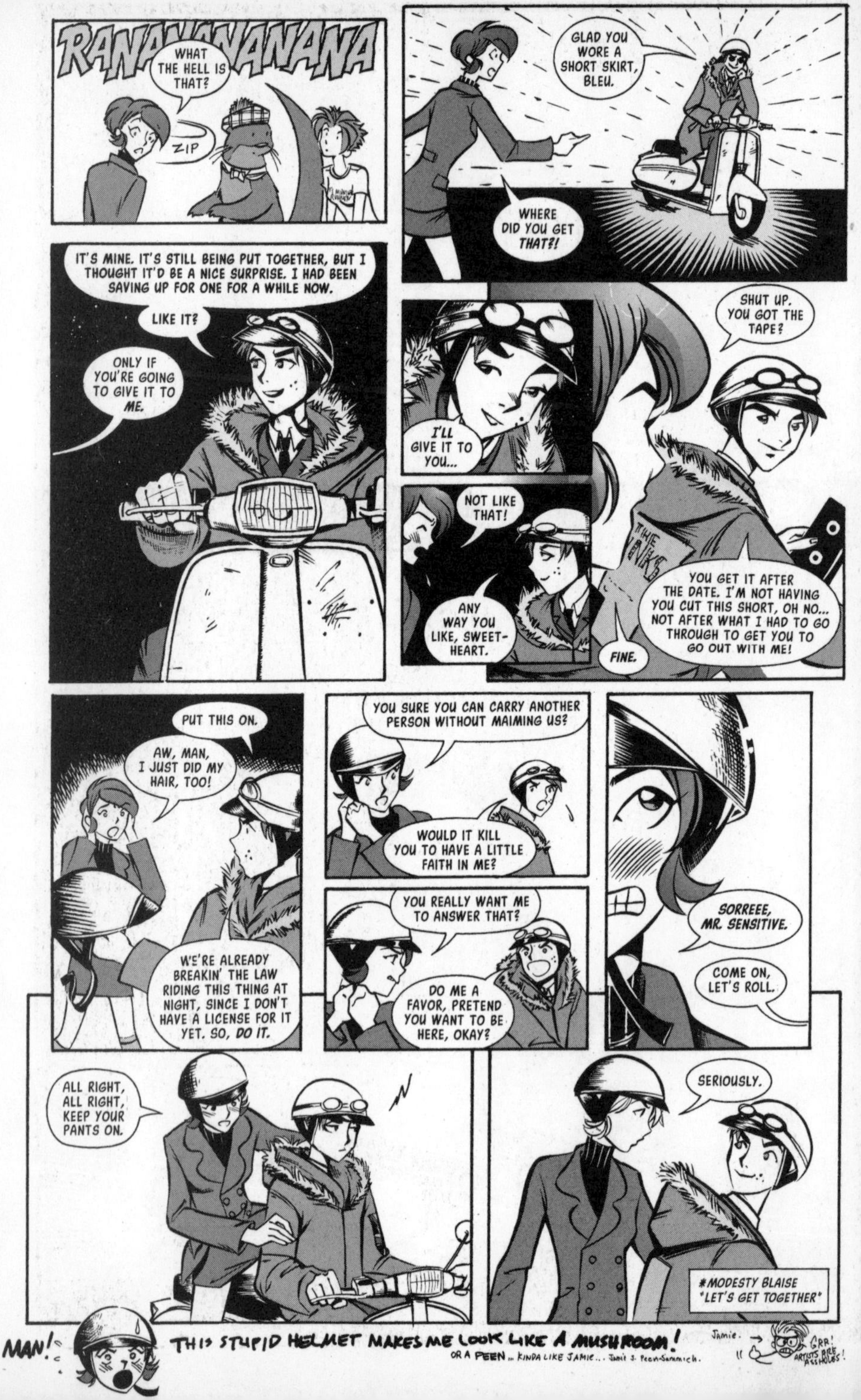
RANANANANANA
WHAT THE HELL IS THAT?
ZIP
GLAD YOU WORE A SHORT SKIRT, BLEU.
WHERE DID YOU GET THAT?!
IT'S MINE. IT'S STILL BEING PUT TOGETHER, BUT I THOUGHT IT'D BE A NICE SURPRISE. I HAD BEEN SAVING UP FOR ONE FOR A WHILE NOW.
LIKE IT?
ONLY IF YOU'RE GOING TO GIVE IT TO ME.
I'LL GIVE IT TO YOU...
NOT LIKE THAT!
ANY WAY YOU LIKE, SWEET-HEART.
SHUT UP. YOU GOT THE TAPE?
YOU GET IT AFTER THE DATE. I'M NOT HAVING YOU CUT THIS SHORT, OH NO... NOT AFTER WHAT I HAD TO GO THROUGH TO GET YOU TO GO OUT WITH ME!
FINE.
PUT THIS ON.
AW, MAN, I JUST DID MY HAIR, TOO!
WE'RE ALREADY BREAKIN' THE LAW RIDING THIS THING AT NIGHT, SINCE I DON'T HAVE A LICENSE FOR IT YET. SO, DO IT.
YOU SURE YOU CAN CARRY ANOTHER PERSON WITHOUT MAIMING US?
WOULD IT KILL YOU TO HAVE A LITTLE FAITH IN ME?
YOU REALLY WANT ME TO ANSWER THAT?
DO ME A FAVOR, PRETEND YOU WANT TO BE HERE, OKAY?
SORREEE, MR. SENSITIVE.
COME ON, LET'S ROLL.
ALL RIGHT, ALL RIGHT, KEEP YOUR PANTS ON.
SERIOUSLY.
*MODESTY BLAISE "LET'S GET TOGETHER"
MAN!
THIS STUPID HELMET MAKES ME LOOK LIKE A MUSHROOM!
OR A PEEN... KINDA LIKE JAMIE... Jamie S. Peen-Sammich.
Jamie.
GRR! ARTISTS ARE ASSHOLES!

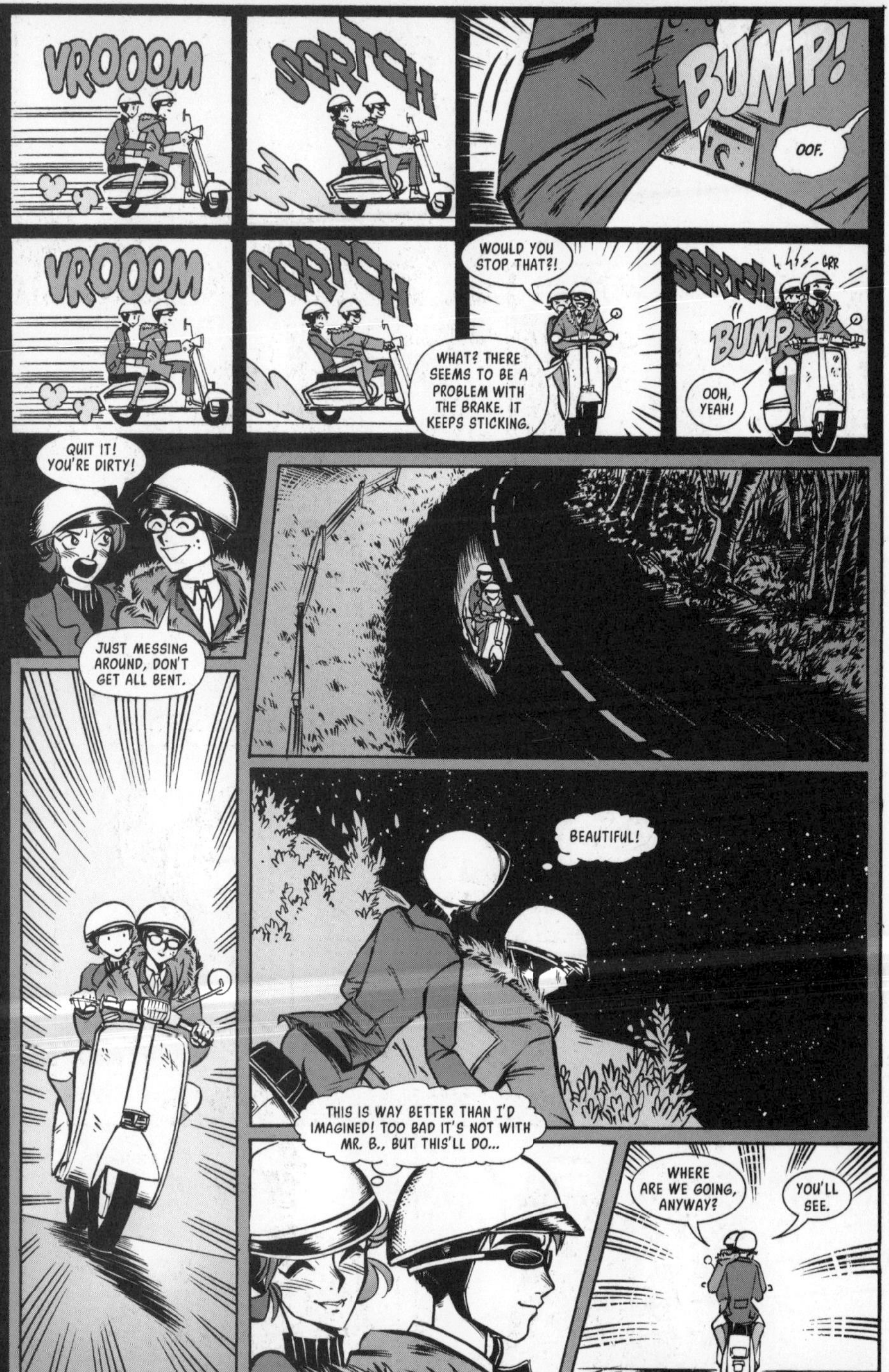
VROOOM
SCRTCH
BUMP!
OOF.
VROOOM
SCRTCH
WOULD YOU STOP THAT?!
WHAT? THERE SEEMS TO BE A PROBLEM WITH THE BRAKE. IT KEEPS STICKING.
SCRTCH
GRR
BUMP
OOH, YEAH!
QUIT IT! YOU'RE DIRTY!
JUST MESSING AROUND, DON'T GET ALL BENT.
BEAUTIFUL!
THIS IS WAY BETTER THAN I'D IMAGINED! TOO BAD IT'S NOT WITH MR. B., BUT THIS'LL DO...
WHERE ARE WE GOING, ANYWAY?
YOU'LL SEE.

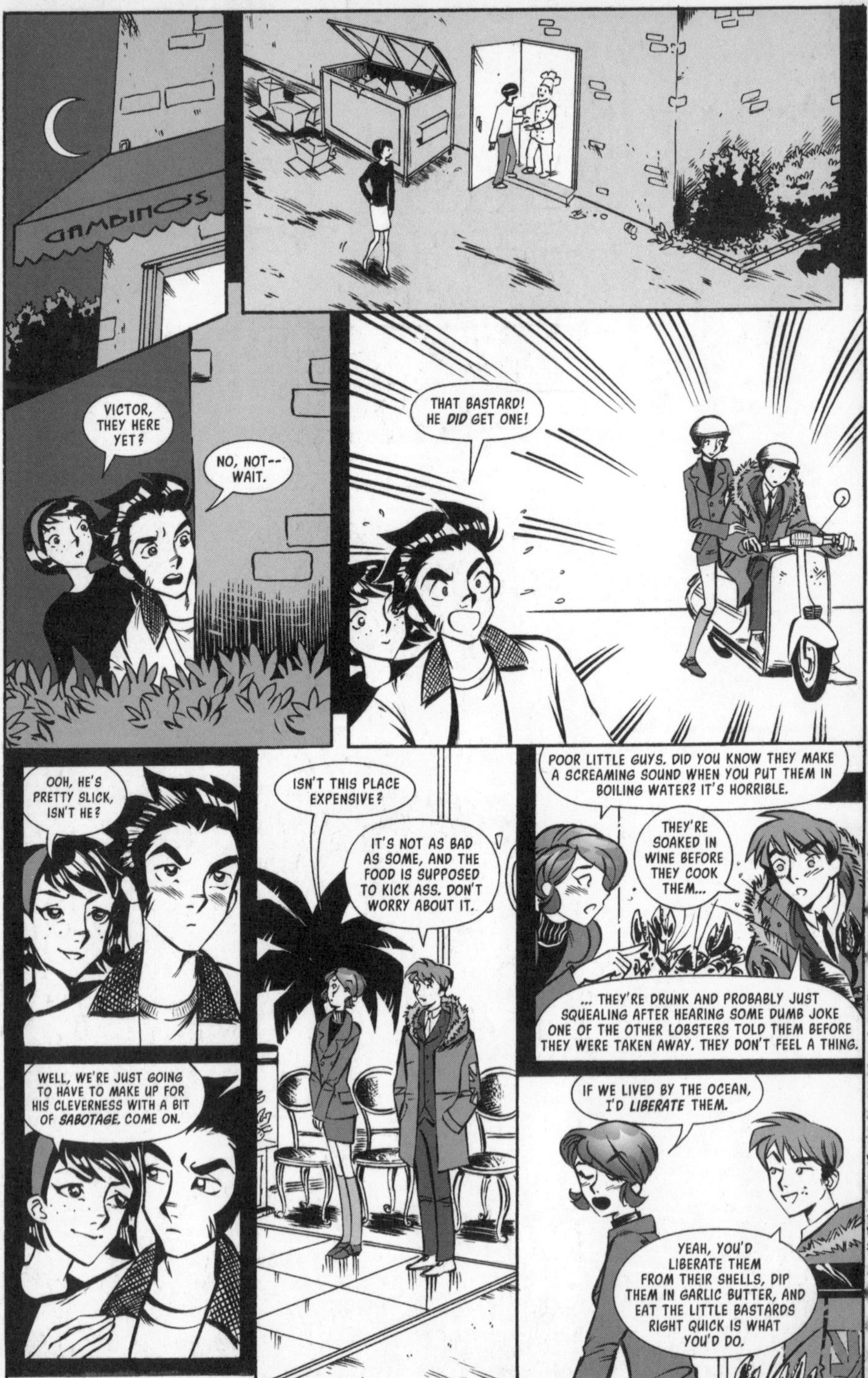
GAMBINO'S
VICTOR, THEY HERE YET?
NO, NOT-- WAIT.
THAT BASTARD! HE DID GET ONE!
OOH, HE'S PRETTY SLICK, ISN'T HE?
WELL, WE'RE JUST GOING TO HAVE TO MAKE UP FOR HIS CLEVERNESS WITH A BIT OF SABOTAGE. COME ON.
ISN'T THIS PLACE EXPENSIVE?
IT'S NOT AS BAD AS SOME, AND THE FOOD IS SUPPOSED TO KICK ASS. DON'T WORRY ABOUT IT.
POOR LITTLE GUYS. DID YOU KNOW THEY MAKE A SCREAMING SOUND WHEN YOU PUT THEM IN BOILING WATER? IT'S HORRIBLE.
THEY'RE SOAKED IN WINE BEFORE THEY COOK THEM...
... THEY'RE DRUNK AND PROBABLY JUST SQUEALING AFTER HEARING SOME DUMB JOKE ONE OF THE OTHER LOBSTERS TOLD THEM BEFORE THEY WERE TAKEN AWAY. THEY DON'T FEEL A THING.
IF WE LIVED BY THE OCEAN, I'D LIBERATE THEM.
YEAH, YOU'D LIBERATE THEM FROM THEIR SHELLS, DIP THEM IN GARLIC BUTTER, AND EAT THE LITTLE BASTARDS RIGHT QUICK IS WHAT YOU'D DO.

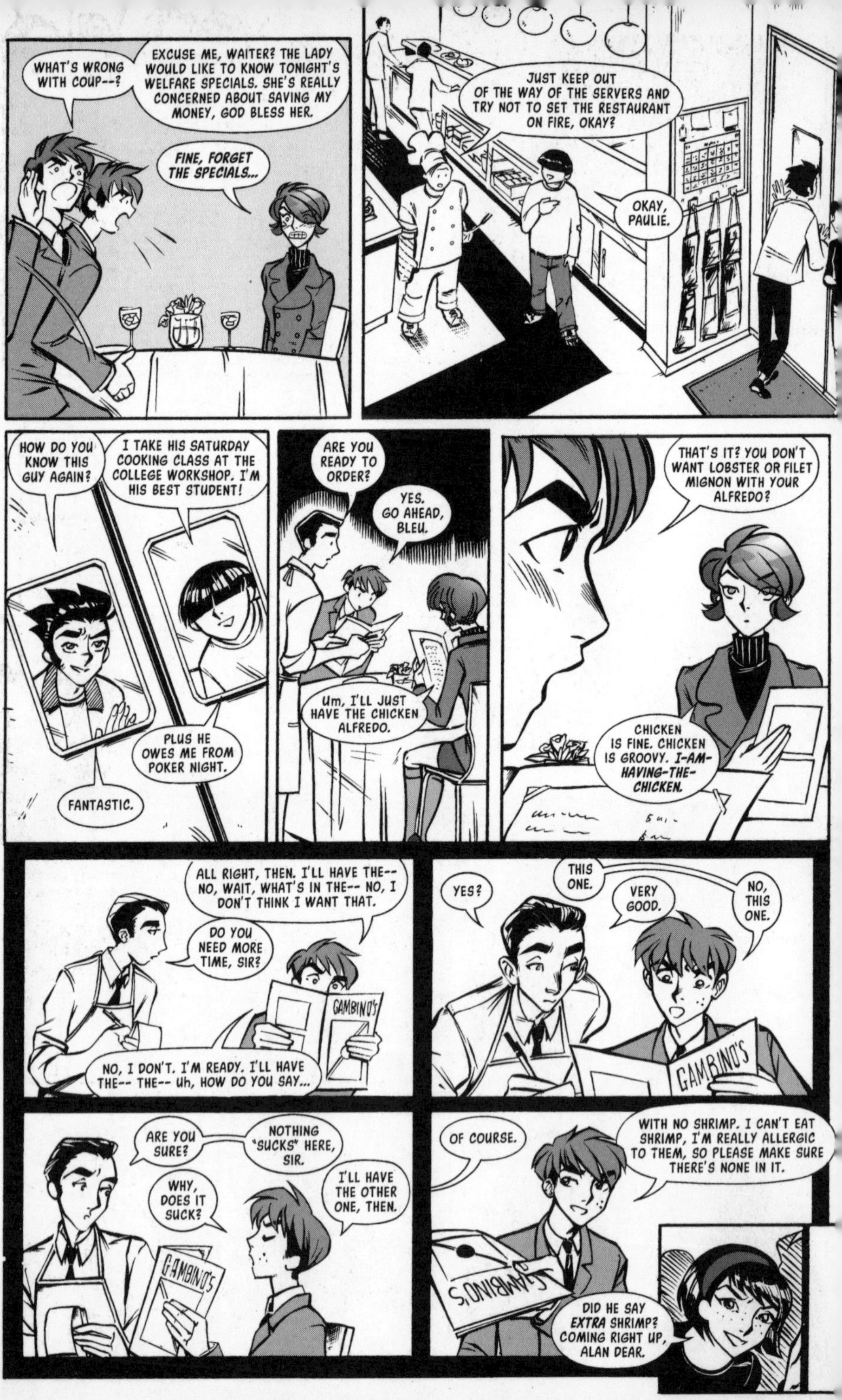

WHAT'S WRONG WITH COUP--?
EXCUSE ME, WAITER? THE LADY WOULD LIKE TO KNOW TONIGHT'S WELFARE SPECIALS. SHE'S REALLY CONCERNED ABOUT SAVING MY MONEY, GOD BLESS HER.
FINE, FORGET THE SPECIALS...
JUST KEEP OUT OF THE WAY OF THE SERVERS AND TRY NOT TO SET THE RESTAURANT ON FIRE, OKAY?
OKAY, PAULIE.
HOW DO YOU KNOW THIS GUY AGAIN?
I TAKE HIS SATURDAY COOKING CLASS AT THE COLLEGE WORKSHOP. I'M HIS BEST STUDENT!
PLUS HE OWES ME FROM POKER NIGHT.
FANTASTIC.
ARE YOU READY TO ORDER?
YES. GO AHEAD, BLEU.
Um, I'LL JUST HAVE THE CHICKEN ALFREDO.
THAT'S IT? YOU DON'T WANT LOBSTER OR FILET MIGNON WITH YOUR ALFREDO?
CHICKEN IS FINE. CHICKEN IS GROOVY. I-AM-HAVING-THE-CHICKEN.
ALL RIGHT, THEN. I'LL HAVE THE-- NO, WAIT, WHAT'S IN THE-- NO, I DON'T THINK I WANT THAT.
DO YOU NEED MORE TIME, SIR?
NO, I DON'T. I'M READY. I'LL HAVE THE-- THE-- Uh, HOW DO YOU SAY...
GAMBINO'S
YES?
THIS ONE.
VERY GOOD.
NO, THIS ONE.
GAMBINO'S
ARE YOU SURE?
NOTHING "SUCKS" HERE, SIR.
WHY, DOES IT SUCK?
I'LL HAVE THE OTHER ONE, THEN.
GAMBINO'S
OF COURSE.
WITH NO SHRIMP. I CAN'T EAT SHRIMP, I'M REALLY ALLERGIC TO THEM, SO PLEASE MAKE SURE THERE'S NONE IN IT.
DID HE SAY EXTRA SHRIMP? COMING RIGHT UP, ALAN DEAR.

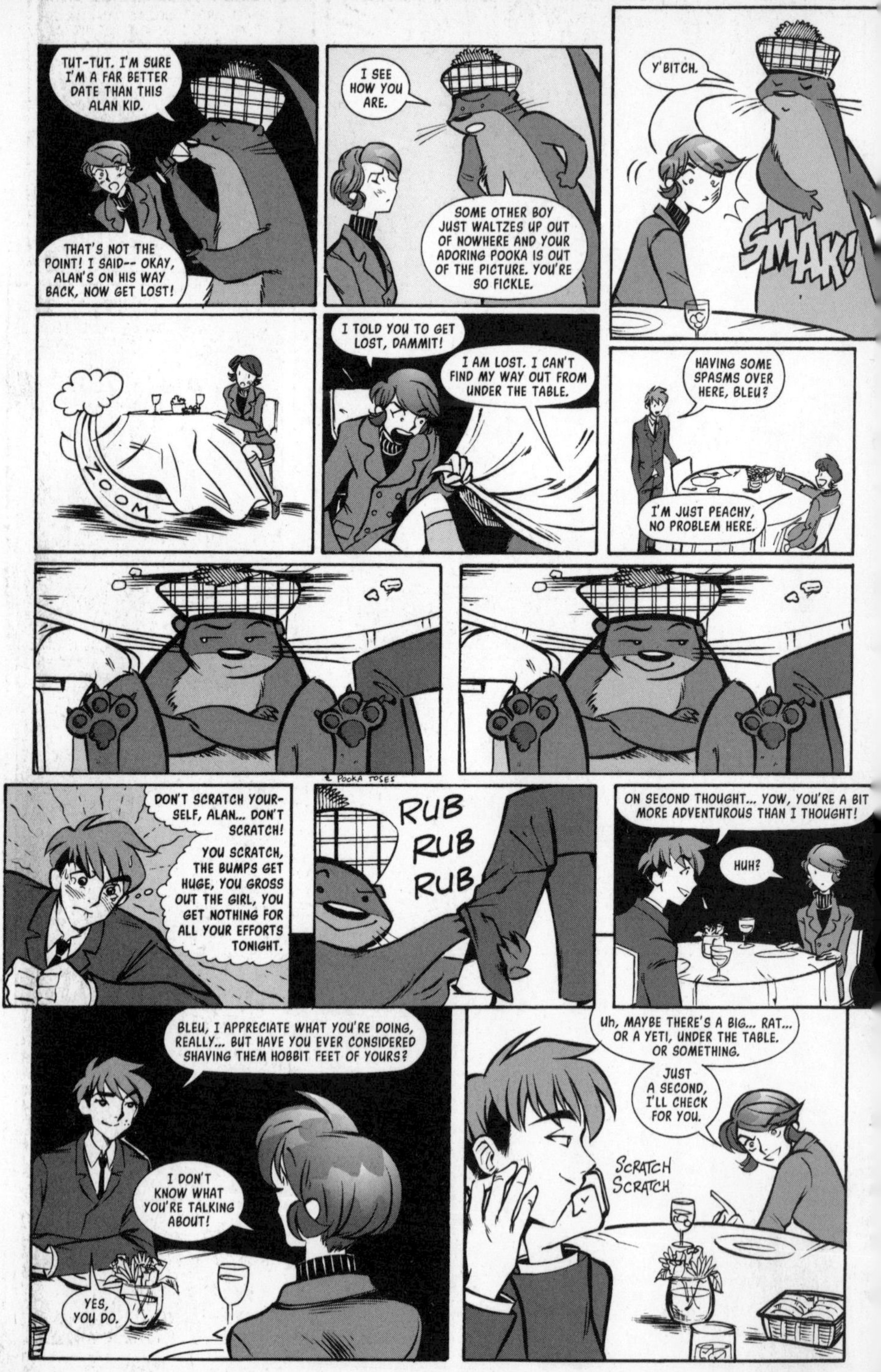
TUT-TUT. I'M SURE I'M A FAR BETTER DATE THAN THIS ALAN KID.
THAT'S NOT THE POINT! I SAID-- OKAY, ALAN'S ON HIS WAY BACK, NOW GET LOST!
I SEE HOW YOU ARE.
SOME OTHER BOY JUST WALTZES UP OUT OF NOWHERE AND YOUR ADORING POOKA IS OUT OF THE PICTURE. YOU'RE SO FICKLE.
Y'BITCH.
SMAK!
ZOOM
I TOLD YOU TO GET LOST, DAMMIT!
I AM LOST. I CAN'T FIND MY WAY OUT FROM UNDER THE TABLE.
HAVING SOME SPASMS OVER HERE, BLEU?
I'M JUST PEACHY, NO PROBLEM HERE.
DON'T SCRATCH YOURSELF, ALAN... DON'T SCRATCH!
YOU SCRATCH, THE BUMPS GET HUGE, YOU GROSS OUT THE GIRL, YOU GET NOTHING FOR ALL YOUR EFFORTS TONIGHT.
POOKA TOSES
RUB
RUB
RUB
ON SECOND THOUGHT... YOW, YOU'RE A BIT MORE ADVENTUROUS THAN I THOUGHT!
HUH?
BLEU, I APPRECIATE WHAT YOU'RE DOING, REALLY... BUT HAVE YOU EVER CONSIDERED SHAVING THEM HOBBIT FEET OF YOURS?
I DON'T KNOW WHAT YOU'RE TALKING ABOUT!
YES, YOU DO.
Uh, MAYBE THERE'S A BIG... RAT... OR A YETI, UNDER THE TABLE. OR SOMETHING.
JUST A SECOND, I'LL CHECK FOR YOU.
SCRATCH
SCRATCH

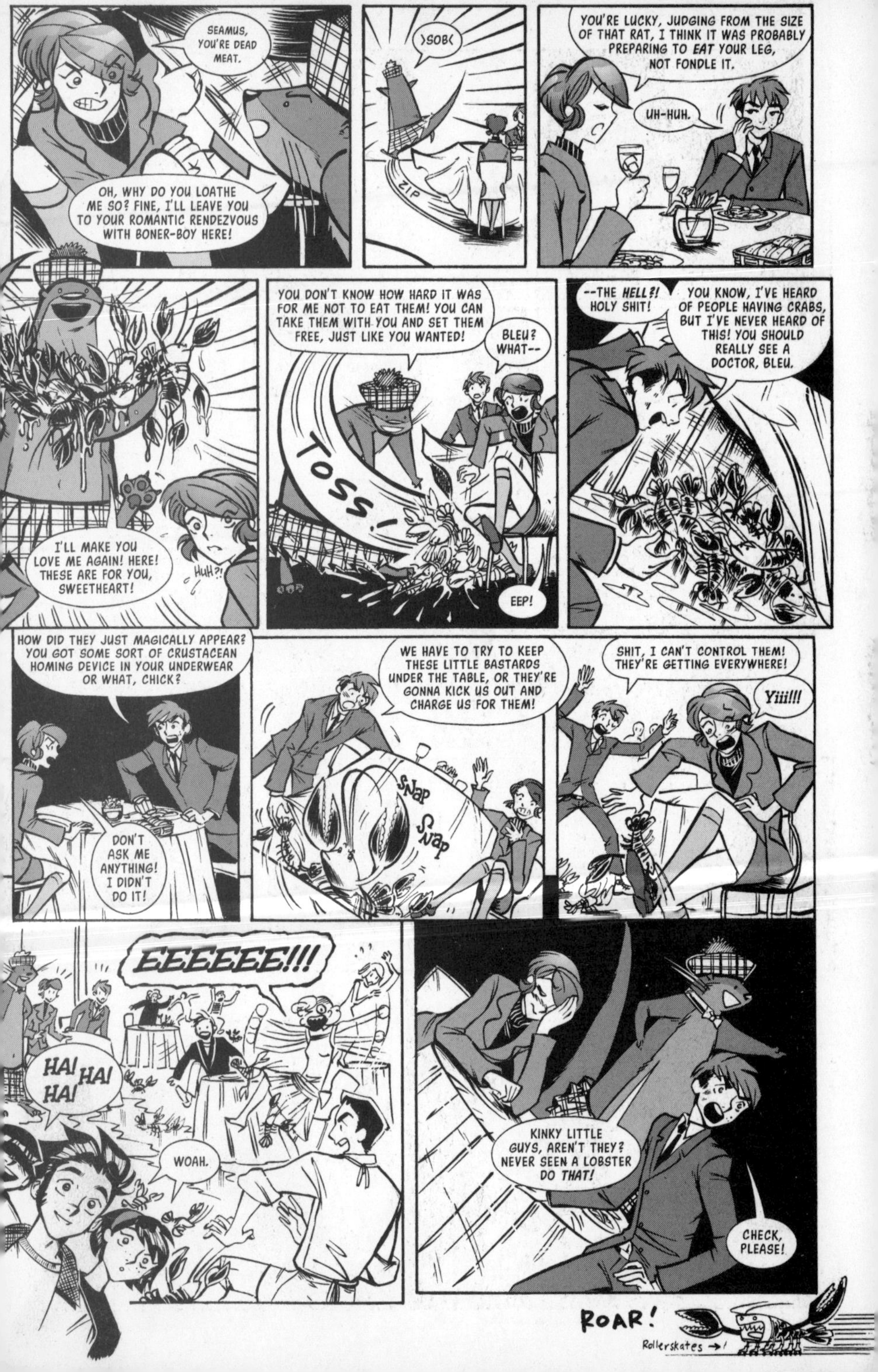
SEAMUS, YOU'RE DEAD MEAT.
OH, WHY DO YOU LOATHE ME SO? FINE, I'LL LEAVE YOU TO YOUR ROMANTIC RENDEZVOUS WITH BONER-BOY HERE!
›SOB‹
ZIP
YOU'RE LUCKY, JUDGING FROM THE SIZE OF THAT RAT, I THINK IT WAS PROBABLY PREPARING TO EAT YOUR LEG, NOT FONDLE IT.
UH-HUH.
I'LL MAKE YOU LOVE ME AGAIN! HERE! THESE ARE FOR YOU, SWEETHEART!
HUH?!
YOU DON'T KNOW HOW HARD IT WAS FOR ME NOT TO EAT THEM! YOU CAN TAKE THEM WITH YOU AND SET THEM FREE, JUST LIKE YOU WANTED!
BLEU? WHAT--
TOSS!
EEP!
--THE HELL?! HOLY SHIT!
YOU KNOW, I'VE HEARD OF PEOPLE HAVING CRABS, BUT I'VE NEVER HEARD OF THIS! YOU SHOULD REALLY SEE A DOCTOR, BLEU.
HOW DID THEY JUST MAGICALLY APPEAR? YOU GOT SOME SORT OF CRUSTACEAN HOMING DEVICE IN YOUR UNDERWEAR OR WHAT, CHICK?
DON'T ASK ME ANYTHING! I DIDN'T DO IT!
WE HAVE TO TRY TO KEEP THESE LITTLE BASTARDS UNDER THE TABLE, OR THEY'RE GONNA KICK US OUT AND CHARGE US FOR THEM!
SNAP
SNAP
SHIT, I CAN'T CONTROL THEM! THEY'RE GETTING EVERYWHERE!
Yiii!!!
EEEEEE!!!
HA! HA! HA!
WOAH.
KINKY LITTLE GUYS, AREN'T THEY? NEVER SEEN A LOBSTER DO THAT!
CHECK, PLEASE!
ROAR!
Rollerskates

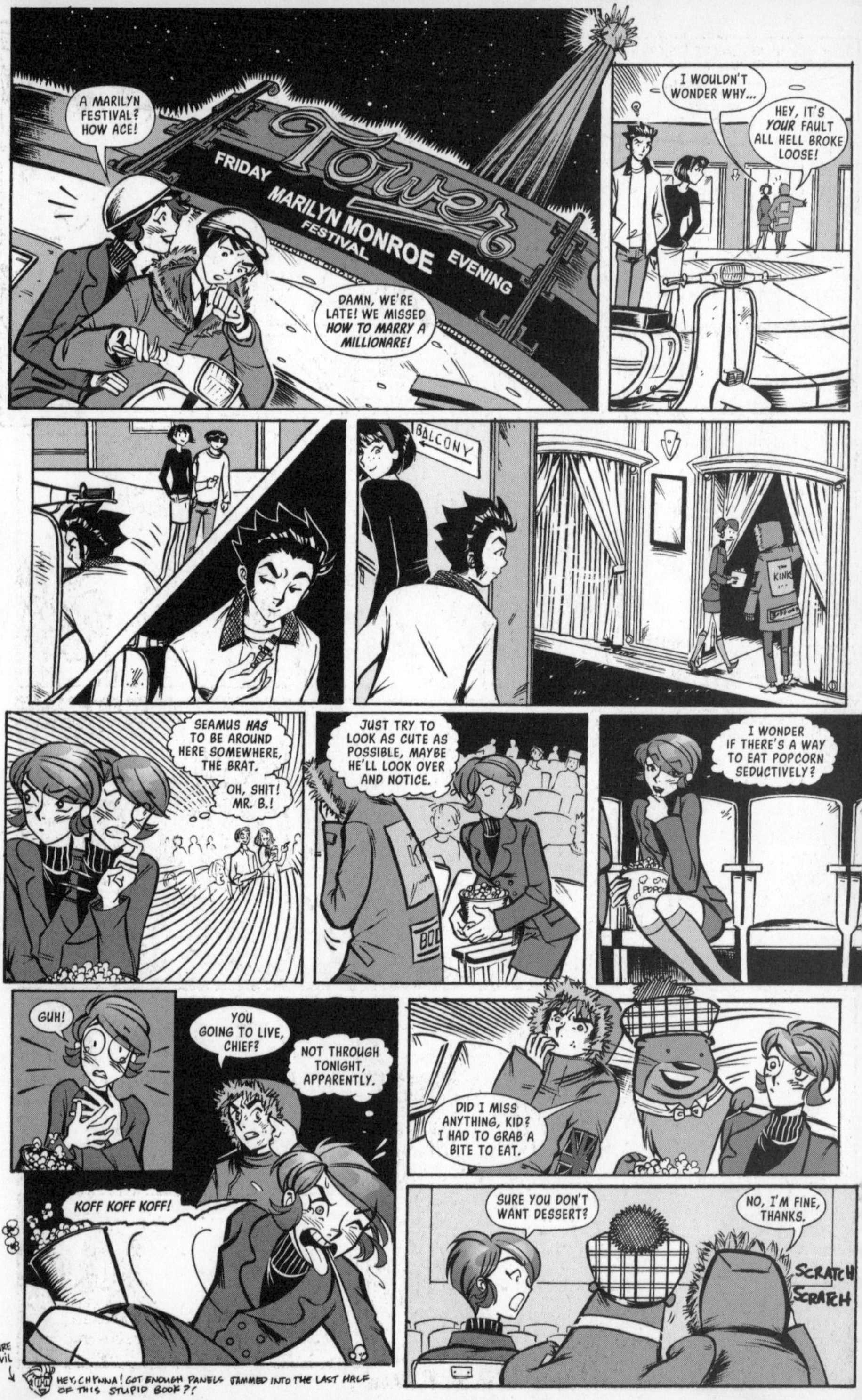
A MARILYN FESTIVAL? HOW ACE!
Tower
FRIDAY MARILYN MONROE FESTIVAL EVENING
DAMN, WE'RE LATE! WE MISSED HOW TO MARRY A MILLIONARE!
I WOULDN'T WONDER WHY...
HEY, IT'S YOUR FAULT ALL HELL BROKE LOOSE!
BALCONY
THE KINKS
SEAMUS HAS TO BE AROUND HERE SOMEWHERE, THE BRAT.
OH, SHIT! MR. B.!
JUST TRY TO LOOK AS CUTE AS POSSIBLE, MAYBE HE'LL LOOK OVER AND NOTICE.
I WONDER IF THERE'S A WAY TO EAT POPCORN SEDUCTIVELY?
GUH!
YOU GOING TO LIVE, CHIEF?
NOT THROUGH TONIGHT, APPARENTLY.
KOFF KOFF KOFF!
DID I MISS ANYTHING, KID? I HAD TO GRAB A BITE TO EAT.
SURE YOU DON'T WANT DESSERT?
NO, I'M FINE, THANKS.
SCRATCH
SCRATCH

PURE EVIL

HEY, CHYNNA! GOT ENOUGH PANELS JAMMED INTO THE LAST HALF OF THIS STUPID BOOK?!

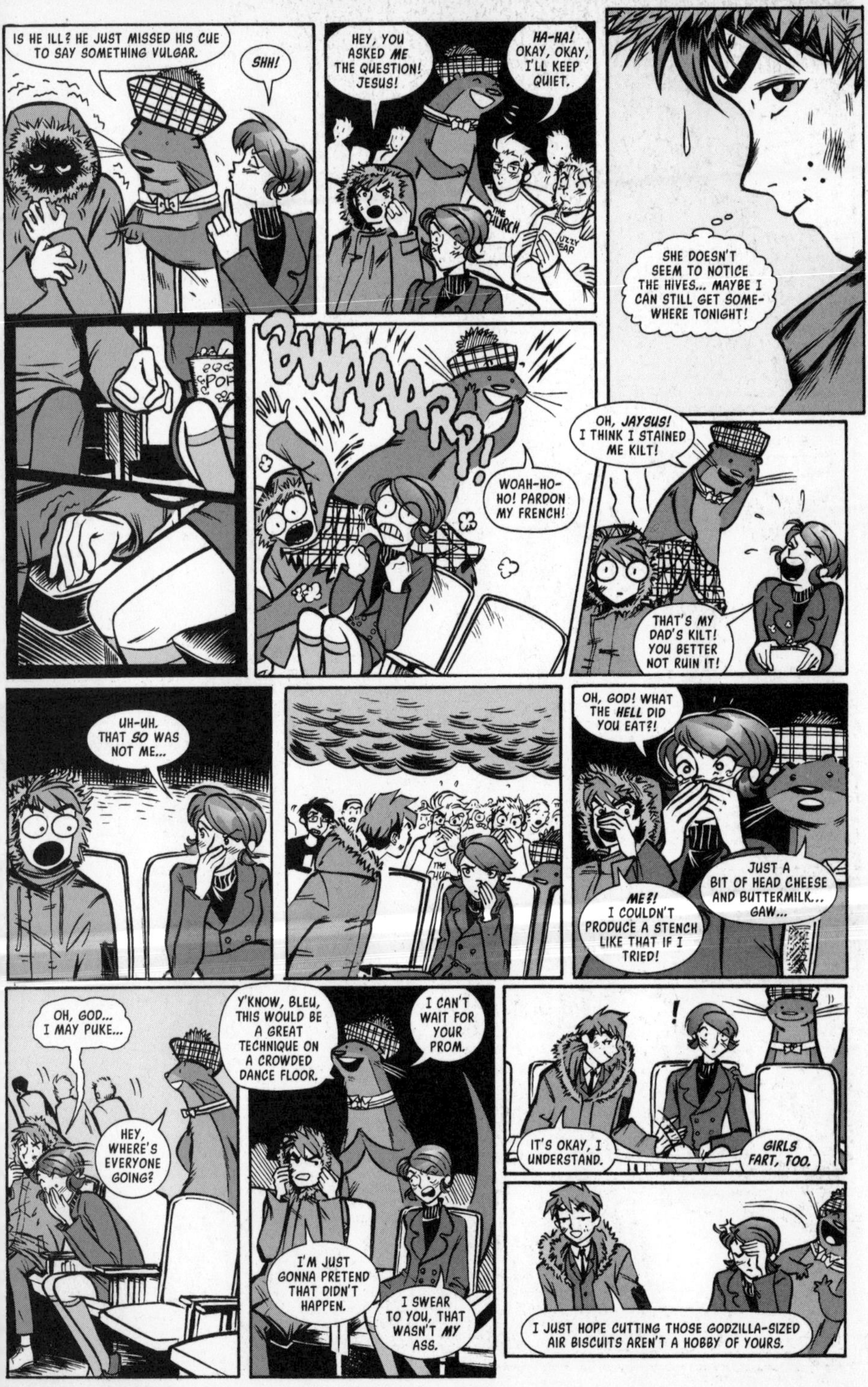

IS HE ILL? HE JUST MISSED HIS CUE TO SAY SOMETHING VULGAR.
SHH!
HEY, YOU ASKED ME THE QUESTION! JESUS!
HA-HA! OKAY, OKAY, I'LL KEEP QUIET.
THE CHURCH
SHE DOESN'T SEEM TO NOTICE THE HIVES... MAYBE I CAN STILL GET SOME-WHERE TONIGHT!
POP
BWAAARP!
WOAH-HO-HO! PARDON MY FRENCH!
OH, JAYSUS! I THINK I STAINED ME KILT!
THAT'S MY DAD'S KILT! YOU BETTER NOT RUIN IT!
UH-UH. THAT SO WAS NOT ME...
OH, GOD! WHAT THE HELL DID YOU EAT?!
ME?! I COULDN'T PRODUCE A STENCH LIKE THAT IF I TRIED!
JUST A BIT OF HEAD CHEESE AND BUTTERMILK... GAW...
OH, GOD... I MAY PUKE...
HEY, WHERE'S EVERYONE GOING?
Y'KNOW, BLEU, THIS WOULD BE A GREAT TECHNIQUE ON A CROWDED DANCE FLOOR.
I CAN'T WAIT FOR YOUR PROM.
I'M JUST GONNA PRETEND THAT DIDN'T HAPPEN.
I SWEAR TO YOU, THAT WASN'T MY ASS.
!
IT'S OKAY, I UNDERSTAND.
GIRLS FART, TOO.
I JUST HOPE CUTTING THOSE GODZILLA-SIZED AIR BISCUITS AREN'T A HOBBY OF YOURS.

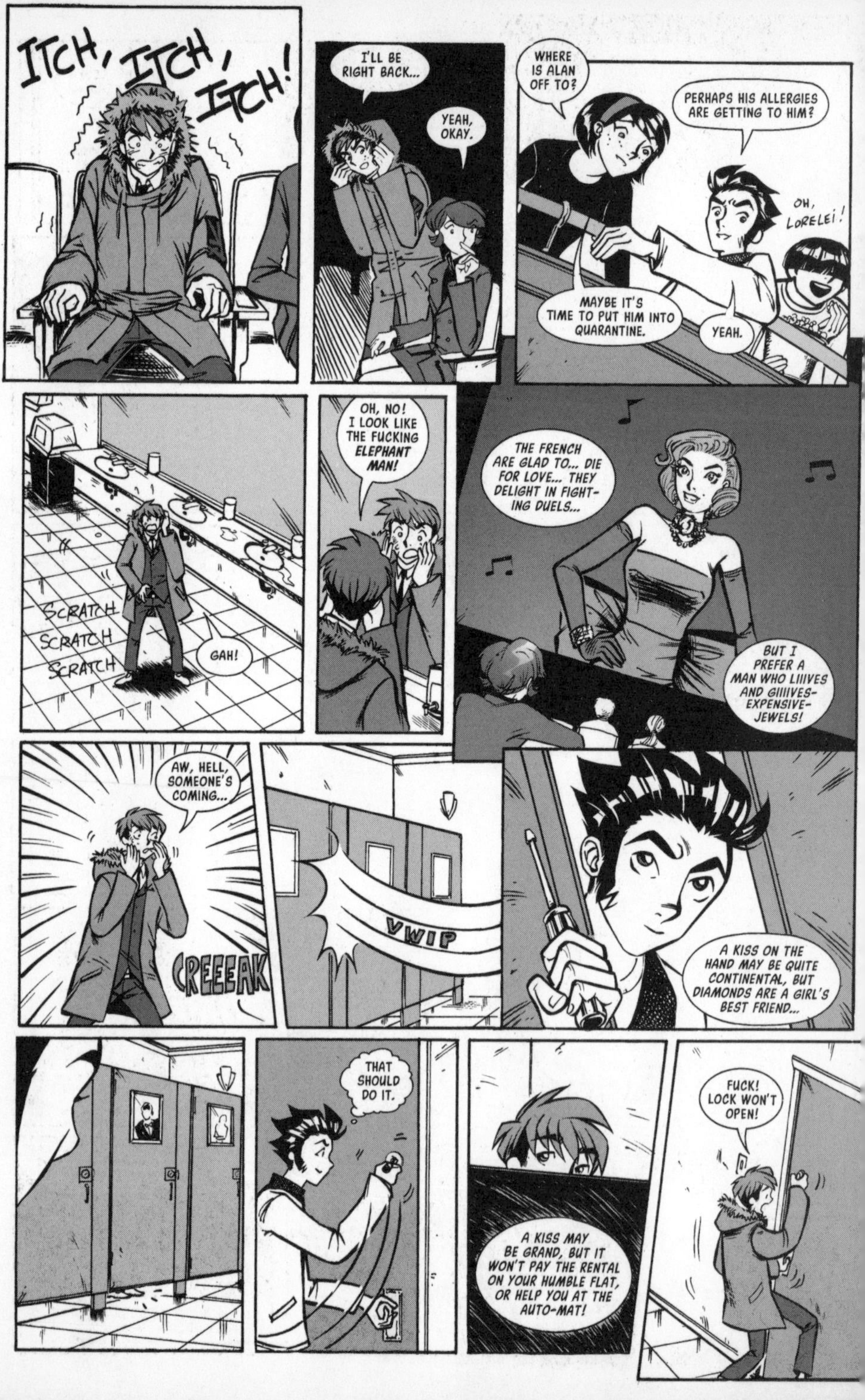
ITCH, ITCH, ITCH!
I'LL BE RIGHT BACK...
YEAH, OKAY.
WHERE IS ALAN OFF TO?
PERHAPS HIS ALLERGIES ARE GETTING TO HIM?
OH, LORELEI!
MAYBE IT'S TIME TO PUT HIM INTO QUARANTINE.
YEAH.
SCRATCH SCRATCH SCRATCH
GAH!
OH, NO! I LOOK LIKE THE FUCKING ELEPHANT MAN!
THE FRENCH ARE GLAD TO... DIE FOR LOVE... THEY DELIGHT IN FIGHT-ING DUELS...
BUT I PREFER A MAN WHO LIIIVES AND GIIIVES-EXPENSIVE-JEWELS!
AW, HELL, SOMEONE'S COMING...
CREEEAK
VWIP
A KISS ON THE HAND MAY BE QUITE CONTINENTAL, BUT DIAMONDS ARE A GIRL'S BEST FRIEND...
THAT SHOULD DO IT.
A KISS MAY BE GRAND, BUT IT WON'T PAY THE RENTAL ON YOUR HUMBLE FLAT, OR HELP YOU AT THE AUTO-MAT!
FUCK! LOCK WON'T OPEN!

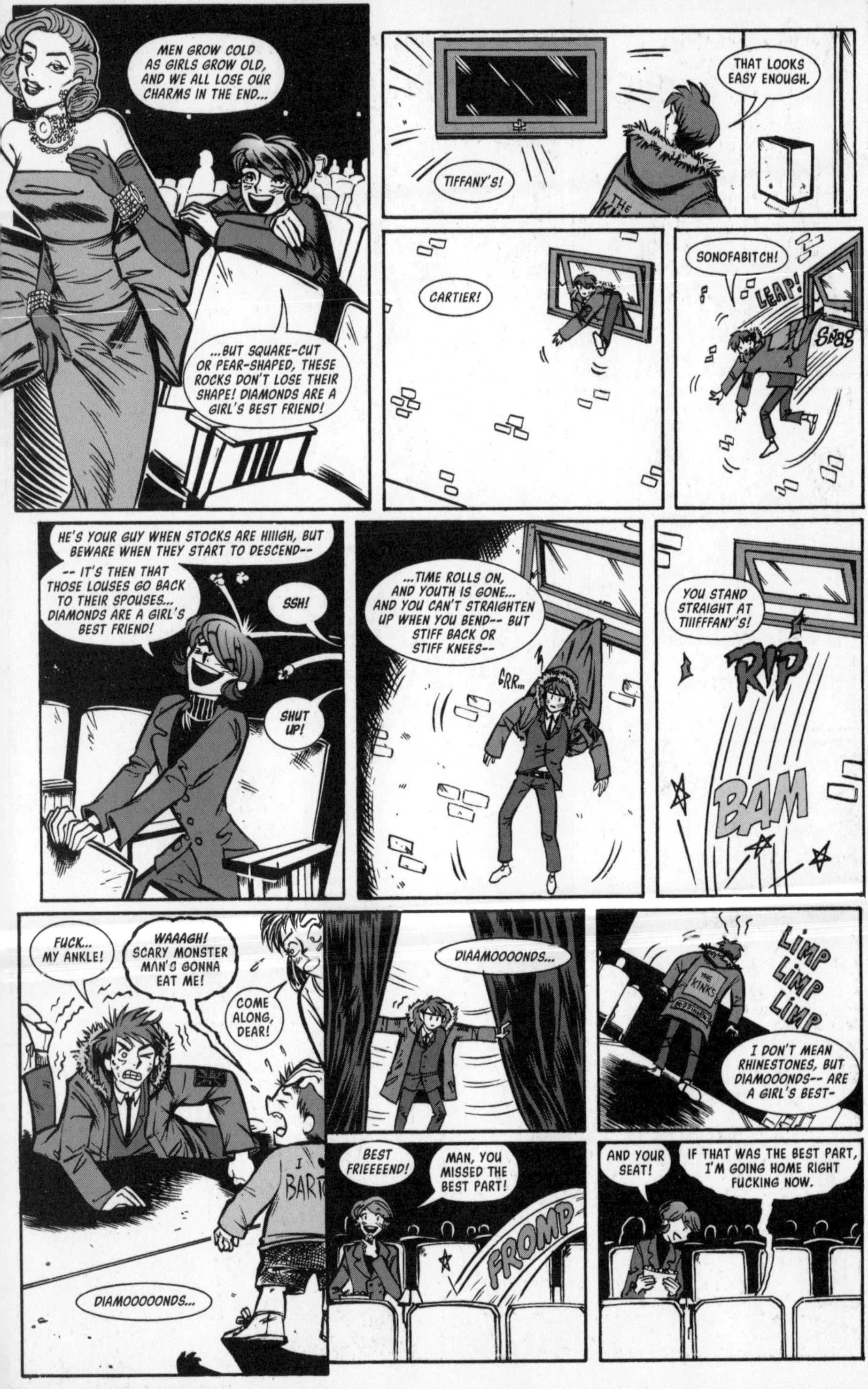
MEN GROW COLD AS GIRLS GROW OLD, AND WE ALL LOSE OUR CHARMS IN THE END...
...BUT SQUARE-CUT OR PEAR-SHAPED, THESE ROCKS DON'T LOSE THEIR SHAPE! DIAMONDS ARE A GIRL'S BEST FRIEND!
TIFFANY'S!
THAT LOOKS EASY ENOUGH.
CARTIER!
SONOFABITCH!
LEAP!
SNAG
HE'S YOUR GUY WHEN STOCKS ARE HIIIGH, BUT BEWARE WHEN THEY START TO DESCEND--
-- IT'S THEN THAT THOSE LOUSES GO BACK TO THEIR SPOUSES... DIAMONDS ARE A GIRL'S BEST FRIEND!
SSH!
SHUT UP!
...TIME ROLLS ON, AND YOUTH IS GONE... AND YOU CAN'T STRAIGHTEN UP WHEN YOU BEND-- BUT STIFF BACK OR STIFF KNEES--
GRR...
YOU STAND STRAIGHT AT TIIIFFFANY'S!
RIP
BAM
FUCK... MY ANKLE!
WAAAGH! SCARY MONSTER MAN'S GONNA EAT ME!
COME ALONG, DEAR!
DIAMOOOOONDS...
DIAAMOOOONDS...
LIMP LIMP LIMP LIMP
THE KINKS
I DON'T MEAN RHINESTONES, BUT DIAMOOONDS-- ARE A GIRL'S BEST-
BEST FRIEEEEND!
MAN, YOU MISSED THE BEST PART!
FROMP
AND YOUR SEAT!
IF THAT WAS THE BEST PART, I'M GOING HOME RIGHT FUCKING NOW.

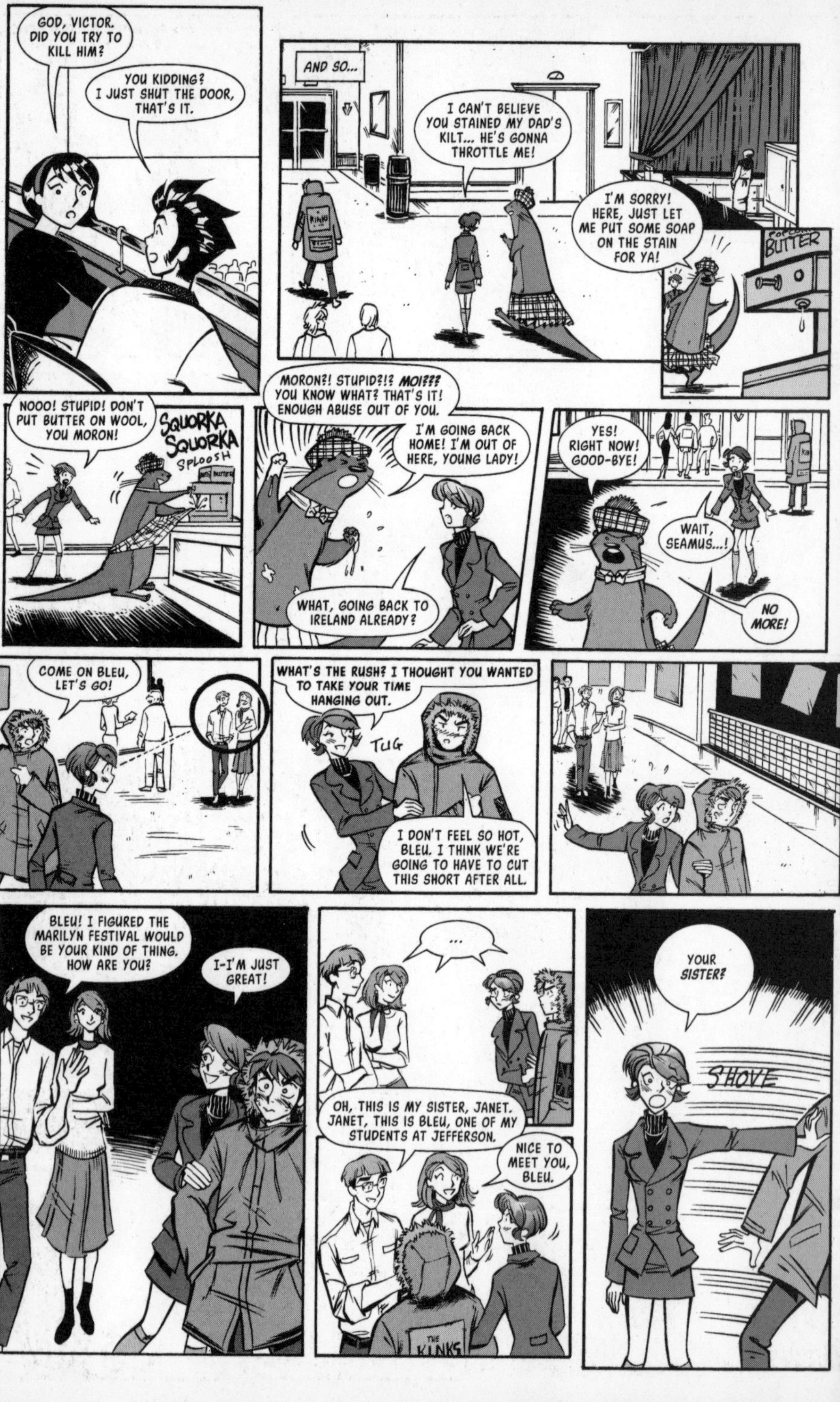
GOD, VICTOR. DID YOU TRY TO KILL HIM?
YOU KIDDING? I JUST SHUT THE DOOR, THAT'S IT.
AND SO...
I CAN'T BELIEVE YOU STAINED MY DAD'S KILT... HE'S GONNA THROTTLE ME!
I'M SORRY! HERE, JUST LET ME PUT SOME SOAP ON THE STAIN FOR YA!
BUTTER
NOOO! STUPID! DON'T PUT BUTTER ON WOOL, YOU MORON!
SQUORKA SQUORKA
SPLOOSH
MORON?! STUPID?!? MOI??? YOU KNOW WHAT? THAT'S IT! ENOUGH ABUSE OUT OF YOU.
I'M GOING BACK HOME! I'M OUT OF HERE, YOUNG LADY!
WHAT, GOING BACK TO IRELAND ALREADY?
YES! RIGHT NOW! GOOD-BYE!
WAIT, SEAMUS...!
NO MORE!
COME ON BLEU, LET'S GO!
WHAT'S THE RUSH? I THOUGHT YOU WANTED TO TAKE YOUR TIME HANGING OUT.
TUG
I DON'T FEEL SO HOT, BLEU. I THINK WE'RE GOING TO HAVE TO CUT THIS SHORT AFTER ALL.
BLEU! I FIGURED THE MARILYN FESTIVAL WOULD BE YOUR KIND OF THING. HOW ARE YOU?
I-I'M JUST GREAT!
...
OH, THIS IS MY SISTER, JANET. JANET, THIS IS BLEU, ONE OF MY STUDENTS AT JEFFERSON.
NICE TO MEET YOU, BLEU.
THE KINKS
YOUR SISTER?
SHOVE

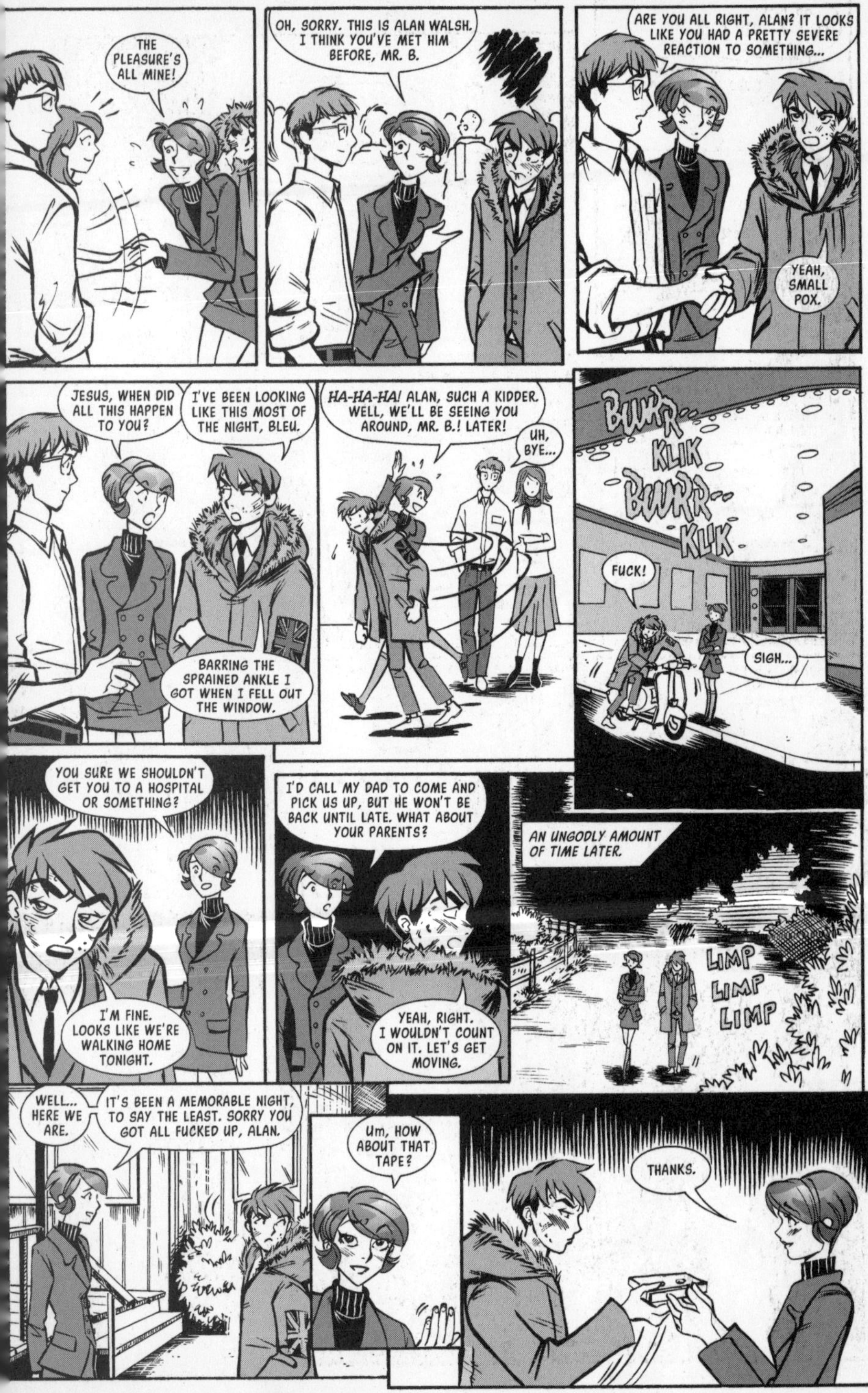
THE PLEASURE'S ALL MINE!
OH, SORRY. THIS IS ALAN WALSH. I THINK YOU'VE MET HIM BEFORE, MR. B.
ARE YOU ALL RIGHT, ALAN? IT LOOKS LIKE YOU HAD A PRETTY SEVERE REACTION TO SOMETHING...
YEAH, SMALL POX.
JESUS, WHEN DID ALL THIS HAPPEN TO YOU?
I'VE BEEN LOOKING LIKE THIS MOST OF THE NIGHT, BLEU.
BARRING THE SPRAINED ANKLE I GOT WHEN I FELL OUT THE WINDOW.
HA-HA-HA! ALAN, SUCH A KIDDER. WELL, WE'LL BE SEEING YOU AROUND, MR. B.! LATER!
UH, BYE...
BUKR... KLIK BUKR... KLIK
FUCK!
SIGH...
YOU SURE WE SHOULDN'T GET YOU TO A HOSPITAL OR SOMETHING?
I'M FINE. LOOKS LIKE WE'RE WALKING HOME TONIGHT.
I'D CALL MY DAD TO COME AND PICK US UP, BUT HE WON'T BE BACK UNTIL LATE. WHAT ABOUT YOUR PARENTS?
YEAH, RIGHT. I WOULDN'T COUNT ON IT. LET'S GET MOVING.
AN UNGODLY AMOUNT OF TIME LATER.
LIMP LIMP LIMP
WELL... HERE WE ARE.
IT'S BEEN A MEMORABLE NIGHT, TO SAY THE LEAST. SORRY YOU GOT ALL FUCKED UP, ALAN.
UM, HOW ABOUT THAT TAPE?
THANKS.

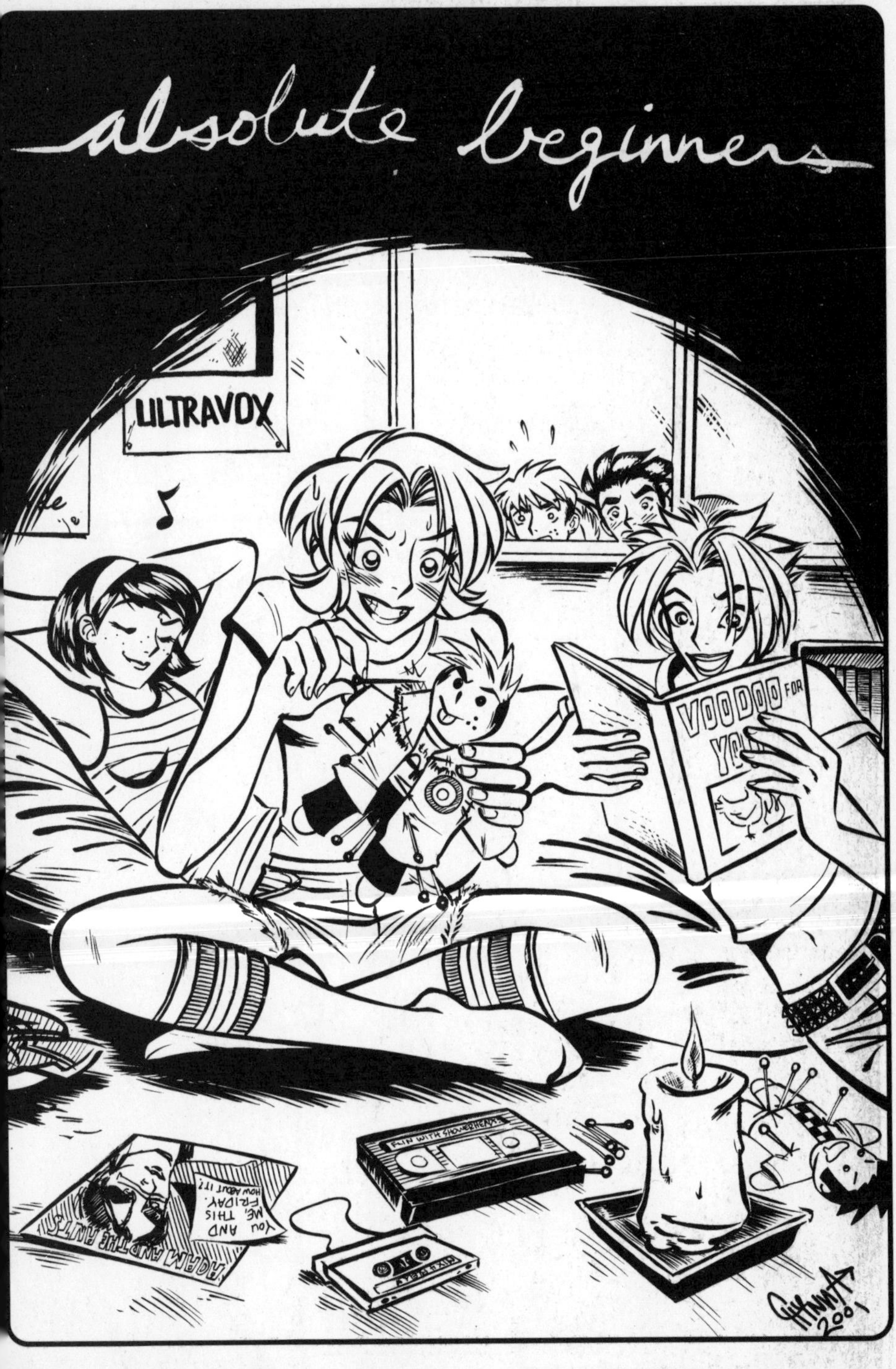
absolute beginners
ULTRAVOX
VOODOO FOR
FUN WITH SHOWERHEADS
YOU AND ME, THIS FRIDAY. HOW ABOUT IT?
ADAM AND THE ANTS
CHYNNA 2001

Fuck the internet. Fuck it in the ear.

Not since the days of the gold rush have so many charged after so little. Like the Russian army of old running from their enemies and burning the ground behind them so that it wouldn't be useable to the conquerors that followed, the initial online pirates snatched all the precious gems and left the rest of us exclaiming, a la Charlie Brown, "I got a rock!" (How's that for a complex sentence of mixed metaphors, children?)

So it was that Chynna Clugston and myself stepped into the cyber world, ready to produce a continuing *Blue Monday* serial comprised of episodes of three to five minutes. We wrote six, only to be told that there was no money left and all efforts were to be halted. In our giddiness, we weren't prepared for the rubble and devastation that was the world wide wipeout. There was a virtual earthquake and the superhighway collapsed. We had comedy, but no one was laughing.

The goal was, roughly, to tell the story of the first miniseries, *The Kids Are Alright*. What follows is what we came up with—a plan to get the ball rolling, introducing the kids and leading us into our main plot. If you've read *The Kids Are Alright*, you'll recognize a lot of the elements we pilfered. You'll also see us having a bit of fun and playing with the format we were given. We wanted it to be wacky, and for each episode to have a lot of energy so people would come back and watch the next one. And in the end, it was a good time for us, e-mailing scripts back and forth, arguing over lines, insulting each other in the way we are (in)famous for.

Still, we didn't get paid for these scripts. So we publish them here to give two fingers to the internet. Coz, you know, fuck the internet. Fuck it in the ear.

-- Jamie S. Rich,
bad cover version

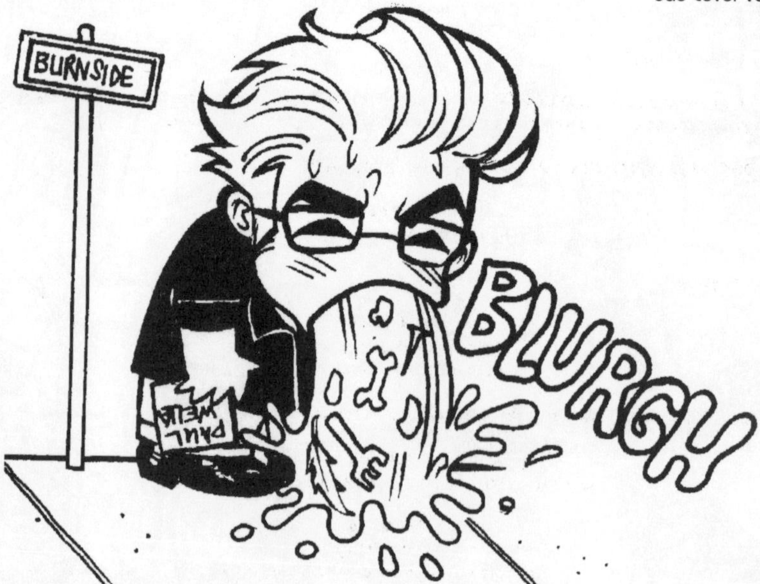
BURNSIDE
PAUL WELLER
BLURGH

P.S. The nightmarish vision of Bleu waking up in the second episode is based on what Chynna looked like one morning when we spent the night at Scott Morse's house. I kid you not! It was frightening! Like a Def Leppard groupie after taking a bath with the hair dryer.

BLUE MONDAY: THE KIDS ARE ALRIGHT

online animation
by Chynna Clugston & Jamie S. Rich

Episode 1

INT: KARAOKE BAR

DARKNESS.

A spotlight suddenly snaps on.

VICTOR GOMEZ, in black suit and fedora, stands on a bare stage. Behind him is a satin curtain, in front of him a microphone. He clears his throat.

In the bottom left of the screen, SUPER-DEFORMED CLOVER CONNELLY pops up. This will be the first we see of this storytelling device—essentially the same as the little margin cartoons in the comics. Her voice should be slightly distorted—a little like a Chipmunk version of Clover—to go with the image.

S-D CLOVER
Ladies and gents...introducing Victor fakkin' Gomez!

S-D Clover sinks away.

A ska beat kicks in. Victor begins to do a sort of wooden skank, kind of like that dancing guy from Mighty Mighty Bosstones if he were a marionette puppet. Victor begins to sing The Specials' "Rudi, A Message to You" in that tuneless way of folks who think they can sing but really can't.

VICTOR
Stop your messing around, better think of your future.
Rudeeee...a message to you, Rooodee.
A message to you...

Spotlight out. DARKNESS.

Spotlight on. Regular-sized CLOVER CONNELLY is in Victor's spot, wearing a Cramps T-shirt, cut-off shorts, plaid stockings. She glares at the audience, gives a Billy Idol sneer.

SUPER-DEFORMED ERIN O'NEILL pops up in the lower right corner.

S-D ERIN
And for our next number...Clover Connelly!

S-D Erin sinks away.

CLOVER
(singing, a little too emotive)
I touch you once, I touch you twice.

It's OMD's "If You Leave," famous as the lovesong from Pretty In Pink.

CLOVER
I won't let go at any price. I need you now, like I need—

HECKLER
(from offstage)
What are ya? Some kind of little Miss Mary?

Clover stops singing. She looks to the voice angrily.

CLOVER
What? What you fuckin' sayin' ta me?

(o.s.)
Sing a real song, you stupid girl!

Clover leaps into the audience after the heckler, fists flying.

CLOVER
I'll murder ya, ya sheep-shagging poofta!

Spotlight out. DARKNESS.

Double spotlight snaps on. On the left, ALAN WALSH in parka; on the right, ERIN O'NEILL in headband and striped top.

Alan holds two fingers behind Erin's head and sticks out his tongue.

SUPER-DEFORMED VICTOR pops up on the left.

S-D VICTOR
And now, two for the price of one. Alan Walsh...

S-D Victor disappears to be replaced by S-D Clover on the right.

S-D CLOVER
...and Erin "The Hardy Tarty" O'Neill.

S-D Clover off.

Bonnie Tyler's "Total Eclipse of the Heart" kicks in.

ALAN
(loud and high-pitched)
Turn arrrround, Bright Eyes!

ERIN
(not bad, but small next to Alan)
Every now and then I fall apart.

ALAN
Turrrn around, Bright Eyyyyyyes!

ERIN
(disintegrates into laughter)
Every now and then...hahahaha...

ALAN
(more shouting than anything)
Turn around, Bright Eyes!!!

Lights out. DARKNESS.

SUPER-DEFORMED ALAN WALSH appears on the left.

S-D ALAN
And finally, the moment you've been waiting for...
(throwing out his arm while sliding off)
...Bleu! L! Finnegannnnnn!

Lights on. BLEU L. FINNEGAN is center stage wearing a white shirt and tie, short black skirt, white thigh-high stockings, and bird's-egg blue shoes. The Who's "The Kids Are Alright" comes in loud.

BLEU

(animated—think Billy Idol and Iggy Pop)
I don't mind, other guys dancin' with my girrrrl...
That's fine, and I know them all pretty welllll....
And I know that sometimes I go out of my mind
Better leave them behind...because the Kids Are Alright!
The Kids Are Alright!!!!
(arms in air, bowing)
Thank you! You're too kind! Thank you!

S-D Alan and S-D Victor pop up bottom left. The instrumental of the music continues.

S-D ALAN/S-D VICTOR
(in unison, shouting)
BLUE MONDAY!

As they say it, the words BLUE MONDAY appear in the upper left (think Japanese commercials).

S-D Erin pops up in the right, but not in the exact corner (leaving room for S-D Clover).

S-D ERIN
The Kids Are Alright!

THE KIDS ARE ALRIGHT appears upper right.

S-D Clover comes in, bottom right.

S-D CLOVER
(snotty)
Pfft! More like "The Song Remains Deranged."

Bleu, still center stage, throws a hand in the air and gives the V-sign with two fingers.

BLEU
It's ace!

FADE TO BLACK...

Episode Two

EXT: GRAVEYARD—EVENING

ERIN, CLOVER, and BLEU are lounging around in the graveyard, gripped with *ennui*.

SUPER-DEFORMED ERIN appears in the lower left.

S-D ERIN
Friday!

S-D Erin sinks out of sight.

BLEU
(laying backwards over a tombstone)
This sucks. This town sucks. Everything sucks. There's never nothin' to do.

CLOVER
Someday we'll die and be free!

BLEU
Something needs to happen. Something big.

ERIN
Rather than complain about not having anything fun to do, why not create some fun?

CLOVER
How the hell you suppose we bleedin' do that?

BLEU
I know!
(she sits up in a light-bulb-over-head pose)
Let's fuck with the boys.

INT: SUPERMARKET – EVENING

Inside shot, supermarket doors opening. The girls come barreling in.

BLEU
This'll be great.

ERIN
The best ever.

CLOVER
The gits! They'll never know what hit 'em!

They all laugh as they come straight at the camera, until their heads fill the screen and...

CUT TO:

EXT: ALAN'S HOUSE – NIGHT

The girls, dressed all in black, skulk around outside ALAN'S HOUSE.

CLOVER
Cool! Alan's parents are gone, and the lights aren't on, so the lamebrains are
out causing trouble somewhere.

BLEU
All *right!* Let's get to it.

ERIN
(holding up a roll)
Toilet paper, anyone?

FADE:

CLOSE-UP: Erin's hands rubbing Vaseline on a window.

SUPER-DEFORMED BLEU
(in lower left)
Vaseline on the windows and doorknobs!

FADE:

Bleu dips a tampon into a jelly-jar full of red liquid.

SUPER-DEFORMED ERIN
(in lower right)
Tampons dipped in cherry punch...

Diagonal split down screen. Bleu continues dipping as five or six of the soaked tampons slam against the front door.

S-D ERIN
...and tossed on the door.

114

SUPER-DEFORMED CLOVER
(lower left)
Now, *that's* unnecessary.

Split screen gives away to a full shot of the door, as S-D Erin disappears.

S-D BLEU
(replacing Erin)
Plus a few eggs for good measure.

BACKGROUND FADE:

S-D Clover remains lower left as S-D Bleu disappears and a CLOSE-UP of Erin's hands squirting canned whipped cream into a condom.

S-D CLOVER
Condoms filled with whipped cream left around the yard!

S-D Clover disappears.

FADE:

EXT: ALAN'S HOUSE – NIGHT

FULL SHOT, all the girls dancing around a tree, throwing toilet paper and laughing.

FADE:

INT: BLEU'S ROOM – MORNING

The girls are conked out in Bleu's messy room—posters on wall, a floor covered in clothes, magazines, food boxes, etc. Bleu is sprawled out on the bed, and Clover and Erin are on the floor. Clover snores.

SUPER-DEFORMED ALAN and SUPER-DEFORMED VICTOR come up in the lower right, looking extremely pissed. Little anger lines are above their heads.

S-D ALAN/S-D VICTOR
(in unison)
The next day, while the little skanks sleep...

The door flies open. It's Bleu's dad, MR.FINNEGAN.

MR. FINNEGAN
All right, girls! Wakey-wakey! It's eight o'clock and we've got to get a move
on if we're going to go to the Walsh's house!

Bleu lifts her head. The side of her hair that has been against the pillow stands straight up. We see she is sleeping with her all-important Oscar doll.

BLEU
Huh? What?

MR.FINNEGAN
Some vandals trashed the Walsh place, and I volunteered you girls to help the
boys clean up.

Mr.Finnegan exits. Clover and Erin wake-up and glare at Bleu.

BLEU
Well, that didn't go as planned.

CLOVER
Who should I maim first? You, or yer Da?

Episode Three

EXT: ALAN'S HOUSE – MORNING

ERIN, BLEU, and CLOVER are in the yard—raking up condoms, pulling toilet paper out of the tree, general cleaning. Also, general grumbling.

CLOVER
Stupid boys. I'll gut them and feed them their own intestines. Dork boy haggis.

BLEU
It's not fair. Alan and Victor aren't even here.

ERIN
Keep whinin', Finnegan. This is all your fault.

PULL BACK: as they're grumbling, we move back across the yard to behind some bushes. There, ALAN and VICTOR are waiting and watching.

ALAN
Victory is sweet, my friend, but somehow this isn't enough.

VICTOR
Just what I was thinking...

EXT: ALAN'S HOUSE—MORNING

Back on the girls.

Bleu is picking up one of the condoms with two sticks.

BLEU
Mannn, this is nasty. How did we even come up with this?

ERIN
(holding out trash bag for Bleu)
I dunno. I think it was Clover's big idea.

CLOVER
(off screen)
Fakk off!

The condom slips and falls on Bleu's shoe.

CLOVER
Ugh! I know it's whipped cream, but that shit is sick!
ERIN
(bending down)
Wait! That condom's yellow! We bought clear ones. Mint flavor, remember?

Bleu blinks, processing the info.

BLEU
You mean...?
(freaking out)
AAAAAAAAAAAAAAA!!!!

EXT: ALAN'S HOUSE/BEHIND BUSHES—MORNING

In the distance, over the bushes, the girls give up.

116

CLOVER
(in distance)
Fergit this. Let's get something to eat.

ALAN
C'mon, let's follow 'em.

EXT: LUCKY BURGER – DAY

The boys are skulking around a parked car, watching as the girls enter the joint. They then head towards the back of the restaurant.

ALAN
Monkeyboy's working today, right?

VICTOR
Uh-huh.

ALAN
Good. You know those panty shots of Clover he wants so bad?

VICTOR
Oh, yeah…those're sweet. Right up the skirt.

ALAN
Now's his chance to earn 'em…

INT: LUCKY BURGER'S KITCHEN – DAY

MONKEYBOY shows Alan and Victor where the girls' burgers are waiting.

SUPER-DEFORMED ERIN comes down out of the top right of the screen. She's upside down.

S-D ERIN
A few minutes later…

MONKEYBOY
That's their order there. I better not get fired for this.

ALAN
Oh, it'll be worth it for a permanent glimpse at Clover's knickers.

VICTOR
Trust us.

MONKEYBOY
(practically drooling)
Whattaya going to do? Spit in 'em?

ALAN
(smirking)
Oh, nothing that cross.

Alan and Victor reach in their pants and pull out handfuls of pubic hair.

SFX
Rrrrrrrip!

MONKEYBOY
Hahahahahah! That's so fucked up! I wanna do one!

INT: LUCKY BURGER EATING AREA – DAY

Monkeyboy announces the order number over the loudspeaker.

MONKEYBOY
Order number >heh-heh< sixty-nine.

CLOVER
(grabbing the tray)
Ha bloody ha. Took long enough.

Monkeyboy snickers in the background as Clover walks away with the infected burgers. She sits the tray on the table where Bleu and Erin are waiting.

BLEU
Gawd! That took a lifetime! I'm starving!

ERIN
I'll say.

CLOSE-UP: Bleu bites in and starts chewing.

CLOSE-UP: Erin also takes a big bite and chews happily.

CLOSE-UP: Clover digs in, but as soon as it is in her mouth, her face falls. Something's wrong.

CLOSE-UP: Bleu freezes.

CLOSE-UP: The bitten-into burger, pubes sticking out of every end.

BLEU
Yargh!
(tosses burger, hitting Clover)
Pube burger!!!!

Clover looks at hers and throws it away from her as fast as she can.

CLOVER
Gross!

FULL-SHOT: We are behind the girls. The boys are outside, through the window, laughing. Victor gives them the finger, Alan waves. In the foreground, Erin keeps munching.

CLOVER
(shaking her fist)
You're fakkin' dead, you bloody mongoloids!

CLOSE-UP: Erin takes another bite.

ERIN
(mouth full)
It's not so bad. Tasted kinda spicy, actually.

Wah-wah.

FADE OUT:

Episode Four

EXT: ALAN'S HOUSE—DAY

The girls storm up towards Alan's house...think the sort of insistent, angry walk that might be accompanied by the Wicked Witch theme music from *The Wizard of Oz.* CLOVER has changed, in as much as she is now all dolled-up in full girl make-up gear.

BLEU
(putting a hand on Clover's shoulder)

Are you sure about this? Things might just get worse!

CLOVER
(perturbed)
What? You can't be serious. They can't just get away with this.

CLOSE-UP: We now really see Clover's made-over self, and she is holding up a copy of *Cheeky* magazine. (Maybe it should have Andi Watson or Scott Morse on the cover, with the headline "Inside Guys Inside Comics.")

CLOVER
Besides, I didn't get m'self dolled up to look eighteen for the mere pleasure of the sweaty magazine clerk drooling over me. Now, let's go...

The girls approach the front door and knock on it. MRS.WALSH comes out.

MRS.WALSH
Yes?

BLEU
(acting all sweet and girlie – stress *acting*)
Hi, Mrs.Walsh. Is Alan home?

MRS.WALSH
I'm sorry. He and Victor just left.

BLEU
Oh, no. He was supposed to give me some reference material for a school project.

MRS.WALSH
Well, if you want to search for it in that disaster area he calls a room, be my guest.

BLEU/CLOVER/ERIN
Thank you!

INT: ALAN'S ROOM—DAY

The girl's enter Alan's room, to find porn everywhere. Centerfolds are on the wall, stacks of magazines are on the floor, etc. Plus, dirty clothes, scattered CDs, school stuff, Coke cans, etc.
Bleu is stunned and dismayed, Erin looks amused, and Clover is downright indignant.

ERIN
See, told you. They're mad for it.

CLOVER
Jesus, Mary, 'n' Joseph—would ya like some bedroom with your porn?

Bleu ceremoniously takes the first poster off the wall.
BLEU
(giggling)
They're going to be so pissed...

EXT: ALAN'S HOUSE—DAY

ALAN and VICTOR return to the house, and they see the girls taking off in the distance—just their backs, but it's obvious they are carrying things.

ALAN
...so I says to her, "Baby, that's a meal, not a snack." Hahahahaha.

VICTOR
(seeing the girls)
Holy shit! Look!

ALAN
What the hell were they doing here?

VICTOR
I dunno, but I doubt it's good. Come on...

The boys run to the house.

INT: ALAN'S ROOM – DAY

The boys burst in. The room has changed. Naked men now replace the naked women on the walls. Alan freaks!

ALAN
AAAAAAAAA!!!!!!

VICTOR
Looks like your walls came out of the closet, man.

ALAN
(tossing things around, turning the room upside down)
That's not funny. That's so not funny. Where's my porn? Those harlots took it.
They took it all! Where's my favorite issue of Cherry?

VICTOR
Be cool, man. All is not lost. For once, I have an idea.
(picking up the phone and dialing)
Hi, Mr.Finnegan?...Is Bleu there?...No? That's too bad. You see...

FADE:

INT: BLEU'S ROOM—DAY

The girls enter Bleu's room with sodas and bags from a record store.

SUPER-DEFORMED VICTOR appears in the bottom left.

S-D VICTOR
Later, when the girls get home...

BLEU
Clover, you're a genius. I'm still pissing myself. Alan's going to lose
his lower intestine when he sees his porn gone.

ERIN
I just hope my parents don't find the boxes in the attic.

Clover puts her bags down on Bleu's bed and notices a piece of paper sitting on Bleu's pillow. Her expression goes blank.

CLOVER
Uh...Bleu? You didn't put your Oscar stuffed animal somewhere else today, did you?

BLEU
No, why?

CLOVER
(getting angry)
I think the boys have been here.

Clover snatches up the note, and Bleu and Erin huddle around her. It's a patchwork note, put together from

newspaper clippings—typical movie ransom type stuff.

120

CLOVER
(reading out loud)
"To Chicks, We got your little doll 'Occy' and Clover's precious *Some Kind of Wonderful*
video tape. Erin's lucky her parents still have us banned from the house. We know these
are your most treasured possessions, so if you want to see this crap ever again, meet
us at the graveyard at midnight. Bring the porn and some Jell-O or everything burns!"
(crumpling up note)
Those evil twats! I'll rip their eyes out and dance on 'em!

BLEU
(eyes growing large with tears)
Occy? How could they do this to Occy? Have they no heart?

ERIN
(sly smirk)
Don't worry. We'll get the stuff back...and beat them at their own game all at
the same time. They've won nothing yet.

SUPER-DEFORMED CLOVER appears in the lower right. She is wearing a soccer uniform with the word "HOOLI-
GAN" and the numeral "1" on it.

S-D CLOVER
Bring it on!

Episode Five

EXT: GRAVEYARD – NIGHT

OCCY, the Oscar the Grouch doll, hangs from a tree on a noose. He wears a T-shirt with his name scrawled on
it. The surroundings resemble some sort of Wiccan ceremony—a pentagram, candles, skulls. Next to Occy, a
videotape can be seen clearly. Both Occy and the videotape have matches sticking out of them. Occy is also
bound and gagged. Gregorian chants play in a boom box in the background.

SUPER-DEFORMED BLUE comes up on the screen, wearing a monk's habit.

S-D BLEU
Midnight at the graveyard!
(sinking out of site, waving hands ominously)
Ooooooooh...

ERIN, CLOVER, and BLEU step through the graveyard gate. They see the display. Clover has a cardboard box
and it's got the word "PORN" written on it in marker.

CLOVER
What the bloody 'ell...??

BLEU
Are those matches? They stuck matches on our stuff! Poor Occy!

CLOVER
How pathetic! This is the worst case of trying too hard I've ever seen.

ALAN
(off screen)
That may be...

ALAN and VICTOR step out of the shadows on the opposite side of the ritual circle.

ALAN
...but I believe you owe us something.

Clover lifts the box of porn over her head.

CLOVER
Fork over the Occy and the movie or your smut burns, wankers!

BLEU
(stepping forward, holding magazine and zippo)
And this will be the first to go!

Alan and Victor look shocked.

ALAN
(whispers)
Dude, that's my prize *Cherry*. How'd she know that was my fave?

VICTOR
(whispers)
Maybe because it was in a stain-resistant, mylar cover hanging over your bed?

Alan relents and retrieves the doll and the video. Erin steps forward to get them.

ALAN
Okay, okay! Don't do anything rash! Here…Now give us the porn!

Clover drops the box on the ground.

CLOVER
Later, losers.

Clover squirts lighter fluid into the box, and Bleu lights a match and drops it. Clover is also giving the boys the two-finger salute (the British version of flipping the bird). As the girls exit, the boys dive for the box and desperately try to put out the flames—committing the fatal mistake of blowing on them and fanning them, making the box ignite further.

ALAN/VICTOR
Noooooooooooooo!!!!!!

VICTOR
Not the best porn collection in the world!

They dump the box over and start stomping out the fire. Alan grabs a magazine and shakes the last of the flame out. He notices the periodical is not what he expects it to be.

ALAN
Hey, wait a minute! *Better Homes and Gardens*?!?!?

VICTOR
(sifting through the pile)
Those little strumpets! It's a whole box of them! This isn't the porn at all!

SUPER-DEFORMED ERIN, CLOVER, and BLEU all pop up simultaneously, tongues sticking out, middle fingers in the air.

S-D GIRLS
Nyaaaahhhhh!

The S-D girls sink back down.

Victor kicks the wreckage. Ash and cinders fly!

ALAN
(yelling into the forest)

We'll get you yet, you dirty sluts!!!! Just you wait! No one messes with my porn!!!

EXT: FOREST – NIGHT

The girls run through the forest, laughing maniacally, waving their retrieved treasures around.

ALAN
(off screen)
NO ONE!!!!

The girls run over a hill, leaving a picturesque view of the forest, moon in the sky. Super-Deformed Bleu dances on from the left, does a little jig across the screen.

S-D BLEU
(singing)
Dooo-dooo-dooo-doooo (etc., some kind of made up melody)

She moves off the right...

FADE OUT.

Episode Six

FADE IN:

INT: HIGH SCHOOL GYM – NIGHT
The gym is full of kids, mingling, talking. No one is really dancing. A DJ spins records.

We pan through the crowd. Catch snippets of conversations.

HEAVY METAL DUDE
Ha-ha! Bleu rejected you! Told ya!

CHICK
Who's she waiting for? Prince Charming?

PREPPIE BOY
I asked Bleu to dance, and she said "No"! No one ever says that to me!

CHICK #2
Omigod, no way!

We find BLEU sitting off by herself, against the wall, kicking her feet. She sighs.

BLEU
This dance sucks. All these stupid Fresburger boys keep asking me to shake it, when all I want, for once in my miserable life, is for an ace looker to come and give me a twirl. Is that so much to ask? I don't even know why I bother...

DAMON
(off screen)
Bleu?

Bleu looks up and claps her hands over her mouth in shock. DAMON ALBARN and GRAHAM COXON from the band BLUR have come over to her. (We can supply reference, or if it would be better to go with parody versions for legal reasons, they can be DARIEN and GARY from FADE.)

DAMON
I was wondering if you'd like to dance wiff me.

GRAHAM
Buggar! I was going to ask her that! Save one for me, will ya, Bleu-Luv?

BLEU
(stars and hearts floating around her head)
Holy shit! You're Damon and Graham from Blur—only, like, my favorite band!
Oh. My. God.

Damon sweeps Bleu out onto the floor. She blushes. Chick and Chick #2 watch from the background.

DAMON
My, you are a cutie...

CHICK
What-ever....

CHICK #2
Bitch!

A hand reaches in from off screen and taps Damon on the shoulder. Its owner clears his throat. Bleu's eyes go big as she sees him.

BLEU
Paul Weller! From The Jam!

It is indeed PAUL WELLER (or, if necessary, WELLS PAUL from THE JELLY). He's wearing a suit and looking very *Quadrophenia*.

PAUL
Why not give it over to someone who knows what he's doing, kid?

DAMON
(annoyed)
If you think you can handle it, geezer.

Paul wedges himself between the two.

BLEU
Today can't get much better than this!

PAUL
You know, I'm old enough to be your—

BLEU
(putting a finger to his lips, both stern and kind of turned off)
Shh! Don't say that! It'll ruin the moment.

The next voice we hear is a cheesy radio DJ's voice, but it comes through the body of ADAM ANT, in full *Kings of the Wild Frontier* regalia. (This will lead to Bleu waking up and realizing she is being influenced by the radio.)

DJ VOICE
(off screen)
Heads up, Ant fans! Don't finalize your plans yet!

Adam appears between them in an explosion of divine light. Paul immediately jumps back.

PAUL
Ponce!

ADAM/DJ
Adam Ant is coming to town!

BLEU
(leaping on Adam)
Adam, my love! You don't know how long I've waited for this moment!

ADAM/DJ
Hold up a second! Tickets went on sale this morning, and they're already sold out! Sorry!

Adam steps back from Bleu and disappears into dark clouds (the opposite of when he came).

BLEU
No, no! This can't be happening! Nooooooo—

CUT TO:

INT: BLEU'S BEDROOM-MORNING

Bleu sits straight up in bed. Occy falls to the floor.

BLEU
--oooooooooooo!!!!

There is a radio on a stand by the bed.

RADIO/DJ
That's right. Adam Ant himself is coming to Fresburger, and your only chance to get tickets now is by listening to KFAB! You should've gotten up earlier!

Radio begins to play "Goody Two Shoes." Bleu grabs the radio and begins slamming it on the table.

BLEU
No, no, no! Why couldn't you have told me this before?! You're evil, evil, EVIL! Aaaaaaaa!

Bleu breaks down into exaggerated crying.

SUPER-DEFORMED CLOVER appears in the bottom right.

S-D CLOVER
(rolling eyes)
Well, here we go...How pathetic!

An angry SUPER-DEFORMED BLEU, dressed like Adam Ant circa *Prince Charming*, leaps into action on the left.

S-D BLEU
I wanna see Adam! I have to!!! Ohhhhhh...
(sobs)

S-D CLOVER
(mock concern)
We know, dear. You poor thing.
(winking and saluting to the audience)
Vive le rock!

BLACK:

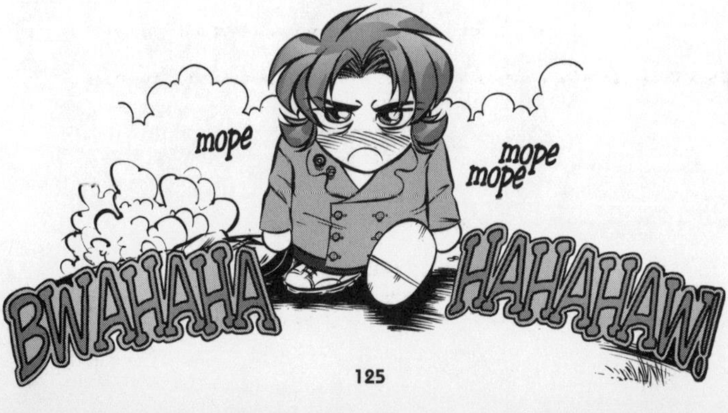
mope
mope
mope
BWAHAHA
HAHAHAW!

HI THERE.
WE'VE RECIEVED A FEW COMPLAINTS THAT OUR MORONIC CREATOR CHYNNA HAS NEGLECTED TO REINTRODUCE US PROPERLY, SO THE CAST OF BLUE MONDAY DECIDED TO REMEDY THE SITUATION.
WE APOLOGIZE FOR THE CONFUSION. ENJOY!
SOUNDTRACK: HUMAN LEAGUE "MIRROR MAN"
HEY, CLOVER CONNELLY! WHAT'S UP?
HOY, BLEU L. FINNEGAN! I'M JUST WAITIN' FOR...
...ALAN WALSH AND VICTOR GOMEZ TO SHOW UP!
REALLY, CLOVER?
YES, BLEU!
AND LOOK! IT'S ERIN O'NEILL!
HI, BLEU! HI, Clover!
HI, ERIN!
...AND RISSA MEADE IS HERE, TOO!
HI, BLEU, CLOVER, AND ERIN!
HI, RISSA!
UH-OH, BLEU. DON'T LOOK NOW, BUT...
MR. BISHOP IS WALKING TO CLASS! (as if you didn't know.)
OOH, MR. BISHOP!
HIYA!
BUT WHERE'S MONKEYBOY?
RIGHT HERE IN THE TREE! HEY, BLEU, CLOVER, ALAN, VICTOR, ERIN, RISSA AND MR. BISHOP!
DON'T FORGET TOM, PATRICK, AND TRAVIS!
HEY, BLEU, CLOVER, ALAN, VICTOR, ERIN, RISSA, MR. BISHOP AND MONKEYBOY!
HEY!!!!!!!
HEY, MONKEYBOY!
ALRIGHTY, THEN! WE HOPE THIS HAS HELPED A BIT! THANKYOUVERYMUCH!

For Marty Nissen

Who was funny, clever, a fabulous artist, and always great company. A great lover of Dixieland Jazz, he often worked as a DJ along with his job as a graphic designer. Kicked ass in WWII, too.

Thanks for the support and dirty jokes, Marty... I can't believe you aren't with us anymore.

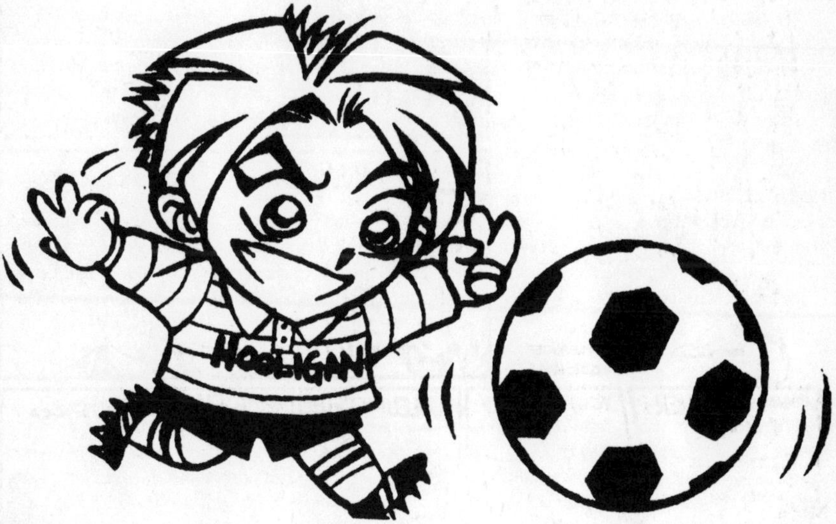
HOOLIGAN

Acknowledgements

Special thanks to the usual gang of idiots, my gagmen (whether voluntarily or not)--Jon "Spanky" Flores, Lissa "Tigolbiddies" Read, Chris Denton-Cheese & Co.; the crew at Penny Lane, Rob & Brandie, Jeremiah, Irving, Aaron, etc.; just about everybody I mentioned in the first trade; shout-outs to some new additions to the world—Jasmine Hurley and Clara Ivy Tinsley-Watson; also wedding congrats to Shane & Lisa, Judd & Pam, Scott & Dani, Evan & Sarah (just about everyone got married or squirted out a puppy this year, so forgive me if I missed someone—I'm under the influence of too much chimichanga at the moment and am out of my senses). Thanks also to Bart Mendoza; Awkward; all the crazy kids at San Diego Comic Con this year, especially the one who fell off the curb while shouting nice things in my direction; AFO's Dade and Jackie; Fred; Sherrie & Larry; the VIZ kids (you rock!); TokyoPop' Sequential Tart's wonderful, uh, tarts; Spinnerrack's Eric & co.; Grayhaven Magazine's Andrew and Barry; Shougn; Ken Smith; Brian Bendis, Ralph Macchio & Smitty; Keith and his flaming pubes; Nutty Neiko (Hi! Hi! Hi!); Jenny & the Pharaohs; Sean Bright; (who is newly married as well!); Jamie McElvie, who looks *extremely* American; Jenny and her cat Avienda (who is messing up my shit as I write this); Keith Wood and Cara Niece; the fun-loving fools in my house: Buster, Mr. Darcy, Teagan, Ben, and of course Guy, who else...Joe Nozemack, FuzzyBear Luscious Jones, and Jamie S. Rich, too, I guess.

Now, scratch that last one. >:)

- Chynna – San Diego, 2003

Bio

Chynna Clugston is the Queen of Hearts. Born in the early part of the century, she started a career as a film actress at the tender age of 14, back in the golden days of silent movies. She worked with Fatty Arbuckle, Mary Pickford, and Buster Keaton before being drummed out of the business for never speaking her real lines and only telling dirty jokes. Astute audience members with a talent for reading lips had complained.

In the years that followed, Chynna remained an influential member of the arts community, inspiring Clara Bow's "It Girl" look and inventing the flapper. Once, F. Scott Fitzgerald was asked how his wife, Zelda, felt about being portrayed as Daisy Buchanan in *The Great Gatsby*, and in a moment of intense inebriation, the writer responded, "Zelda...*pffft!* That bitch is Chynna!" Shortly after WWII, however, Chynna grew weary of the life of a public spectacle and withdrew to a nunnery.

Ms Clugston next surfaced at the height of the '60s British rock-and-roll invasion. Though her participation was not widely reported, eagle-eyed music fans have spotted her in photographs with Keith Moon, Steve Marriott, David Bowie, Peter Noone, and other stars of the era. When '70s FM cockrock and super-sensitive singer-songwriter treacle took over the airwaves, she once again disappeared, waiting for a better cultural climate to launch her devious plan on an unsuspecting public.

That plan was *Blue Monday*, a psychokinetic farce fueled by teenage hormones and a love for everything flash. Since its initial publication, Chynna has become a comic-book sensation, earning herself nominations from the Friends of Lulu, Russ Manning Awards, Harvey Awards, and the Eisners. Spreading the love around, she's also done illustrations for Dark Horse's *Buffy The Vampire Slayer* comics, collaborated with Jen Van Meter and Christine Norrie on the first two *Hopeless Savages* series, contributed illustrations to the novel *Cut My Hair* (written by her editor and greatest admirer, Jamie S. Rich), teamed her characters up with Paul Dini's in *Jingle Belle's Cool Yule*, and worked with Brian Michael Bendis on an issue of Marvel Comics' *Ultimate Marvel Team-Up*. Her most recent work includes the *It Girl* story in Mike Allred's *The Atomics: Spaced Out & Grounded in Snap City* (published by Oni in October 2003) and her own, stand-alone miniseries, *Scooter Girl*, currently in progress. She will be returning to *Blue Monday* in 2004.

Chynna currently resides in San Diego, CA, where she refuses to ever file her CDs properly or wash out her Pepsi glass.

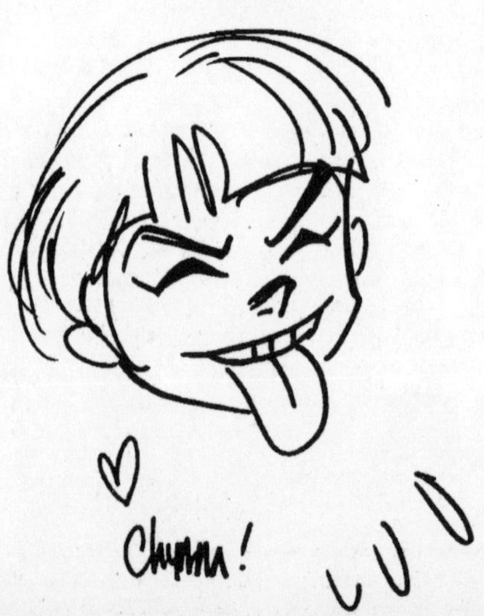
Chynna!